SPIRITUALITY OF
THE OLD TESTAMENT

VOLUME III

Cross and Crown Series of Spirituality

LITERARY EDITOR

Reverend Jordan Aumann, O.P., S.T.D.

NUMBER 24

Spirituality of the Old Testament

Paul-Marie of the Cross, O.C.D.

Translated by ELIZABETH McCABE

VOLUME III

B. HERDER BOOK CO.

15 & 17 South Broadway, St. Louis 2, Mo.

AND *2/3 Doughty Mews, London, W.C.1*

This is a translation of *L'Ancien Testament, source de vie spirituelle,* fourth edition, by Paul-Marie de la Croix, O.C.D., published by Desclée de Brouwer & Cie, Paris.

NIHIL OBSTAT:
   J. S. Considine, O.P.
   Censor Deputatus

IMPRIMATUR:
   ✠ Rt. Rev. Msgr. George L. Casey
   Vicar General
   Archdiocese of Chicago

November 6, 1962

To Mary, Queen and Beauty of Carmel.
May she make fruitful in our souls
the words which she kept in her heart.

❀ CONTENTS

Part III Divine Pathways

PART III

Divine Pathways

Chapter 1

❦ FAITH

THE JOURNEY TO GOD

Lead me in the eternal way.[1]
And they shall all be taught of God.[2]

An essential action animates the context of the Old Testament: that action whereby God, not content with manifesting Himself, stoops to mankind with condescension, brings about a true descent toward man, and thus opens to humanity a road of love by which He will induce mankind to come and meet Him.

This action can be perceived all through the Bible. We see God revealing Himself to men, multiplying His kindness to His people, continuing man's education with mercy and reviving it tirelessly. Better still, divine goodness comes to fetch humanity at the heart of its misery, communicates with it in spite of man's ingratitude and infidelities, walks with humanity and shows it the road to be followed to bring about its salvation. Men, therefore, do not have to

[1] Ps. 138:24.   [2] Isa. 54:13; John 6:45.

3

discover for themselves roads to God, but must follow those which God first took to come to them, roads along which He calls and signals to them. This explains the security and permanence of these divine paths.

But love is already at work in the Old Testament. In the New, it shows itself completely and is fulfilled, but it retains the same nature. The love of God for each of us has always been and will always be a predilection. Nevertheless, what love—even a divine one—would resign itself to give always, without making sure that its gift is received; to wait always, without receiving anything in return? No matter how feeble, how imperfect or how poor, man's answer is always necessary to the very life of love. "Love calls for love." And the sacred text shows us God's people trying to reply to the love that entreats them, and making their way toward the Promised Land.

The Exodus, a major event in the Old Testament, seems even more focal when we discover that it is an image of another exodus, of another pilgrimage: that of the soul on its way to the promised land of union with God.

As on Easter night, along the road to Emmaus, our Lord will rejoin His disciples and travel with them. He who is the Way will explain the Scriptures to them; He who is the Truth will give Himself as nourishment; He who is Life will simply resume what He had done for His people all during the Old Testament, but this time in order to accomplish it.

In the Bible there are spiritual roads: that of faith, thanks to which man, illuminated by the light of revelation, believes in Him who speaks and advances toward Him; that of wisdom, which teaches man to judge earthly values sanely, and to use them in his search for a God, a search which the soul indeed experiences and tastes through the gift of divine wisdom; that of suffering, which, hurling man into the crucible and testing him as gold is tested by fire, transforms him little by little until he becomes capable of that union toward which God never stops drawing him, and of which he already tastes the first fruits here.

These roads are not arbitrary structures or figments of the imagination. They are as solidly indicated in the sacred text as the road of Egypt toward Chanaan. God Himself traced them and assures us they will have an endlessly renewed efficacy. In his search for God, in his response to the call of divine love, man should always use them.

In order to follow these exacting roads, man must deepen his faith, question the world around him, study his own heart, put all the resources of his spirit into action, be willing to pass through the crucible of suffering, steer his soul to the high seas, in short, pledge himself entirely. These roads also exact God's kind and efficacious action, which never ceases to exert itself alongside man's action and penetrates his inward being.

Indeed, necessary though they be, the efforts and searchings of man would come to no conclusion without the gift of faith. Without divine wisdom, human wisdom would remain sterile. Purifying sufferings would be without supernatural fruitfulness if there were no divine visits to bring them to life and transform them. Only divine action allows man to set sail for the unknown and secretly desired shores of union with God. On the spiritual level, the whole Bible appears as an immense Jacob's ladder by which God comes down to man and man climbs to God.

On these paths of faith, wisdom and purifying suffering, the light is doubtless still hidden from us. Doubtless, too, on the individual level as on the group level, the failures and loss of ground seem innumerable. Nevertheless, it was by these paths of God that the chosen people were gradually drawn toward the light. This light by which the men of the Old Testament were secretly visited came, in fact, from the expected rays of redemptive grace.

Finally, the magnetism of Christ in the Old Testament explains the spiritual ascent of humanity, whose steps the Bible retraces and whose paths the Bible shows us; human paths and divine paths, which the Christian within the Church—and the Church herself—benefiting from the full light of Christ, must lengthen and follow to their end.

NECESSITY OF FAITH

Now faith is the substance of things to be hoped for, the evidence of things that appear not. For by this the ancients obtained a testimony.[3]

Go thy way. Thy faith hath made thee whole.[4]

The just shall live in his faith.[5]

This is the victory which overcometh the world: our faith.[6]

Man needs faith in order to receive divine revelation. In the Old Testament faith appears as a road along which God communicates with man, and along which man walks toward God.[7] "Go forth out of thy country, and from thy

[3] Heb. 11:1–2.   [4] Mark 10:52.   [5] Hab. 2:4.
[6] I John 5:4.

[7] The New Testament is an echo of the Old: "But without faith it is impossible to please God. For he that cometh to God must believe that He is; and is a rewarder to them that seek Him" (Heb. 11:6).

kindred, and out of thy father's house, and come into the
land which I shall show thee." [8]

Faith is required from the time of the first revelation.
Though a gift of God, it is also man's reply to the God
who speaks and makes Himself known to him. There are
abundant examples of faith in the history of Israel, but
the patriarchs, and especially Abraham, our father in the
faith, are the most heroic examples. "Abraham believed
God and it was reputed to him unto justice." [9] When St.
Paul wishes to give examples of faith, he takes them above
all from the days of the patriarchs:

By faith Abraham obeyed to go out into a place which he was
to receive for an inheritance. And he went out, not knowing
whither he went. By faith he abode in the land, as in a strange
country, dwelling in cottages, . . . for he looked for a city
that hath foundations; whose builder and maker is God. By
faith also Sara herself, being barren, received strength to conceive seed, even past the time of age. . . . By faith also of
things to come, Isaac blessed Jacob and Esau. . . . By faith
Moses, when he was grown up, denied himself to be the son
of Pharao's daughter, rather choosing to be afflicted with the
people of God than to have the pleasure of sin for a time. . . .
By faith he celebrated the Pasch and the shedding of the blood.
. . . By faith the Israelites passed through the Red Sea. . . .
By faith the walls of Jericho fell down. . . . And what shall
I yet say? For the time would fail me to tell of Gedeon, Barac,
Samson, Jephthe, David, Samuel, and the prophets.[10]

This faith, which Christ will demand as a condition not
only of the miracle which He wishes to perform [11] but of

[8] Gen. 12:1.   [9] Gen. 15:6.   [10] Heb., chap. 11.

[11] Cf. Matt., chaps. 8, 9. "And He wrought not many miracles
there, because of their unbelief" (Matt. 13:58).

the soul's salvation ("Thy faith hath made thee safe" [12]), is no less indispensable in the Old Testament. The prophets often recalled this fact to that forgetful people: "If you will not believe, you shall not continue." [13]

Faith proves itself necessary in order to know and approach God. This the Bible definitely teaches, and the sacred text gives us innumerable examples throughout the history of Israel. The holy book is not only a witness to the existence and necessity of faith in Israel, it emphasizes as well the double function faith carries out for us. The first is to make us believe in God and adhere to His word. In this respect it fills excellently the role of a path to Him; it even does more, since it unites us truly to Him. The second is to make us discover its object.[14] The obscurity with which God remains veiled in faith does not stop us from being able to speak of "the eyes of faith."

On one side as on the other, on the subjective as on the objective level, progress is possible. On the subject's side, the adherence to faith can make progress in purity and in depth. The object, on its side, can be more intimately and less inadequately known. In both cases, faith will have fulfilled for the soul her function as a road and itinerary to God. Faith will have brought man closer to God, and will have united them.

Before finding out how faith appears as God's road in the Old Testament, one must answer at least briefly the question which springs to mind: Can we speak of authentic faith in a case where even Christ's name, the name which

[12] Luke 7:50.   [13] Isa. 7:9.
[14] As Peter did when he confessed his belief in Christ (Matt. 14:33; 16:16).

alone saves us and gives us eternal life, is unknown? But
was it unknown? Christ's name certainly was, but His
presence and His action were alive in the Old Testament.
"Search the Scriptures; for you think in them to have life
everlasting. And the same are they that give testimony of
Me." [15] "For if you did believe Moses, you would perhaps
believe Me also; for he wrote of Me." [16]

The constituents of Israel's faith are definitely less rich
than ours, but that which this people do not yet possess
through faith, they already possess through hope. And better still, they hold tightly together the two virtues, which
were not made to be separated. Israel's faith seems full
of hope, entirely turned toward a Savior and based on the
conviction that salvation is found only in Him. Would that
Christians, deep in the heart of their belief in the existence
of the Savior, cherished a hope as vital, as warm, as ardent
as that of Israel.

The study of faith in the Old Testament rarely gives us

[15] John 5:39.

[16] John 5:46. The Bible bears the Word of God and its unity
is created by this Word. From the opening lines, the Word expresses itself, announces its coming, and one day the Evangelists
will proclaim the redemptive work of this same Word made flesh.
The Person of the Word, like the Persons of the Father and the
Holy Ghost, acts throughout the two Testaments. It was in these
divine Persons, hidden though they were, that the men of old
placed their faith; from Them they drew the life they have handed
down to us. From the time of the Old Testament, every word
spoken by God to men has its source in the Word. Clinging to
this Word through faith, Israel clings to Christ and thus receives
eternal life. It is not surprising therefore that in its ways and development, the faith of Israel shows qualities which make it like
ours, since now and at that time its foundation and its end are the
same as ours.

the chance to pronounce Christ's name. However, this name underlies all the texts we are about to meet. A brotherhood and a spiritual alliance bind us to those who prepared in faith and hope the coming of the Messiah, to those to whom St. Paul would one day say belonged "the adoption as of children and the glory and the Testament and the giving of the Law and the service of God and the promises . . . of whom is Christ, according to the flesh." [17] At the threshold of our research, it is good for us to be aware of this.

THE FORMATION OF FAITH

[These observances] . . . are a shadow of things to come, but the body is of Christ.[18]

Revelation gave to the men of the Old Testament the contents of their faith. The truths which they had to believe were few. They knew nothing of the Trinity, the Incarnation, the Redemption, grace or the sacraments. Even man's last end had not been revealed in a specific manner. Nevertheless, their faith, which had arrived at a transcendent and rewarding God, was, as St. Paul affirms, an authentic faith.[19] This faith depended especially upon the word of God as preserved in the sacred books.

But God, coming to the help of this newborn and still imperfect faith, did not deliver His word without adding manifestations and signs to it. Their role in the development of faith was to be a capital one. Thanks to them, the road of faith would become richer, more definite and more accessible to man.

[17] Rom. 9:4.   [18] Col. 2:17.
[19] "For by this the ancients obtained a testimony" (Heb. 11:2, 6).

The role of the signs is to make the divine message authentic.[20] They underline its meaning as much in the New as in the Old Testament. Christ will use signs and will not fail to accomplish what was spoken of Him in the Scriptures, so that men will know that He is sent by God and will believe in His word. However, He Himself will refuse to display signs when there is danger of their being bandied about by man's worldly curiosity.[21] At such times He will speak of the day when signs will no longer be necessary; when faith will be sufficient to itself and more and more purely based on the word.[22] "Blessed are they who have not seen and have believed." [23]

But the Old Testament is not yet ready for this. Signs are numerous and continual and form faith's conscious support.[24] Particularly throughout the Exodus God multiplied signs for Israel. The psalms refer to signs and recall them ceaselessly to a forgetful and ungrateful people. "Remember His marvellous works which He hath done." [25] "Who

[20] Hear the man blind from birth in the Gospel: "Why, herein is a wonderful thing, that you know not from whence He is. . . . Unless this Man were of God, He could not do anything" (John 9:30).

[21] "And Herod, seeing Jesus, was very glad, because he hoped to see some sign wrought by Him. But He answered him nothing" (Luke 23:8, 9). "This generation is a wicked generation. It asketh a sign, and a sign shall not be given it, but the sign of Jonas" (Luke 11:29).

[22] "Faith then cometh by hearing; and hearing by the word of Christ" (Rom. 10:17).

[23] John 20:29.

[24] We have already pointed out that in revelation the signs were joined to the word. Now we must bring to light the specific role they play in the development and deepening of faith.

[25] Ps. 104:5.

shall declare the powers of the Lord?" [26] "They forgot God, who saved them, who had done great things in Egypt, wondrous works in the land of Cham." [27] "He sent forth signs and wonders in the midst of thee, O Egypt." [28] A servant of God, King Ezechias, asked for a sign through the mediation of the prophet Isaias: "What shall be the sign that the Lord will heal me?" [29] Moreover, God did not hesitate to send signs forcibly to those who would have willingly done without them, such as Pharao; or to those who, through indifference or fear, had no intentions of conforming to the divine plan.

And the Lord spoke again to Achaz, saying: Ask thee a sign of the Lord thy God, either unto the depth of hell, or unto the height above. And Achaz said: I will not ask and I will not tempt the Lord. And he said: Hear ye therefore, O house of David: Is it a small thing for you to be grievous to men, that you are grievous to my God also? Therefore the Lord Himself shall give you a sign. Behold a virgin shall conceive and bear a Son; and His name shall be called Emmanuel.[30]

Shall we say that such a profusion of signs is required for a faith still in its infancy, and that the "adult" faith— which Christ demands from constant hearts and for which He promises happiness—is a naked faith? It is good to take note here of the fact that signs will never completely disappear; they will remain necessary, at least to justify belief.[31] Besides, the word itself is a sign to the spirit. The Word made flesh is the truest sign of all. But no matter of what kind nor how brilliant they may be, signs will never

[26] Ps. 105:2.   [27] Ps. 105:22.   [28] Ps. 134:9.
[29] IV Kings 20:8.   [30] Isa. 7:10–14.
[31] Even in our day the Church is characterized by miracles.

take from faith its hidden character, which is fully supernatural and commendable.

In the Old Testament, signs not only emphasize and
announce the divine presence or divine action; they "signify" as well. Indeed, from the beginning of revelation,
they have had a double mission: to justify belief and to
shape faith itself. The latter mission is of such great importance that its consequences are still felt today. Our faith
is a legacy from and bears the imprint of the spiritual direction which the Old Testament gave it.

In the Old Testament many signs serve as symbols. In
a specific way they teach man what God is in Himself.
They help him to become aware of divine reality and divine ways in a more accessible, less inadequate manner.[32]
Though they are material, they develop in the man of faith
inclinations which are definitely more spiritual and more
in accord with the object of his faith.[33]

The role of symbolic signs as means of instruction appears most clearly in Exodus. Nowhere else does faith find
such an assistant to help it make progress and perfect
itself. This book, therefore, ought to be examined with
particular attention, for the entire Exodus is a sign and a
symbol. St. John in his Gospel, his Apocalypse, and his
Epistle hints that in Exodus we find the type of the mystery
of our faith and of Christian life. The symbolic value of

[32] We cannot ignore the fact that even in the New Testament
the Holy Ghost—to take one example—appeared in the form of
a dove (John 1:32; Luke 3:22) or as tongues of fire (Acts 2:3),
and that Christ spoke of Him as an invisible breath (John 3:8).

[33] Thus, Christ will unveil to the Jews the mystery hidden in the
miracle of the manna, sign and symbol of a wholly spiritual mystery
(John, chap. 6).

the signs contained in Exodus are therefore of highest importance.

Do not be surprised that material signs should give faith its form and enrich and perfect revelation through their symbolism, for revelation speaks to beings involved in the material. This is true of us and was even more so of the Semites, a people whose character is fundamentally concrete.

Because of its abstract nature, a concept doubtless possesses a purity which makes it suitable for spiritual use, but it runs the risk of touching and awakening only the spirit and of leaving the other faculties unmoved, especially those faculties which man derives from his sensual nature. And yet it is these very faculties which allow man to capture and exploit symbolic signs, which are a particularly rich and provocative means to knowledge of spiritual reality.

In the education of the Hebrew people, God hardly ever used concepts. Quite the opposite; He used images, signs and symbols abundantly. His revelations and teachings were always given through His "lessons of things," with an admirable mastery and assurance. It is worthy of note that these material symbols, so far removed by their nature from the spiritual realities they were supposed to suggest or evoke, when used by God were able to give to faith some of its most significant, most dynamic and, on the whole, least inadequate data. Today as well, through these same symbols whose use divine choice permits, faith continues to be enlightened and formed. In fact, through them we become more aware of the nature and characteristics of faith; we perceive as well how God educates faith and how He deepens it.

Among the signs which the Old Testament offers us we find: the cloud, the pillar of light and of shadow, the fire, all of which recur frequently and which we can call major signs. They are the elements which make up "theophanies," they accompany and are almost identified with Yahweh's glory. They play a particularly important part in the deepening of faith and truly work to shape it.

In most of the biblical narrative, cloud and glory are united. The cloud is mentioned in almost all the theophanies of Exodus and in many other passages of the Old Testament as well: "And the seventh day he called Moses out of the midst of the cloud. . . . The cloud covered the tabernacle of the testimony, and the glory of the Lord filled it." [34] Inspired by the account of Exodus, the psalmist says: "Yahweh bowed the heavens, and came down; and darkness was under His feet. . . . Clouds and darkness are round about Him." [35] The sacred authors have tried to describe the cloud. A few have recalled its shadowy aspect: "And He made darkness His covert, His pavilion round about Him; dark waters in the clouds of the air." [36] Others have recalled its luminous nature. There are even texts where these two elements, at first sight irreconcilable, are united: "And it was a dark cloud and enlightening the night." [37]

This impression of strange mystery grows because of the very nature of the cloud. We cannot in fact think of a more

[34] Exod. 24:16; 40:32.   [35] Ps. 17:10; 96:2.
[36] Ps. 17:12.   [37] Exod. 14:20.

intangible reality. Without shape or definite outline, the cloud defies description. But by this very fact it escapes the danger of representation which God continually opposes in the Old Testament. "You shall not make any graven images," is said again and again to the Hebrews. The cloud at least leaves no image in man's mind. Appearing usually at the peak of a mountain, it draws man's eyes from earth and offers him, in the sky itself, an almost immaterial reality. Of course, the cloud is still a perceptible representation, but so free of material qualities that it finds itself on the doorstep of the spiritual, and eminently suited to express spiritual mysteries. Can one find among perceptible symbols, one as spiritual and as suited to this people in its infancy? And does this not prove spontaneously to man the connection that exists between the cloud in which God hides, and the nature of the knowledge through faith which is asked of man? This people, to whom representation of any kind was so often forbidden and from whom the mysterious presence hides Himself behind intangible signs, finds itself not only preserved from error, but also orientated in a positive manner toward a true knowledge of faith.

The cloud has another characteristic; the sacred texts speak of it as "shadowed on one side and on the other illuminating the night." This complex nature, this opposition, which the sacred authors not only do not try to avoid but emphasize, will allow the soul to reach the depths of faith. Nothing represents the knowledge of faith more clearly than this "light and shadow" which evokes irresistibly the biblical account.

Was it possible by means of symbols to capture in a more

certain and balanced manner the union of light and obscurity at the core of faith? Mystics and theologians in
turn will make use of this symbol of light and of obscurity.
They will speak of the great shadows and the dark night
of faith; they will also speak of the "eyes of faith." Souls
experiencing faith will also refer instinctively to these images to express something of what they feel. Thus, they
will all help us to realize with what unfailing assurance
God, from the beginning of the religious history of mankind, had chosen signs most capable of revealing to man
the characteristics of faith.

The history of Israel alone is sufficient to show us how
precious the sign of the cloud was to souls, helping them
penetrate the knowledge of faith. In fact, Israel's mission
was to bring the light, and then to spread it to the world.
God was therefore obliged to give Israel the means for this,
and to safeguard her against constantly recurring distortions and perversions of the religious meaning. Moreover,
He had to overcome the obstacles due to the interior state
of these men of Israel, "stiff-necked and with uncircum-
cised hearts."

Faith was therefore made obscure so that both the mind
and the heart would be obliged to search deeply. Indeed,
a profound faith implies that the spirit has engaged the
flesh in sad combat, and has finally won.[38] It also implies
that fidelity has been able to keep itself alive at the heart
of crucifying trials. The long and painful crossing of the
desert became for Israel the moment at which she realized
the obscurity of faith, and became for faith the means of

[38] "And this is the victory which overcometh the world: our
faith" (I John 5:4).

growing in depth. God plunged the Egyptians, chasing the Hebrews, into physical darkness: "But over them only was spread a heavy night, an image of that darkness which was to come upon them. But they were to themselves more grievous than the darkness." [39] They were in fact unable to perceive anything except the matter of the signs; but it was not so for the Hebrews: "Thy saints had a very great light." [40]

Israel has above this a sublime mission to fill. She is the trustee of the divine commandments, and alone among the nations possesses truth and stands in the light: "The Egyptians heard their voices indeed, but did not see their shape. And they that before had been wronged gave thanks. . . . The others indeed were worthy to be deprived of light and imprisoned in darkness, who kept Thy children shut up, by whom the pure light of the Law was to be given to the world." [41] This light which illumines Israel is spiritual and must become more so each day: "For, behold, darkness shall cover the earth and a mist the people; but the Lord shall arise upon thee and His glory shall be seen upon thee. And the Gentiles shall walk in thy light, and kings in the brightness of thy rising." [42]

And also, while the idolatrous and pagan peoples, deprived of a faith in the true God, understand only the material side of the trials which strike them, Israel discovers their significance and spiritual meaning. Her faith feeds on them and becomes purified and fortified through them. True faith is her inheritance. To come into it, she must first follow a dry road and go through a dark night. She

[39] Wisd. 17:20.   [40] Wisd. 18:1.   [41] Wisd. 18:2, 4.
[42] Isa. 60:2.

must allow herself to be totally captured and moved by the Spirit and, in her ignorance of divine paths, she will have to plunge into the unknown—a hard and laborious wandering!

God's people are not, as Egypt is, surrounded by shadows, but still they carry them within, and before them stretches the mysterious shadow of the cloud. On leaving Egypt, Israel thinks only of obtaining her independence and making sure of prosperity. Her faith is real but as yet does not know the profoundness of obscurity; therefore trial comes terribly. Deprived of all human help, dragged by their leader for forty years through a burning desert, where hunger and thirst make themselves cruelly felt, the Hebrews must lean for support on the word of God alone, which is unpredictable and mysterious.

The flesh will not refrain from complaining about the spirit. The Bible has recorded the naive recriminations of this people who began to regret "the fish that we ate in Egypt, free cost," [43] and we see discontent giving birth to rebellion and even to an almost general apostasy (Exod., chap. 32). From this long and difficult trial, necessary to deepen the faith of Israel and establish it in unshakeable confidence, only two men, Josue and Caleb, emerged victorious. The people seemed only to wander in the desert, however. In reality they were constantly led by Yahweh. But only the men of faith realized this.

"He found him in a desert land, in a place of horror, and of vast wilderness. He led him about and taught him; and He kept him as the apple of His eye. As the eagle enticing her young to

[43] Num. 11:5.

fly, and hovering over them, He spread his wings; and hath taken him and carried him on His shoulders.[44]

And the Lord went before them to shew the way by day in a pillar of a cloud, and by night in a pillar of fire; that He might be the guide of their journey at both times.[45]

Therefore they received a burning pillar of fire for a guide of the way which they knew not; and Thou gavest them a harmless sun of a good entertainment.[46]

These quotations point out in a timely way another quality of the cloud. It appears here in the form of a pillar, and this pillar advances, guiding and leading the people of God through the desert. The sacred authors had definitely stated that "Yahweh was in the cloud." If He is now in the pillar of cloud it is in order to walk with it before Israel. Seeing this pillar before them and receiving from it the order to follow wherever it goes, the people understand that faith is not only a knowledge of God, nor even light and shadow, but also a road. This was especially made evident in the Exodus. During this long and important period, it was by means of the pillar of cloud that God led His people. Everyone could see then, through this sensible sign, that divine fidelity did not fail: "There never failed the pillar of the cloud by day, nor the pillar of fire by night, before the people." [47] "So it was always." [48]

But God demanded that His faithfulness be repaid. And at least on this point the conduct of Israel is an excellent example. In fact, the sacred authors tell us:

If at any time the cloud removed from the tabernacle, the children of Israel went forward by their troops. If it hung over, they remained in the same place.[49]

[44] Deut. 32:10–12.   [45] Exod. 13:21.   [46] Wisd. 18:3.
[47] Exod. 13:22.   [48] Num. 9:16.   [49] Exod. 40:34, 35.

And when the cloud that covered the tabernacle was taken up, then the children of Israel marched forward; and in the place where the cloud stood still, there they camped. . . . But if it remained over the tabernacle for two days or a month or a year, the children of Israel remained in the same place and marched not. But immediately, as soon as it departed, they removed the camp.[50]

A month . . . a year, the time judged necessary by God for the accomplishment of His work in these hard and often rebellious hearts. And thus they formed the habit of depending on God alone ("The Lord alone was his leader" [51]) and the faith of Israel strengthened itself.

And then, from whom if not from God would this people have learned the surest road to reach far-off Chanaan? They received no explanations from their leaders as to these long trips, these endless halts in inhospitable, arid and desolate places. To those who are willing to follow such a road, God assures His assistance. Without fear their souls can lean on this hidden presence; even though it leaves them in the obscurity of faith, a luminous pillar leads them on the road of life. "Who is there . . . that hath walked in the darkness, and hath no light? Let him hope in the name of the Lord and lean upon his God." [52]

The pillar of cloud and the shadowed brightness which it shed guided Israel through the desert. They helped her form an exact idea of faith. Since God is said to have "gone before Israel in a pillar of cloud and of fire," we must understand that invisibly, under the veils of faith, God Himself walks with the soul.

The pillar of cloud also prevented Israel from seeing in

[50] Num. 9:17, 22.   [51] Deut. 32:12.   [52] Isa. 40:10.

faith nothing but a road toward a motionless and far-off light. It led Israel to understand that faith never ceases to act on the soul, enlightening and transforming it; in a way it is God walking with the soul. Like the pillar of cloud, faith is a walking road. It is already for Israel what one day on the road to Emmaus Christ would be for the disciples: the one who guides without making Himself known; the one who, while exterior darkness rises, brings to the soul an interior light which illumines it, burns and transforms it, and leads it on; the one who shows that He is the road to follow, the living Way. "I am the Way." [53]

Through their symbolism, the cloud as well as the pillar of light and shadow bring to faith a remarkably enriching depth. In spite of this, another aspect of faith, however, has yet to be brought to light, and this will be accomplished by the symbol of fire, which is the richest of them all in spiritual meaning. Through it we advance in knowledge, not only of faith but of God Himself and of the soul which is joined to Him by faith. Numerous quotations show fire closely united to the manifestations of Yahweh's glory:

And you came to the foot of the Mount, which burned even unto heaven; and there was darkness, and a cloud and obscurity in it.[54]

And all Mount Sinai was on a smoke, because the Lord was come down upon it in fire.[55]

For behold the Lord will come with fire, and His chariots are like a whirlwind.[56]

The fire seems distinct from the cloud. And yet they are very often joined together: "For the cloud of the Lord

[53] John 14:6.   [54] Deut. 4:11.   [55] Exod. 19:18.
[56] Isa. 66:15.

hung over the tabernacle, . . . a fire by night." [57] "By night, (the cloud had) as it were, the appearance of fire." [58] The fire springs from the heart of the cloud. To the sacred authors, cloud and fire display successively or simultaneously different aspects of one unique and divine reality.[59]

The sign of fire will enter into the history of Israel under many different though constant forms. Sometimes it symbolizes the purifying action of faith and sometimes its transforming action. It evokes the power and activity of God, no less than the burning ardor of His love. The entire Old Testament is marked with this sign. Joined to divine manifestation, fire appears more especially at the great moments in the life of the people of God and of His faithful servants. Thus, Abraham sees a burning furnace and a brand of fire pass mysteriously between the two halves of the victim offered as a holocaust.[60] Moses becomes aware of God's presence at the sight of the bush which burns without being consumed.[61] The divine fire penetrates, purifies and fortifies the faith of Elias, Isaias, Ezechiel and so many others.

But God wanted the faith of the entire people to be enlightened and inflamed by the sign of fire. The whole of the history of Israel, especially at the most decisive moments, is marked by divine fire and carries its traces. As

[57] Exod. 40:36.   [58] Num. 9:16.

[59] The New Testament also refers frequently to the symbol of fire. If fire is often used to recall eternal punishment (Matt., chaps. 13, 18), it is used just as much to speak of divine action: "He shall baptize you in the Holy Ghost and fire" (Matt. 3:11), or to refer to Christ's mission among men: "I am come to cast fire on the earth. And what will I, but that it be kindled?" (Luke 12:49).

[60] Gen. 15:12–17.   [61] Exod. 3:2.

far back as its past goes, Israel sees fire associated with divine action. The cherubim guard with swords like flames of fire the gates of paradise from which Adam and Eve were driven. Yahweh punishes the wicked towns with fire. But it is especially at the time of the Exodus that fire bears witness to divine action and justifies the people's faith. Everyone in Israel saw and followed the pillar of fire that burned at night and lit up the road. "For the cloud of the Lord hung over the tabernacle a fire by night, in the sight of all the children of Israel." [62] It was in front of all the people that fire, instrument of God's justice, swallowed up Abiron and his companions, who had failed to believe in the divine word.[63] Much later, all the people called together by Elias on Carmel will see fire fall from heaven and consume the victim.[64]

But fire is not only the sign of God's justice, striking those who are far from the true faith. It is in itself a revelation of the divine nature, of a depth and a power which speak more than words; a revelation which it impresses upon minds and hearts with a unique strength. So fire is for the people the supreme divine manifestation.

God never speaks so clearly as through fire; and it is also by fire that the people answer Him. Fire is truly a language between God and His creature. Fire precedes the Lord and announces His coming: "A fire shall go before Him." [65] It shows in a miraculous manner, when necessary, that God accepts what has been offered to Him: "And behold a fire, coming forth from the Lord, devoured the holocaust and

[62] Exod. 60:36.   [63] Num. 16:35.   [64] III Kings 18:38.
[65] Ps. 96:3.

the fat that was upon the altar; which when the multitude
saw, they praised the Lord, falling on their faces." [66] In
the sacrifice of Elias on Carmel, fire is not only the sign
sent by God; it really becomes a symbol of the true God:

> Call ye on the names of your gods, and I will call on the
> name of my Lord; and the God that shall answer by fire, let
> him be God. . . . And when it was now time to offer the
> holocaust, Elias the prophet came near and said: O Lord God of
> Abraham, and Isaac, and Israel, shew this day that Thou art
> the God of Israel. . . . Hear me. . . . Then the fire of the
> Lord fell, and consumed the holocaust, and the wood, and the
> stones, and the dust, and licked up the water that was in
> the trench. And when all the people saw this, they fell on
> their faces. And they said: The Lord He is God; the Lord
> He is God.[67]

And when the people wish to speak to Yahweh, they
use God's own language without hesitation. Better than
any word, the flame which consumes the holocaust and
rises to the sky, will tell the Lord of the repentance, the
prayer, the adoration of Israel.

In man's relations with God in the Old Testament, fire,
therefore, has a privileged place. God was certainly not
ignorant of the fact that fire lent itself to myth and that
distortions could result from this. In order to prevent this,
He monopolized it to His own profit, making of fire one
of the symbols of His nature and His action: "The Lord
thy God is a consuming fire, a jealous God." [68]

The personality of the Messiah, toward whom goes all

[66] Lev. 9:24.   [67] III Kings 18:24, 36–39.   [68] Deut. 4:24.

the hope of Israel, will have the same characteristics.[69] Up
to the end of the Old Testament, fire will be given as characteristic of the Messiah and divine action:

The light of Israel shall be as a fire, and the Holy One thereof
as a flame.[70]

Behold I send My angel, and he shall prepare the way before My face. And presently the Lord whom you seek, and the
angel of the Testament whom you desire shall come to His
Temple. Behold He cometh. . . . And who shall be able to
think of the day of His coming? And who shall stand to see Him?
For He is like a refining fire and like the fuller's herb. And He
shall sit refining the silver and cleansing it, and He shall purify
the sons of Levi and shall refine them as gold and as silver.[71]

The Precursor replies to the prophet by evoking the
action of the divine fire which he has come to announce:

Bring forth therefore fruit worthy of penance. . . . For now
the axe is laid to the root of the trees. Every tree therefore that
doth not yield good fruit shall be cut down and cast into the
fire. I indeed baptize you with water unto penance; but He that
shall come after me is mightier than I, whose shoes I am not
worthy to bear. He shall baptize you in the Holy Ghost and in
fire.[72]

Through these symbols men will come to understand
that the soul which approaches God will be purified as
though by a fire. They will equally understand that, like
a devouring fire, the jealousy of God's love will burn the
soul which He desires, and that nothing will be able to

---

[69] Christ Himself will say, speaking of His mission: "I am come
to cast fire on the earth. And what will I, but that it be kindled?"
(Luke 12:49).

[70] Isa. 10:17.   [71] Mal. 3:1–3.   [72] Matt. 3:8–11.

extinguish this fire: "For love is strong as death, jealousy as hard as hell. The lamps thereof are fire and flames. Many waters cannot quench charity, neither can the floods drown it." [73] Thus, through fire, the warm and vigorous, enlightening and exhilarating but also purifying and consuming nature of faith is revealed to us.

Man sees through the symbol of fire something of the divine life, dazzling, impetuous and flashing, capable of setting all things on fire without losing any of its substance. Such is the burning bush which, under Moses' eyes, burned without being consumed; such was the vision of Ezechiel, when fire appeared as the supreme symbol of an infinite life, infinitely mysterious.

And I saw, and behold a whirlwind came out of the north, and a great cloud, and a fire infolding it . . . and in the midst thereof the likeness of four living creatures. . . . This was the vision running to and fro in the midst of the living creatures, a bright fire and lightning going forth from the fire. And the living creatures ran and returned like flashes of lightning. [74]

Elsewhere this living image of fire calls perfectly to mind the many states through which faith causes the soul to pass. As though under the action of a fire which is both light and heat, the soul is successively enlightened, inflamed, purified and devoured by faith. Like fire, faith melts the soul. Faith lights up and catches fire at the flaming contact of divine fire; it burns with ardor. Thanks to this powerfully symbolic sign, the soul understands that live faith unites it to God and makes it share in His life, that faith is ardent reality, supremely active.

[73] Cant. 8:6, 7.   [74] Ezech. 1:4–14.

It is easily seen how these signs, by the richness of their symbolism, helped the men of the Old Testament to discover the true meaning of faith and to penetrate to its depths. Under God's action and guidance, the perceptible itself, working in the service of the spiritual, did not fail in its mission. The people of Israel, so often allowed to look upon Yahweh's glory, discerned through the signs which announced this glory what God expected of them and with what qualities their faith was to be marked.

Doubtless, few of them profited from the divine teaching to plunge into the depths of faith; few made of this teaching a road of meekness, a path to God; and few perhaps were those who attained that ardent faith, that living faith, which the divine fire was sent to reveal to them. However, several men were able to penetrate to the heart of the mystery of faith and to live it fully. They are still our models today, and we cannot appreciate their example too greatly.

PRIVILEGED WITNESSES OF THE FAITH

Remember your prelates who have spoken the word of God to you; whose faith follow, considering the end of their conversation.[75]

Among the men whose lives the Bible relates, some are obviously presented to us as models. These are the men whose faith remains with us as an instruction and a light. In this group, none are as imposing as Abraham, Moses and Elias.[76] They are true giants of faith in the Old Testament. It is possible, however, to show that each one of these men

[75] Heb. 13:7.

[76] See how the Epistle to the Hebrews praises the faith of Abraham and of Moses (Heb., chap. 11), as does Ecclesiasticus 44:4.

brought to light in a special manner a particular important aspect of faith, whose privileged witnesses they have remained throughout the centuries.

Abraham is really "our father in the faith." When God calls him from the land of idols to an unknown country,[77] it is to test his soul by faith and also to plant deep faith in this people who are to be born of the patriarch. Therefore, in calling Abraham by his name, God is already calling each one of us by ours. "The seed of Abraham My friend; in whom I have taken thee from the ends of the earth, and from the remote parts thereof have called thee, and said to thee: Thou art My servant. I have chosen thee and have not cast thee away. . . . Fear not, for I have redeemed thee, and called thee by thy name. Thou art Mine." [78]

Abraham sees God as his unique good, the good which is above all others. "Go forth out of thy country, and from thy kindred, and out of thy father's house, and come into the land which I shall show thee." [79] Through faith, Abraham knows his God, and his God is sufficient to him. For His sake he leaves all that he loved, and obedient to this first call, the patriarch will hear many others. Yahweh's voice will become familiar to his heart, planting a growing faith in his soul. A steady relationship will be established between God and himself. The nomad's humble life will be transformed.

When, at the threshold of his tent, Abraham is visited by God, without hesitation he recognizes and adores his Lord in the man he receives as a chosen friend. "The Lord appeared to him in the vale of Mambre as he was sitting at the door of his tent, in the very heat of the day. And when

[77] Heb. 11:8.   [78] Isa. 41:9; 43:1.   [79] Gen. 12:1.

he had lifted up his eyes, there appeared to him three men standing near him; and as soon as he saw them, he ran to meet them from the door of his tent, and adored down to the ground. And he said: Lord if I have found favor in Thy sight, pass not away from Thy servant." [80] Because he always enters fully into God's plans, his own life is disrupted over and over again by mysterious and unforeseen divine intervention. But God finds in him the living faith which He needs, and Abraham's response to grace is strong enough for God to make of him the "father of us all in faith." [81]

Abraham believed God and it was reputed to him unto justice.[82]

Now to him that worketh, the reward is not reckoned according to grace but according to debt. But to him that worketh not, yet believeth in Him that justifieth the ungodly, his faith is reputed to justice. . . . For not through the Law was the promise to Abraham that he should be heir of the world, but through the justice of faith. . . . Therefore is it of faith, that according to grace the promise might be firm to all the seed; not to that only which is of the Law, but to that also which is of the faith of Abraham, who is the father of us all.[83]

Nowadays belief in one God is so widespread that it is no longer the upsetting, unheard of fact that it really was for Abraham's contemporaries. Pioneer of the monotheistic religion, first missionary, Abraham will be called upon to give proof of his faith. He will show faultless fidelity and, supported by the divine word, will sacrifice everything. "Fear not, Abram, I am thy protector, and thy reward

[80] Gen. 18:1–3.　　[81] Rom. 4:16.　　[82] Gen. 15:6.
[83] Rom. 4:4–16.

exceeding great. . . . I am the almighty God; walk before
Me, and be perfect." [84]

Be perfect! This is what Abraham must accomplish before God and before man, as a unique sign of the truth
which he has received. No doubt he had human weaknesses;
the stratagem he used when dealing with Pharao is not
free from human diplomacy, but who will reproach Abraham for it when God Himself seems to vouch for him in
similar circumstances? Does the Lord not say to Abimelech:
"He shall pray for thee and thou shalt live"? [85] It is impossible to judge such acts by the norms of our Christian
morality.

Abraham's integrity remains a model, as does his love
of peace, shown by a profound spirit of conciliation: "Abram
therefore said to Lot: Let there be no quarrel, I beseech
thee, between me and thee, and between my herdsmen and
thy herdsmen; for we are brethren. Behold the whole land
is before thee; depart from me I pray thee. If thou wilt go
to the left hand, I will take the right; if thou choose the
right hand, I will pass to the left." [86] His charity flies to
help his brother in danger. "Which when Abram had heard,
to wit, that his brother Lot was taken, he numbered of the
servants born in his house, three hundred and eighteen well
appointed, and pursued them to Dan." [87]

Splendidly disinterested, he refuses the goods offered
him by the king of Sodom in return for his collaboration:
"That from the very wool thread unto the shoe latchet, I
will not take of any things that are thine, lest thou say: I
have enriched Abram. Except such things as the young

[84] Gen. 15:1; 17:1.   [85] Gen. 20:7.   [86] Gen. 13:8–9.
[87] Gen. 14:14.

men have eaten, and the shares of the men that came with me; these shall take their shares." [88]

For a long time his behavior does not seem to receive any rewards. He is deprived of the posterity which God had promised to him, and to which he will pass on his faith: "I shall go without children; and the son of the steward of my house is this Damascus Eliezer." [89] From this we understand how sorrowful, though constantly serene, was the quality of faith in Abraham. God, who never stops making him great promises and showing him an undreamed of future, asks him nevertheless to lean on His word alone, to believe in the impossible: "Lift up thy eyes and look from the place wherein thou now art, to the north and to the south, to the east and to the west. All the land which thou seest, I will give to thee, and to thy seed forever. And I will make thy seed as the dust of the earth; if any man be able to number the dust of the earth, he shall be able to number thy seed also." [90] But to the promises are added tragic forebodings: "Know thou beforehand that thy seed shall be a stranger in a land not their own, and they shall bring them under bondage, and afflict them, four hundred years." [91]

At last the day comes when God replies to his most ardent wish and gives him the beloved son on whom rest the hopes of the covenant, but only in order soon to ask Abraham to sacrifice him with his own hands: "After these things, God tempted Abraham, and said to him: Abraham! And he answered: Here I am. He said to him: Take thy

[88] Gen. 14:23–24. [89] Gen. 15:2. [90] Gen. 13:14–17.
[91] Gen. 15:13.

only-begotten son Isaac, whom thou lovest, and go into the land of vision; and there thou shalt offer him for a holocaust." [92]

Strengthened by God, the faith of Abraham does not falter: "(Wisdom) knew the just, and preserved him without blame to God, and kept him strong against the compassion for his son." [93] The divine will, so disconcerting, so baffling to the man without ardent faith, was to Abraham the unique, perfect, adorable expression of the impenetrable plans of a God whom he knew to be all powerful. "Because thou hast done this thing, and hast not spared thy only-begotten son for My sake, I will bless thee . . . and in thy seed shall all the nations of the earth be blessed because thou hast obeyed My voice." [94]

Did Abraham understand the fullness of that prophecy? If we refer to Christ's words: "Abraham your father rejoiced that he might see My day. He saw it and was glad," [95] it would seem that he had at least some knowledge and had been filled with light in return for so much faith. The time has come, in fact, when Abraham believes, with a certitude rooted in an inexpressible experience, that the covenant of old concluded with Yahweh will be accomplished.

My covenant is with thee; and thou shalt be a father of many nations. . . . And I will bless Sara, and of her I will give thee a son, whom I will bless; and he shall become nations, and kings of people shall spring from him. . . . And I will make of thee a great nation, and I will bless thee, and magnify thy name; and thou shalt be blessed.[96]

[92] Gen. 22:1, 2.   [93] Wisd. 10:5.   [94] Gen. 22:16–18.
[95] John 8:56.   [96] Gen. 17:4; 17:16; Gen. 12:2.

Abraham is not ignorant of the role assigned to him. He knows he must be the father of a great people, of a countless people: "And I will multiply thee exceedingly." [97]

In spite of this, he continues to lead the simple and harsh life of a nomad. It is in this humble and occasionally crucifying fidelity to the divine voice, which makes itself heard through all the circumstances of his life, that Abraham bears witness and day by day builds up that unshakeable faith which he will transmit to his descendants: "He kept the law of the Most High and was in covenant with Him. In his flesh he established the covenant, and in temptation he was found faithful. Therefore by an oath He gave him glory in his posterity." [98]

From this time on, the covenant is sealed in suffering and blood. God prints the sign of this supernatural life, which will forever make all believers brothers in faith, on the men of Abraham's race through circumcision. The blessing which rests on them has come down to us.[99]

At the end of a long life, the patriarch can go to his rest. Faith set love on fire in Abraham's heart, and this love is turned at all times to a God who seems to repay this ardor with interest. "Abraham, . . . being proved by many tribu-

---

[97] Gen. 17:2.   [98] Ecclus. 44:20–21.

[99] "Neither are all they that are the seed of Abraham, children. . . . That is to say, not they that are the children of the flesh are the children of God; but they that are the children of the promise are accounted for the seed" (Rom. 9:7–8). "And if you be Christ's, then are you the seed of Abraham, heirs according to the promise" (Gal. 3:29). "And the Scripture, foreseeing that God justifieth the Gentiles by faith, told unto Abraham before: In thee shall all nations be blessed. Therefore they that are of faith shall be blessed with faithful Abraham" (Gal. 3:8–9).

lations, was made the friend of God." [100] He was also made the father of all those who will enter after him into the great night of faith and will remain faithful.

While the Old Testament shows us in Abraham the type of believer tested and faithful to his belief, we see in Moses, "a man exceeding meek above all men that dwelt upon earth," [101] the fertile soil where grace will make faith fruitful; where grace will make faith increase into a shaft of light which, until the time of Christ, will be the world's torch. Strength, gentleness and fidelity will be closely allied in Moses' soul, allowing him to bring to men, with an incontestable authority, the great message of divine transcendence and divine kindness.

His praises, sung by Ecclesiasticus, help us to see this great figure sculptured by God: [102]

Moses was beloved of God and men; whose memory is in benediction. He made him like the saints in glory and magnified him in the fear of his enemies, and with his words he made prodigies to cease. He glorified him in the sight of kings and gave him commandments in the sight of His people and shewed him His glory. He sanctified him in his faith and meekness and chose him out of all flesh. For He heard him and his voice, and brought him into a cloud. And He gave him commandments before His face and a law of life and instruction, that he might teach Jacob His covenant and Israel His judgment.[103]

---

[100] Jud. 8:22.   [101] Num. 12:3.

[102] The Epistle to the Romans also makes us see the historical and religious importance of Moses: "Death reigned from Adam unto Moses, even over them also who have not sinned" (Rom. 5:14).

[103] Ecclus. 45:1–6.

In spite of exceptional gifts, Moses was at the beginning a poor and fearful creature like all men. The revelation of Horeb, which makes Moses secure in the knowledge and contemplation of truth, at the same time causes him to feel his basic weakness. The burden he has received from God crushes him. "I will send thee to Pharao, that thou mayest bring forth My people, the children of Israel out of Egypt. . . . I beseech thee, Lord, I am not eloquent from yesterday and the day before; and since Thou hast spoken to Thy servant, I have more impediment and slowness of tongue. . . . I beseech thee, Lord, send whom Thou wilt send." [104] He will carry this weakness many times to God's feet, along with the sins of his people, the inconstant men who were placed in his hands. He will offer their profound misery with his own, and will thus become the image of the divine Mediator [105] to whom God will listen and whose prayer He will grant without measure. Mediator with regard to Israel's sin: "Either forgive them this trespass, or if Thou do not, strike me out of the book that Thou has written. . . . If I have found grace in Thy sight, O Lord, I beseech Thee that Thou wilt go with us (for it is a stiff necked people) and take away our iniquities and sin, and possess us." [106]

He is mediator of the grace which will accompany his people: "And the Lord said to Moses: This word also, which thou hast spoken, will I do. For thou hast found grace before Me, and thee have I known by name." [107] He is mediator of the strength that will save Israel:

[104] Exod. 3:10; 4:10, 13.
[105] Moses is called "prince and redeemer" (cf. Heb., chap. 8; Acts 7:35).
[106] Exod. 32:32; 34:9.   [107] Exod. 33:17.

And when Moses lifted up his hands, Israel overcame; but if he let them down a little, Amalec overcame. And Moses' hands were heavy; so they took a stone, and put under him, and he sat on it; and Aaron and Hur stayed up his hands on both sides. And it came to pass that his hands were not weary until sunset. And Josue put Amalec and his people to flight, by the edge of the sword.[108]

Even when he can no longer carry the burden of this multiple and insubordinate people, he remains their representative before God, as is shown in these words addressed to him by one of his followers: "Be thou to the people in those things that pertain to God, to bring their words to Him; and to shew the people the ceremonies and the manner of worshipping, and the way wherein they ought to walk, and the work that they ought to do." [109]

Indeed, Moses is chosen by God mainly to be the messenger of the divine words; the command, "Speak to the children of Israel," is repeated to him all through his life. And if prodigious events are brought about by God, it is to give authority to the messenger: "Lo, now will I come to thee in the darkness of a cloud, that the people may hear Me speaking to thee, and may believe thee forever." [110] "By this you shall know that the Lord hath sent me to do all things that you see, and that I have not forged them of my own head." [111]

[108] Exod. 17:11–13.   [109] Exod. 18:19–20.   [110] Exod. 19:9.

[111] Num. 16:28. St. Paul shows us how faith guided Moses in his actions: "By faith Moses, when he was grown up, denied himself to be the son of Pharao's daughter, rather choosing to be afflicted with the people of God than to have the pleasure of sin for a time, esteeming the reproach of Christ greater riches than the treasure of the Egyptians. For he looked unto the reward. By faith he left Egypt, not fearing the fierceness of the king. For

The divine word is the completely spiritual gift which God wishes to communicate to souls through his intermediary, so that it might live in their hearts. "The word is very nigh unto thee, in thy mouth and in thy heart, that thou mayest do it." [112] So it is logical that Ecclesiasticus should say: "With his words he made prodigies to cease," [113] thus showing that from henceforth the word of God will find its way into hearts, above all by faith and not by signs and wonders.

Moses is the legislator of a spiritual law, not conceived by man but received from the divine hands: "The two tables of the testimony . . . made by the work of God. The writing also of God was graven in the tables." [114] He is the head of a great nation which must be perpetuated until the end of time, but above all he is the inspired herald of the religion of the true God. "Hear, O Israel. The Lord our God is one God." [115] He possesses unique knowledge and experience [116] in this religion; and no one seems to have entered so early into divine friendship. The sacred author wished to show us this when he depicted Moses bearing about him a reflection of the divine brightness whose rays had touched him.

And . . . Moses . . . knew not that his face was horned from the conversation of the Lord. And Aaron and the children

he endured, as seeing him that is invisible. By faith he celebrated the Pasch" (Heb. 11:24–28).

[112] Deut. 30:14.   [113] Ecclus. 45:2.   [114] Exod. 32:15–16.
[115] Deut. 6:4.

[116] St. Paul realized that Moses knew not only the mystery of God's free election (Rom. 9:15) but also the meaning of a justice and a salvation by faith which are superior to deeds and the Law (Rom. 10:5, 10).

of Israel seeing the face of Moses horned were afraid to come near. . . . And he put a veil upon his face. But when he went in to the Lord, and spoke with Him, he took it away . . . but he covered his face again, if at any time he spoke to them.[117]

But Exodus bears even more witness to this high level of mystical experience and divine communication by making us share a little in the deep and sweet revelation which was bestowed on Moses, a revelation which allowed him to discover God's own feelings and the richness of His heart. "O the Lord, the Lord God, merciful and gracious, patient and of much compassion, and true, who keepest mercy unto thousands." [118] This revelation comes to life in a quotation from Deuteronomy, in which we hear an echo of the burning and ineffable communication of Sinai: "The Lord thy God is a consuming fire, a jealous God." [119]

If Moses asks Israel to search for the Lord, and if he sees this search as a spiritual necessity for the chosen people, it is because his own lively faith and his experience of God have led him to consider the divine friendship as a supremely desirable possibility. "And when thou shalt seek there the Lord thy God, thou shalt find Him . . . if thou seek Him with all thy heart and all the affliction of thy soul. . . . Because the Lord thy God is a merciful God." [120]

God asked Moses for the total gift and He received it. That is why Moses, in his turn, asks for it with a tireless insistence. He knows only too well that the communication of divine life is attached to it. "Thou shalt love the Lord thy God with thy whole heart, and with thy whole soul, and with thy whole strength." [121]

[117] Exod. 34:29–30, 33–35.   [118] Exod. 34:6, 7.
[119] Deut. 4:24.   [120] Deut. 4:29, 31.   [121] Deut. 6:5.

Yahweh Himself bears witness to Moses' fidelity: "He is most faithful in all My house." [122] His friendship with the Lord is his free and unimaginable reward. "I speak to him mouth to mouth and plainly; and not by riddles and figures doth he see the Lord." [123] "And the Lord spoke to Moses, face to face, as a man is wont to speak to his friend." [124]

Then one day God answered the deepest and boldest prayer which can possibly spring from the human heart: [125]

And Moses said: Shew me Thy glory. He answered: I will shew thee all good, and I will proclaim in the name of the Lord before thee. And I will have mercy on whom I will, and I will be merciful to whom it shall please Me. And again He said: Thou canst not see My face, for man shall not see Me and live. And again He said: Behold there is a place with Me, and thou shalt stand upon the rock. And when My glory shall pass, I will set thee in a hole of the rock, and protect thee with My right hand, till I pass. And I will take away My hand, and Thou shalt see My back parts; but My face thou canst not see. . . . And when the Lord was come down in a cloud, Moses stood with Him, calling upon the name of the Lord.[126]

"Moses was a hundred and twenty years old when he died; his eye was not dim, neither were his teeth removed." [127] Deuteronomy says of his end: "And Moses . . . died there . . . by the commandment of the Lord," [128] and this has been translated by John of St. Thomas: "He

[122] Num. 12:7.   [123] Num. 12:8.   [124] Exod. 33:11.

[125] Christ Himself will point out the value of the revelation made to Moses: "For if you did believe Moses, you would perhaps believe Me also; for he wrote of Me. But if you do not believe his writings, how will you believe My words?" (John 5:46, 47).

[126] Exod. 33:18–23; 34:5.   [127] Deut. 34:7.   [128] Deut. 34:5.

died of the Lord's embrace, because the command from
the divine mouth was like the kiss of God. A kiss which
so strongly marked Moses' soul that he drank and inhaled
in it the whole breath of life, and this, through the power
of spiritual love, tore him from his body." Moses' example
shows what divine friendship can accomplish in a faithful
and entirely dedicated soul. In it we can see the blinding
light which the divine word brings, a light to those who
believe, a darkness to those who deny.

Abraham is a model of tested faith; Moses, a soul who
has received the divine word and has shone with its light.
Elias illustrates another quality of faith symbolized by fire:
that of ardor.

Nothing better evokes the effects of faith working freely
in a soul, stripping it, and making of it a burning brand
which sets on fire everything it touches, than the consuming,
awakening and transforming action of fire. Elias is without
doubt the herald of this ardent, consuming faith, and fire
has remained attached to his memory. "And Elias the
prophet stood up, as a fire; and his word burnt like a
torch." [129] His word is like a fiery sword. "By the word
of the Lord he shut up the heaven; and he brought down
fire from heaven thrice. Thus was Elias magnified in his
wondrous works. And who can glory like to thee?" [130] A
unique aspect of his fiery vocation is that it knew no earthly
fulfilment. "Who wast taken up in a whirlwind of fire, in
a chariot of fiery horses." [131]

And as they went on, walking and talking together, behold a
fiery chariot and fiery horses parted them both asunder; and

[129] Ecclus. 48:1.　　[130] Ecclus. 48:3–4.　　[131] Ecclus. 48:9.

Elias went up by a whirlwind into heaven. And Eliseus saw him, and cried: My father, my father, the chariot of Israel and the driver thereof. And he saw him no more.[132]

A strange man, this Elias the Thesbite. "A hairy man with a girdle of leather about his loins." [133] A man led by the spirit of God. No one knows his hideout and an awful mystery surrounds him. "There is no nation or kingdom whither my lord hath not sent to seek thee. . . . And when I am gone from thee, the spirit of the Lord will carry thee into a place that I know not; and I shall go in and tell Achab, and he not finding thee, will kill me." [134] His strength and the influence of his word are such that Achab himself soon bows his head before the man of God: "And when Achab had heard these words, he rent his garments, and put haircloth upon his flesh and fasted." [135]

On Mount Carmel, Elias, with a glance and by his words, withers the people of Israel and the false prophets assembled there. "How long do you halt between two sides? If the Lord be God, follow Him; but if Baal, then follow him." [136] Before the man who holds out against them, and whom God answers by fire, the entire people fall face downward in the dust and cry out: "The Lord He is God. The Lord He is God." [137] The prophet's whole person, not only his words, bears evidence to the tremendous divine life whose witness and herald he is. "The Lord liveth, the God of Israel, in whose sight I stand." [138]

---

[132] IV Kings 2:11.   [133] IV Kings 1:8.
[134] III Kings 18:10, 12.   [135] III Kings 21:27.
[136] III Kings 18:21.   [137] III Kings 18:39.   [138] III Kings 17:1.

Elias indeed stands before God; he is always wholly in His presence; that is the secret of the burning zeal that devours him. "With zeal have I been zealous for the Lord God of hosts, for the children of Israel have forsaken Thy covenant. They have thrown down Thy altars; they have slain Thy prophets with the sword." [139] And yet St. James, writing of this great prophet whose prayer raised the dead and made fertile rain and consuming fire fall from heaven, tells us that he was only "a man passible like unto us." [140]

When persecuted, Elias admits his troubles, and God has to comfort him.

Then Elias was afraid, and rising up he went whithersoever he had a mind. . . . And he went forward, one day's journey into the desert. And when he was there, and sat under a juniper tree, he requested for his soul that he might die, and said: It is enough for me. Lord, take away my soul, for I am no better than my fathers.[141]

But divine strength is preparing and bringing an amazing awareness to life within him. Suddenly an angel touches him and says:

Arise and eat. He looked, and behold there was at his head a hearth cake, and a vessel of water. And he ate and drank; and he fell asleep again. And the angel of the Lord came again a second time, and touched him, and said to him: Arise and eat, for thou hast yet a great way to go. And he arose, and ate and drank, and walked in the strength of that food forty days and forty nights, unto the mount of God, Horeb. And when he was come hither, he abode in a cave.[142]

[139] III Kings 19:10.   [140] Jas. 5:17.   [141] III Kings 19:3–5.
[142] III Kings 19:5–9.

He complains that he is devoured by zeal, while men are trying to kill him. So the Lord leads him to the place already sanctified by the divine apparition, and there the prophet in his turn receives an indescribable visit from God, whose living presence burns his soul.

Yahweh said: Go forth, and stand upon the Mount before the Lord. And behold the Lord passeth. And a great and strong wind before the Lord overthrowing the mountains, and breaking the rocks in pieces; the Lord is not in the wind. And after the wind, an earthquake; the Lord is not in the earthquake. And after the earthquake a fire; the Lord is not in the fire. And after the fire the whistling of a gentle air. And when Elias heard it, he covered his face with his mantle, and coming forth stood in the entering in of the cave.[143]

This fierce and strong man, eaten up with zeal, is a mystic. He knows how to silence his faculties so that he can listen to God speaking to him in "the whistling of a gentle air." In order to hear Him better, he "covered his face with his mantle," that is to say, he creates night within himself, and, abandoning himself, goes in search of the divine presence. "Coming forth, he stood in the entering in of the cave." [144]

[143] III Kings 19:11–13.

[144] There is a relationship between this passage from the Book of Kings and St. John of the Cross' poem, of which he himself said that it contained all the doctrine which he wished to teach in *The Ascent of Mount Carmel:* "Upon a gloomy night,

> With all my cares to loving ardors flushed,
> (O venture of delight!)
> With nobody in sight
> I went abroad when all my house was hushed."

(*Poems of St. John of the Cross,* translated by Roy Campbell.)

Elias does not keep the divine life, with which he is filled, for himself alone. "And Elias departing from thence, found Eliseus. . . . And when Elias came up to him, he cast his mantle upon him." [145] Others come to join him and, on Mount Carmel, listen to the lessons taught by the prophet. It is probable that Elias often told them that which tradition, following the Sacred Scriptures, still tells those of her sons who, like Elias, are dedicated to the great vocation of solitary contemplation.

And the word of the Lord came to him, saying: Get thee hence, and go toward the east, and hide thyself by the torrent of Carith, which is over against Jordan. And there thou shalt drink of the torrent, and I have commanded the ravens to feed thee there. So he went, and did according to the word of the Lord. And going, he dwelt by the torrent Carith, which is over against the Jordan. And the ravens brought him bread and flesh in the morning and bread and flesh in the evening, and he drank of the torrent.[146]

Hidden in the desert, wrapped up and almost lost in the ocean of divine presence, Elias was refreshed by that torrent whose praises the psalmist will sing: "Thou shalt make them drink of the torrent of Thy pleasure; for with Thee is the fountain of life." [147]

The love with which Elias' soul burned was so ardent that it flames in our sight today like a divine fire.[148] Of

[145] III Kings 19:19.   [146] III Kings 17:2–6.   [147] Ps. 35:9, 10.

[148] Elias' memory was very much alive in the days of the apostles, and was tied up with the messianic promises of Malachias (3:23), which see in him the prophetic figure of Christ. The priests and the scribes will question John the Baptist about him (John 1) and on Calvary, misunderstanding Christ's cry, "Eli, Eli," will think

his work, only this fire remains, and still bears witness to the depth of God's communication with the soul whose faith is stripped and bare. We admire in Elias the harsh outbursts of his jealous faith and the infinitely sweet love found in his faith. He encourages us to climb like he did, with faith united to love, up the mountain of which Psalm 67 speaks: "A mountain in which God is well pleased to dwell." [149]

STAGES IN THE DEVELOPMENT OF FAITH

The God of the people of Israel chose our fathers and exalted the people when they were sojourners in the land of Egypt.[150]

Established by the divine Word on an unshakeable foundation, formed by signs and symbols, the faith was given to Israel from the beginning. It forms the basis for the covenant. It is Abraham's answer to the friendship which God offers him.[151] We see clearly in the Bible that the patriarch became the father of Israel because he was Israel's father in the faith. "He shall become a great and mighty nation, and in him all the nations of the earth shall be

---

that he is calling Elias (Mark 15:34, 36). He appears by Moses' side in the vision on Mount Thabor (Luke 9:30). Christ will recall his work (Luke 4:25–27) and will say of John the Baptist that "He is Elias that is to come" (Matt. 11:14).

[149] Ps. 67:17.   [150] Acts 13:17.

[151] "Therefore is it of faith, that according to grace the promise might be firm to all the seed; not only to that which is of the law, but to that also which is of the faith of Abraham" (Rom. 4:16). "In the promise also of God he staggered not by distrust, but was strengthened in faith, giving glory to God, most fully knowing that whatsoever he has promised, he is able also to perform" (Rom. 4:21).

blessed. For I know that he will command his children, and his household after him to keep the way of the Lord." [152] All the structure of the future rests on him. He carries within himself the faith of Israel and offers a pattern of faith that will never be surpassed.

But the people, whose father in flesh and in faith he was, were far from possessing it to the same extent. In actuality, the dawning of faith in Abraham's tribe, and then in the people of Israel, came about slowly and progressively, under the influence of the spiritual leaders, the patriarchs. Just as Israel, guided by her leaders, made her way laboriously toward the Promised Land, so did she make her way slowly in the faith. There are several stages in this journey, which is an image of ours. There is also a lesson in it, which is enlightening to us and a precious meditation for our spiritual life.

Divine revelation was necessary to make Abraham decide to leave his country, his family and his father's house. He alone receives this revelation. The men who accompany him from Ur into Palestine follow him only because of the tribal laws, and certainly too because his influence and personal value had earned their absolute confidence. For how, indeed, could the members of a poor nomadic tribe have acquired overnight any faith in a God previously unknown to them? Until the day when divine grace would impart this faith to their souls, they believed first of all in their leader, submitting unconditionally to his authority and trusting him to look after their spiritual and material welfare. They applied to him the words which Ruth later was to say to Noemi: "Whithersoever thou shalt go, I will go;

152 Gen. 18:18, 19.

and where thou shalt dwell, I also will dwell. Thy people shall be my people, and thy God my God." [153] And thus it came about that under Abraham's leadership the tribe reached Palestine and adopted the God who became known by the names of their leaders: "God of Abraham, of Isaac and of Jacob."

As Israel's faith was still in its infancy, the patriarchs undertook the religious education of the tribe, while God strengthened the faith by the unexcelled method of sending adversity. First Abraham, and then the whole nation experienced this. Soon the people were to endure the hard slavery of Egypt. By this trial the people were bound more closely together and their faith was developed and preserved. All this suffering taught the people to turn to Yahweh their God and to invoke Him in their affliction.

The children of Israel groaning, cried out because of the works; and their cry went up unto God from the works. And He heard their groaning and remembered the covenant which He made with Abraham, Isaac and Jacob. And the Lord looked upon the children of Israel, and He knew them. [154]

After the sojourn in Egypt, Israel's religious formation had progressed so far that God did not hesitate to let the people face the difficulties of life in the desert. So arduous and irksome was this life, moreover, that God had to lend constant support to their weak faith by multiplying signs and wonders. The true beginning or "baptism" of this faith as confirmed by miracles was the crossing of the Red Sea.

In its first exodus—from Ur to Palestine—the tribe of

[153] Ruth 1:16.   [154] Exod. 2:23–25.

Israel had followed a leader: Abraham. In the second exodus—longer and more painful than the first—the people followed another leader who manifested God's power and constant protection: Moses. The latter's role was vastly different from the former's. Abraham was alone in receiving the grace of faith. The few who followed him received it little by little as they shared his life. Moses, on the other hand, was leader of a nation which already believed, but which he had to lead toward a twofold Promised Land: the earthly land of Chanaan and, far more difficult of attainment, the spiritual realm of personal and living faith. To reach it, the people had to acknowledge a human leader and accept him as the mediator of their total submission to God. Thus, Moses' chief function was to teach this multitude that he was ruling and guiding through the desert that their real leader and guide was not himself, Moses, but was actually God. To do this, he strove little by little to separate the people from their human leader and to strengthen their attachment to God, even though their faith was still feeble. He wore himself out in this hard and thankless task.

Ask of the days of old, that have been before thy time from the day that God created man upon the earth, from one end of heaven to the other end thereof, if ever there was done the like thing, or it hath been known at any time that a people should hear the voice of God speaking out of the midst of fire, as thou hast heard, and lived; if God ever did so as to go and take to Himself a nation out of the midst of nations by temptations, signs and wonders, by fight and a strong hand and stretched-out arm, and horrible visions according to all the things that the Lord your God did for you in Egypt, before thy eyes. That thou mightest know that the Lord He is God, and there is no other besides Him. From heaven He made thee to hear His voice, that He might teach thee. And upon earth He showed thee His exceeding great fire, and thou didst hear His words out of the midst of the fire. Because He loved thy fathers, and chose their seed after them. And He brought thee out of Egypt, going before thee with His great power, to destroy at thy coming very great nations, and stronger than thou art, and to bring thee in, and give thee their land for a possession, as thou seest at this present day. Know therefore this day, and think in thy heart that the Lord he is God in heaven above, and in the earth beneath, and there is no other.[155]

Moses constantly reminded the people that God alone had been their guide. By effacing himself and turning the people toward God, he brought about essential progress in Israel's faith. His unselfish devotion and heroic perseverance in his hard task constitute the true greatness of this giant of the faith. "Not to us, O Lord, not to us; but to Thy name give glory." [156]

If Moses enabled the people to advance along the pathway of faith, it was because he himself walked that path first of all and knew from personal experience its difficulties, obscurities and harsh demands. For God Himself took charge of Moses' education and personally shaped his soul to fit it for the role of mediator. He demanded of Moses constant intensification of effort, total submission to divine commands, and complete adaptability. His intellect was illuminated to enable him to seize and clarify the message

[155] Deut. 4:32–39.

[156] Ps. 113:9. Several times Moses was rejected by the people and his life endangered by rebellion. The deacon Stephen said of him: "And he thought that his brethren understood that God by his hand would save them; but they understood it not" (Acts 7:25).

that he was commissioned to proclaim. God's purpose in requiring that he lead the people through the desert was that Israel might undergo the purification that would prepare for the revelation of the Law. "Go to the people, and sanctify them today, and tomorrow, and let them wash their garments. And let them be ready against the third day; for on the third day the Lord will come down in the sight of all the people upon Mount Sinai." [157]

Even then, in spite of this preparation, only Moses was permitted to approach God and receive His commandments. "And the Lord came down upon Mount Sinai, in the very top of the Mount, and He called Moses unto the top thereof." [158] The people are not capable of receiving the divine message, but need a mediator to transmit it and to reveal its inner meaning.[159] Moses was a figure of Jesus Christ and a figure of the Church. "The people . . . stood afar off, saying to Moses: Speak thou to us, and we will hear; let not the Lord speak to us, lest we die." [160]

However eager Moses was to glorify God, he nonetheless kept reminding Israel of the special mission assigned to him and the authority God conferred upon him.

Keep the commandments of the Lord your God which I command you. . . . The Lord spoke to me, saying: Call together the people unto Me, that they may hear My words, and may learn to fear Me all the time that they live on the earth, and may teach their children. . . . And He commanded me that I should teach you the ceremonies and judgments which you shall do in the land that you shall possess.[161]

[157] Exod. 19:10–11.   [158] Exod. 19:20.
[159] "He that heareth you, heareth Me" (Luke 10:16).
[160] Exod. 20:19.   [161] Deut. 4:2, 10, 14.

The Law given on Sinai was to become the beginning of a new and supremely important stage in the development of faith. While divine transcendence and goodness, as the proper object of all real faith, never ceased being within the reach of alert minds and sensitive hearts, yet on the whole and in spite of so many miracles the faith of the children of Israel never rose above the level of selfish and materialistic attachment.[162] The miracle of the manna, the bread which rained down upon them from heaven, provided evidence of their selfish greed, as was seen later in Christ's multiplication of the loaves.

And when the children of Israel saw it, they said one to another: Manhu! which signifieth: What is this! for they knew not what it was. And Moses said to them: This is the bread which the Lord hath given you to eat. . . . Let every one gather of it as much as is enough to eat: . . . Let no man leave thereof till the morning. And they hearkened not to him, but some of them left until the morning, and it began to be full of worms, and it putrified.[163]

The people needed the knowledge and experience of a new and wholly spiritual reality before their faith could become spiritual and living. In God's plan the Law was the instrument of this process. Generally the Law is considered only in its external aspect, its physical requirements, even the formalism, which, indeed often stemmed from it. There is, on the other hand, a tendency to label it as *the*

[162] The New Testament Israelites showed the same limitations as their Old Testament ancestors. Witness the passage in St. John's Gospel: "Amen, amen I say to you, you seek Me, not because you have seen miracles, but because you did eat of the loaves, and were filled" (John 6:26).

[163] Exod. 16:15–20.

law of fear, and to view it as merely a very imperfect preparation for *the law of love* which, indeed, was destined to supersede it. All too frequent is the failure to consider its positive side, which St. Paul stressed so much, and particularly its role as pedagogue; truly an essential role, especially in its relation to faith. For it is noteworthy that from the time that God revealed the Law to Moses, miracles became rarer and less spectacular. A new regime was being established.

Of course, the Ark containing the tablets of the Law testified that God still dwelt with His people, accompanied them on their journey, continued to look after them with love and omnipotent power. But with the promulgation of the Law, the true presence of God was no longer to be sought in the Ark or in the accompanying miracles but rather within men's hearts. Thenceforth that was the dwelling-place He chose and His presence was continual, because it was interior and totally spiritual.[164] The Law made possible this presence by faith. By the Law Israel knew God's will and learned how to follow it. The Law regulated every minute detail of Israel's moral and social life, in public and in private. Thus the Law required constant practice of obedience and of faith.

Previously faith required mainly an external and collective attitude or a specific response to a particular temporary command of God. But once the Law was given, faith required a total self-commitment of each Israelite, for it touched and ruled each and every one of them from within. It formed a tightly woven pattern in which every

[164] St. Paul stresses Moses' teaching on this point, especially in Romans, chaps. 7 and 9.

element of life was fitted and fixed, so that everything became an occasion for obedience and for faith.[165]

Once the Law was given, the people were no longer asked for individual "acts of faith" on particular occasions but for total acceptance, a habitual state of faith, a life of faith. For those who took part in the Exodus, the Law was inextricably associated with the miracles that occurred when it was promulgated. But in succeeding generations the Law tended to be detached from these material wonders. The people then had to believe in signs that they themselves had not seen and which themselves then became objects of faith. The pre-eminence of the word and of tradition thus became reinforced—faith from hearing. Thus souls entered upon the royal path of true faith.

Israel's history proves that such progress was neither easy nor rapid. Even the first steps in this direction had barely been taken by the end of the Exodus; the whole forty years of purification thus seeming an almost complete failure. Only a tiny minority of the people adhered spontaneously and remained faithful to the divine will as expressed in the Law, while the vast multitude were rebellious. Even Moses weakened at least once and was, therefore, forbidden entry to the Promised Land, which in fact was finally reached by only two of the original travelers: Caleb and Josue.[166]

With Josue begins a new and by no means unimportant stage in the history of faith: God proves Himself *faithful*. The first part of the promise made to Abraham was ful-

[165] In this sense St. Paul could say: "I do not know sin, but by the Law" (Rom. 7:7).

[166] Cf. Num. 32:12.

filled. The truth of God's word was demonstrated by the conquest of the Promised Land as well as by the marvels of the Exodus. "Not so much as one word, which He had promised to perform unto them, was made void, but all came to pass." [167] This decisive proof as well as Josue's guidance induced the people spontaneously to start out on their journey along the pathway of faith. First, on the threshold of the Promised Land, they made a threefold pledge of obedience to their leader: "All that thou hast commanded us we will do; and whithersoever thou shalt send us, we will go. As we obeyed Moses in all things, so will we obey thee also." [168]

Then, at Sichem, in the midst of the conquest, the Law was formally received by the people:

Then Josue built an altar to the Lord the God of Israel in Mount Hebal, as Moses the servant of the Lord had commanded the children of Israel. . . . And he wrote upon stones the Deuteronomy of the Law of Moses, which he had ordered before the children of Israel. And all the people, and the ancients, and the princes and judges stood on both sides of the Ark. . . . He read all the words. . . . He left out nothing of those things which Moses had commanded, but he repeated all before all the people of Israel, with the women and children and strangers that dwelt among them.[169]

There at Sichem also the people solemnly vowed to be true to the renewed covenant: "And the people said to Josue: . . . We will serve the Lord. And Josue said to the people: You are witnesses, that you yourselves have chosen you the Lord, to serve Him. And they answered: We

[167] Jos. 21:43.   [168] Jos. 1:16–17.   [169] Jos. 8:30–35.

are witnesses." [170] But Josue's next words show that at that time only the first commandment implied an absolute obligation and a serious duty. "Now therefore, said he, put away strange gods from among you, and incline your hearts to the Lord the God of Israel. And the people said to Josue: We will serve the Lord our God, and we will be obedient to His commandments." [171]

"Thou shalt not have strange gods in My sight." [172] This was asserted in the Decalogue, and all that was added to faith in the course of subsequent events aimed to make known the omnipotent God, the God of Israel. This was the gist of the first commandment. Since God proved Himself by protecting His people and granting them victory over their enemies, He could more easily obtain from them the act of faith which consisted in ridding themselves of false gods. This principle of faith was clearly perceived and assimilated by the people and it formed a new pattern of religious experience; henceforth the Israelites had the duty to act according to their belief. Their spiritual progress and their corresponding sense of law would depend upon an increasing awareness of the content of faith.

By special divine choice, the Jews received the revelation of a God who was *their own* God—"God of Abraham, of Isaac and of Jacob"—but was also, as events and miracles proved, an omnipotent God, the one and only God. This was the major fact of faith which for centuries was to regulate the people's conduct and even God's sanctions. At the time of the judges there was not much concern over the prescriptions of the Law, even though they had been given to the people at Sichem. In those troubled days of intermi-

[170] Jos. 24:21–22.   [171] Jos. 24:23–24.   [172] Deut. 5:7.

nable clan struggles, each man strove to assure his hold on the land of his inheritance. At the same time the principle of faith in God was assimilated into the life of the people. In all its adventures the infant nation recalled Yahweh's mighty acts of intervention, the events of such a short time ago. This roused the fighters to battle courageously. Religious fervor overturned the altar of Baal and cut down the grove around the altar. At that time in Israel the term *sin* did not refer to any particular lack of justice, purity or brotherly love, but was essentially the sin against faith, sin against the first commandment, that is, idolatry.

God punished only idolatry and seemed hardly to notice how immoral were the crude customs of the people and of the judges themselves.

And an angel of the Lord went up from Galgal to the place of weepers, and said: I made you go out of Egypt, and have brought you into the land for which I swore to your father; and I promised that I would not make void My covenant with you forever, on condition that you should not make a league with the inhabitants of this land, but should throw down their altars.[173]

Thus, the only reproach in those days was idolatry.

And the Lord raised up judges, to deliver them from the hands of those that oppressed them; but they would not hearken to them. . . . And when the Lord raised them up judges, in their days He was moved to mercy. . . . But after the judge was dead, they returned, and did much worse things than their fathers had done, following strange gods, serving and adoring them. . . . And the wrath of the Lord was kindled against Israel.[174]

[173] Judg. 2:1–2.   [174] Judg. 2:16–20.

The chronicles give spirited descriptions of the judges' exploits, which were often somewhat unedifying but in any case displayed the heroes' fearless enthusiasm in the service of Israel's God. Oral tradition was implanted, and with it, the *credo* of Israel: the first commandment of the Law was to fight against strange gods. "In those days there was no king in Israel; but everyone did that which seemed right to himself." [175]

"That which seemed right to himself" undoubtedly meant "that which was to his own interest," for at that time in Israel the only religious duty was faith in the God of Abraham, of Isaac and of Jacob. But deep aspirations were stirring in the multitude; material aspirations, of course, but they were to fit into God's plan. The isolated tribes felt the need to come together under a leader who would assure them greater strength and success in both conquest and defense.

And all the men of Israel said to Gedeon: Rule thou over us, and thy son, and thy son's son, because thou hast delivered us from the hand of Madian. And he said to them: I will not rule over you, neither shall my son rule over you, but the Lord shall rule over you.[176]

It was thought that the Jews, as God's people, should not seek power and order as provided by a human leader. They had consented to God's rule over them and should learn to follow only His purposes.[177] At that point, with the appearance of Samuel, prophecy began to play the

[175] Judg. 21:24.   [176] Judg. 8:22–23.

[177] Israel always claimed to be a free people with no master but Yahweh. The declaration of the highpriests before Pilate, "We have no king but Caesar" (John 19:15), constituted the ultimate apostasy.

predominant role which it was to retain for so long. For
a century the theophanies had ceased and God's voice had
not been heard. "The child Samuel ministered to the Lord
before Heli, and the word of the Lord was precious in
those days, there was no manifest vision." [178] The time was
at hand when the Ark which guided the people in battle
would fall into the hands of the Philistines,[179] an event
which would demand that faith become more deeply rooted,
for God withdrew the material presence of the Ark and
the marvels accompanying it and required instead faith in
His word as received and communicated by those inspired
men, the prophets. Henceforth, to heed them was to be
faithful to Yahweh. The spiritual development of the Jews
depended on their faith in the word of God's chosen servants.

Thus, the rise of prophecy represented a great step forward in the development of faith. What an evolution and
what progress! No longer did it suffice to obey a leader
blindly. The leader himself was likewise bound to obey men
charged with a purely spiritual mission: to transmit God's
orders. By their exhortations these fiery messengers of the
Spirit opposed all improper tendencies and even confounded
purely human argument. God's Spirit resting upon the
prophets and expressed by them became the guide and the
light of Israelites. Thus, their faith entered a safe path of
darkness for the senses, but light for the heart. "And I have
spoken by the prophets, and I have multiplied visions, and
I have used similitudes by the ministry of the prophets." [180]

In its very beginning the prophetic vocation encountered
a double defeat in the person of Samuel, who was a judge

[178] I Kings 3:1.   [179] Cf. I Kings 4.   [180] Osee 12:10.

and a priest as well as a prophet. The monarchy which he wished to prevent was nonetheless established. The first king, by refusing to obey the prophet's orders, led Israel to disaster. But, as happened so often in history, God brought good from evil. The monarchy served God's plan and Saul's example was a lesson for the future. But what was more important was the fact that the monarchy was destined to become an essential element in Israel's progress. "Fear not, you have done all this evil; but yet depart not from following the Lord . . . and the Lord will not forsake His people for His great name's sake." [181] With the establishment of the monarchy, Israel's history advanced toward the phase predicted in God's second promise to Abraham: "I have made thee a father of many nations." [182]

Faith acquired a new dimension as, almost imperceptibly, it turned toward the future to envisage its providential mission, centered upon belief in the Messiah. On the other hand, these more universal views would lead Jewish monotheism to the knowledge that "the God of our fathers" is also the God of the whole earth and belongs to all men. Finally, the deepening knowledge of the faith made possible a stronger practice of its tenets, more faithful observance and better understanding of the Law. The prophets promoted this improvement: "I will teach you the good and right way," said Samuel.[183]

Thenceforth the observance of the first commandment alone no longer sufficed to justify Israel in God's eyes. Though the people as yet ignored the fact that the monarchy was a prefiguration of the eternal kingdom, yet it was the first fraternal community to be formed with religion as its

[181] I Kings 12:20, 22.   [182] Gen. 17:5.   [183] I Kings 12:23.

basis and its purpose. For these directions were laid down for the king:

After he is raised to the throne of his kingdom, he shall copy out to himself the Deuteronomy of this law in a volume. . . . And he shall have it with him, and shall read it all the days of his life, that he may learn to fear the lord his God, and keep His words and ceremonies, that are commanded in the Law. And that his heart be not lifted up with pride over his brethren, nor decline to the right or to the left.[184]

The field of action for effective love increased and developed as the tribes united to form a single nation. A Benjaminite's neighbor was no longer only his brother in the tribe of Benjamin, but also the man of Juda or of Israel. The people enlarged the narrow tribal limits to include the whole nation. But they would have understood little of this ideal, indeed they would barely have been conscious of it, had not God providentially given them an example and a model in David, truly a living commentary on the living faith which God wished His people to have. It seems that merely by scrutinizing the human and deeply religious qualities of their king, the people understood the increased demands of faith and the progress achieved by it. This was a major event in the history of Israel, the climax of the long series of incidents which, since the time of Abraham, had been guiding the people toward their ultimate destiny.

The people loved David; he captivated their attention and became a living book. Like Abraham and Moses, like Elias who was to come soon, David too can be called a man of faith—faith embedded in the totality of everyday life, mighty heroic faith, but also simple, trusting faith, the

[184] Deut. 17:18–20.

faith that is a child's spontaneous impulse. In fact, David's whole self consists of faith and trust in a God whom he loves and of whose love for him he is assured. Even as a child, he ventured forth to the encounter with Goliath, possessing no treasure but faith. In adolescence he formed a strong bond of affection for Jonathan. Zealous faith was the leaven of the friendship between these two deeply religious souls, making it the model of earthly friendships. A supernatural spirit permeates the scene in the forest where the king's son meets the persecuted David: "And Jonathan . . . strengthened his hands in God; and he said to him: Fear not, for the hand of my father Saul shall not find thee, and thou shalt reign over Israel, and I shall be next to thee. . . . And the two made a covenant before the Lord." [185]

When persecuted by Saul, David's only support was his faith. This alone enabled him to see "the anointed of the Lord" in the man pursuing him and to respect the life of the king, who was at his mercy.[186] Only faith prevented his taking vengeance and made him drop his weapon when he heard Abigail speak in the name of God. "And blessed be thou, who hast kept me today from coming to blood, and revenging me with my own hand." [187]

These words give a first glimpse of David's humility; he heeds even the simplest woman when she speaks in the name of Yahweh. Humility, which in God's great servants is the surest sign of living faith, was deeply rooted in David's soul and from the very beginning it was apparent to Yahweh ("For man seeth those things that appear, but the

[185] I Kings 23:17–18.   [186] Cf. I Kings 24:8.
[187] I Kings 25:33.

Lord beholdeth the heart" [188]) in the shepherd who "was
ruddy and beautiful to behold, and of a comely face." [189]
Later his humility would appear on many occasions: in his
dealings with Samuel, in his search for refuge at Najoth in
Ramatha, in his encounter with the prophet Gad ("Till I
know what God will do for me" [190]). He acted only in
obedience to others, trusting God to defend him, even when
his persecutor was delivered into his hands. "And David
said: As the Lord liveth, unless the Lord shall strike him,
or his day shall come to die, or he shall go down to battle
and perish; the Lord be merciful unto me, that I extend
not my hand upon the Lord's anointed." [191] This intense
and modest faith seems to have reached its climax in the
outburst of joy with which he welcomed the holy Ark in
Jerusalem. "And David danced with all his might before
the Lord." [192] That was the supreme moment of spiritual
consolation for him and the reward of that faith which had
been proved by constant and heroic obedience to the direction of the Spirit. His joy surpassed all desire; nor was he
spared the taste of humiliation, for his proud wife Michol
scorned him for dancing half-naked before the people. David
thereupon exclaimed most admirably: "I will both play and
make myself meaner than I have done; and I will be little
in my own eyes; and with the handmaids of whom thou
speakest, I shall appear more glorious." [193] His meaning
was: "God is all; I am nothing."

Everyone knows how terribly David's soul was stained
by sin, but it remained great even in the midst of sin. In
fact, the sin became a means of greater nobility. Far from

[188] I Kings 16:7.   [189] I Kings 16:12.   [190] I Kings 22:3.
[191] I Kings 26:10–11.   [192] II Kings 6:14.   [193] II Kings 6:22.

declining, David's faith increased and sprang forth more ardently from the depths of his misery, yearning toward the God of mercy with a great impulse of limitless trust. We can be grateful that when David adverted to his double crime, spurred by Nathan's intervention, his faith and trust brought forth the humble and admirable lament of the *Miserere:*

> Have mercy on me, O God, according to Thy great mercy. And according to the multitude of Thy tender mercies blot out my iniquity. . . . To Thee only have I sinned, and have done evil before Thee. . . . Thou shalt sprinkle me with hyssop, and I shall be cleansed; Thou shalt wash me, and I shall be made whiter than snow. . . . Create a clean heart in me, O God; and renew a right spirit within my bowels.[194]

So immense was David's faith that even in the depths of his degradation he ventured to ask and hope for a child's heart, a heart made purer through its humility and its surrender to divine mercy.[195] When he contravened God's will by ordering a census of the people without consulting the prophet, God allowed him a choice among various punishments. David answered "I have sinned very much in what I have done. . . . I am in a great strait; but it is better that I fall into the hands of the Lord (for His mercies are many) than into the hands of men." [196]

His heart was so human that it experienced all the weaknesses of a passionate character, but it was so deeply rooted

---

[194] Ps. 50, *passim.*

[195] St. Paul expressed admiration of David's faith: "As David also termeth the blessedness of a man, to whom God reputeth justice without works" (Rom. 4:6).

[196] II Kings 24:10, 14.

in faith that it was touched by grace and almost overwhelmed by the spiritual delights of which a hint is given in a song of thanksgiving. "Who am I, O Lord God, and what is my house, that Thou hast brought me thus far?" [197] He had wished to build a stone temple to his God, but in truth it was God who built a living home for David and blessed his throne forever.

But yet this hath seemed little in Thy sight, O Lord God, unless Thou didst also speak of the house of Thy servant for a long time to come; for this is the law of Adam, O Lord God. And what can David say more unto Thee? For Thou knowest Thy servant, O Lord God; for Thy word's sake, and according to Thy own heart Thou hast done all these great things, so that Thou wouldst make it known to Thy servant. Therefore Thou art magnified, O Lord God, because there is none like to Thee.[198]

This mysterious prediction formed the foundation of all future messianic hope, the expectation of the "Son of David." [199] At first this mysterious illumination delighted the great king's heart, but afterward it became a source of intense suffering. So it was of old with the promises made to Abraham. David's days of gratified faith were followed by days of crucified faith. While David was not asked to sacrifice the son on whom depended the promise, he had to experience still greater suffering than that of the patriarch. He saw the child born of his sin die before his eyes. His two eldest sons also died: the sons who held his hopes for a

[197] II Kings 7:18.   [198] II Kings 7:19–22.

[199] When St. Peter spoke to the Jews, he referred to David's prophecies concerning Christ, the Messiah predicted by Scripture (cf. Acts, chap. 2).

lineage that he now knew to be destined for greatness. Absalom had his brother Amnon assassinated, then tried to usurp the throne, betrayed and persecuted his father, treating him with the most outrageous abuse.[200] There is truly a "passion" of David, a passion in which the great king showed his admirable faith. We may even venture to say that the mighty monarch seems greatest in the troubled episodes of his reign, because then appears his humility— humility being the only virtue that proves that a soul has reached the summit where abjection is even desired and cherished.[201]

If we consider David, we can well understand his immense influence on the development of faith in Israel—an influence that was increased by the psalms which he composed and bequeathed to his people. While he in many ways displayed every human weakness, he was worthy of typifying the supreme Monarch, the King who would some day come to realize the universal expectations. An ever-growing tendency in Israel was to see him as the figure of the King-Messiah, the all-powerful and entirely good king. "I as yet am tender, though anointed king." [202] David had said this of himself and had proved it by his actions. And so, by contact with him or by heart-felt meditation on the legendary figure that the king soon became, Israel deepened the sense of God. Already the Jews were aware of God's greatness, His omnipotence and His dynamic influence. Thanks to David, they acquired or developed their knowledge of divine goodness and mercy which the king extolled because

[200] II Kings 13:28; 18:14.　　　[201] Cf. II Kings 6:22; 16:12.
[202] II Kings 3:39.

of his own experience of these attributes. As often as possible, David set an example of meekness, to the point of receiving these words of praise which, in the mouth of Sarvia's son, Joab, were meant as a reproach: "Thou lovest them that hate thee, and thou hatest them that love thee." [203] How often also did he strive to bring unity to his battling flock, to settle peacefully their conflicts and rivalries. "And he inclined the heart of all the men of Juda, as it were of one man; and they sent to the king, saying: Return thou, and all thy servants." [204]

But his special merit was to reveal in the law of Moses, as yet virtually unknown, the ultimate requirements by pardoning insults and returning good for evil. Saul's grandson, Miphiboseth, who had betrayed David, came to beg his pardon in a long speech, but the king answered simply: "Why speakest thou any more? What I have said is determined; thou and Siba divide the possessions." [205]

David's son had persecuted, betrayed and attacked him, but the king forgot the cruel mistreatment and mourned bitterly when Absalom died. "And the victory that day was turned into mourning unto all the people." [206]

When divine punishment struck the city after the forbidden census had been taken, David offered himself in the place of his people in order that they might be spared. This took place on the thrashing-floor of Areuna, where soon the Temple would be built and where later the Messiah would stand. "And David said to the Lord, when he saw the angel striking the people: It is I; I am he that have

[203] II Kings 19:6.   [204] II Kings 19:13.   [205] II Kings 19:29.
[206] II Kings 19:2.

sinned; I have done wickedly; these that are the sheep, what have they done? Let Thy hand, I beseech Thee, be turned against me, and against my father's house." [207]

David lived his "passion" to make expiation for his sins. "Let him alone that he may curse as the Lord hath bidden him. Perhaps the Lord may look upon my affliction, and the Lord may render me good for the cursing of this day." [208] Without realizing it, David was thus secretly preparing the minds of those who considered suffering a scandal, preparing them to understand the coming Redemption. This enlightenment was, of course, a slow process, but the fact remains that after David, faith had an answer available, or at least the beginning of an answer, to certain questions. Moreover, the requirements of the Law could no longer be eluded. Soon prophecy, having attained its full development, was to utter bitter and fully justified reproaches against Israel. Formerly the people had to be cared for and nourished in the faith like children. David helped them to develop a more robust faith, so that it could venture forth vigorously. He brought faith to dwell in the depths of men's souls, enabling it to acquire the qualities of knowledge and love in a faithful union that is fitting to a child of God living in the Father's kingdom. The life of faith was truly formed and God could henceforth require it of His people.

The Law had hardly been formulated on Sinai and at Sichem when it underwent, as we have seen, a kind of eclipse, so that only its first article was maintained: "Thou shalt not have strange gods before Me." But after the time of David the whole Law appeared as the foundation of the

[207] II Kings 24:17.   [208] II Kings 16:11–12.

holy city, since Jerusalem was not only the seat of royal power but also, as Deuteronomy had commanded, the one and only place for true worship, the place of rest and inheritance. "In the place which the Lord your God shall choose, that His name may be therein. Thither shall you bring all the things that I command you." [209]

At last had arrived the time foreseen by Moses and predicted to the people. "You shall not do there the things we do here this day, every man that which seemeth good to himself. For until this present time you are not come to rest, and to the possession, which the Lord your God shall give you." [210] Once the Jordan was crossed, the Promised Land conquered, and the kingdom of God established, the Israelites could no longer do merely what seemed good to each individual, for at last they had received the sacred inheritance. Henceforth the first commandment—to set aside strange gods—could no longer suffice. Now the people had to begin to experience God, to deepen their life of faith and charity, to offer true worship, to practice the whole Law. The Law found its proper framework in the fixed code of religious duty. It is highly significant that Solomon, in the magnificent prayer for the dedication of the Temple, which somehow initiates this new state of things, proclaims the double accession of worship according to the whole Law, and of the Law according to true worship:

[209] Deut. 12:11.

[210] Deut. 12:8–9. The same meaning is found in Deut. 4:14: "And he commanded me at that time that I should teach you the ceremonies and judgments which you shall do in the land that you shall possess."

O Lord my God . . . open Thy eyes upon this house day and night, . . . that Thou wouldst hear the prayer which Thy servant prayeth in it; hearken then to the prayers of Thy servant and of Thy people Israel. Whosoever shall pray in this place, hear Thou from Thy dwelling place, that is from heaven, and show mercy.

If any man sin against his neighbour, and come to swear against him, and bind himself with a curse before the altar in this house, then hear Thou from heaven, and do justice to Thy servants, so as to requite the wicked by making his wickedness fall upon his own head, and to revenge the just, rewarding him according to his justice.

If Thy people Israel be overcome by their enemies (for they will sin against Thee), and being converted shall do penance, and call upon Thy name, and pray to Thee in this place, then hear Thou from heaven, and forgive the sin of Thy people Israel, and bring them back into the land which Thou gavest to them and their fathers.

If the heavens be shut up, and there fall no rain by reason of the sins of the people, and they shall pray to Thee in this place, and confess to Thy name, and be converted from their sins, when Thou dost afflict them, then hear Thou from heaven, O Lord, and forgive the sins of Thy servants and of Thy people Israel, and teach them the good way, in which they may walk; and give rain to Thy land which Thou hast given to Thy people to possess.

If a famine arise in the land, or a pestilence or blasting, or mildew, or locusts, or caterpillars, or if their enemies waste the country, and besiege the cities, whatsoever scourge or infirmity shall be upon them; then if any of Thy people Israel, knowing his own scourge and infirmity shall pray, and shall spread forth his hands in this house, hear Thou from heaven, from Thy high dwelling place, and forgive, and render to every

one according to his ways, which Thou knowest him to have
in his heart (for Thou only knowest the hearts of the children
of men), that they may fear Thee, and walk in Thy ways all
the days that they live upon the face of the land, which Thou
hast given to our fathers.

If the stranger also, who is not of Thy people Israel, come
from a far country, for the sake of Thy great name, and Thy
strong hand, and Thy stretched-out arm, and adore in this
place; hear Thou from heaven Thy firm dwelling-place, and
do all that which that stranger shall call upon Thee for; that all
the people of the earth may know Thy name, and may fear
Thee, as Thy people Israel, and may know, that Thy name
is invoked upon this house, which I have built.

If Thy people go out to war against their enemies, by the
way that Thou shalt send them, and adore Thee toward the
way of this city which Thou hast chosen, and the house which
I have built to Thy name; then hear Thou from heaven their
prayers, and their supplications, and revenge them.

And if they sin against Thee (for there is no man that sin-
neth not) and Thou be angry with them and deliver them up
to their enemies, and they lead them away captive to a land,
either afar off or near at hand, and if they be converted in
their heart in the land to which they were led captive, and
do penance, and pray to Thee in the land of their captivity,
saying: We have sinned, we have done wickedly, we have
dealt unjustly; and return to Thee with all their heart and
with all their soul, in the land of their captivity, to which they
were led away, and adore Thee toward the way of their own
land which Thou gavest their fathers, and of the city which
Thou hast chosen, and the house which I have built to Thy
name; then hear Thou from heaven, that is, from Thy firm
dwelling-place, their prayers, and do judgment, and forgive
Thy people, although they have sinned; for Thou art my God;

let Thy eyes, I beseech Thee, be open, and let Thy ears be attentive to the prayer that is made in this place.

Now therefore arise, O Lord God, into Thy resting place, Thou and the Ark of Thy strength; let Thy priests, O Lord God, put on salvation, and Thy saints rejoice in good things. O Lord God, turn not away the face of Thy anointed; remember the mercies of David Thy servant.[211]

For the first time the people's solemn consent to fulfill their religious duty was publicly expressed, not merely by an oath rejecting idolatry, but by a kind of humble and fervent acceptance of moral conversion based on a whole body of moral laws. Henceforth, to fail to make progress, to remain at a standstill, will constitute an infidelity. Men will be expected to act like children of God, so that worship according to the spirit and according to the whole extent of the moral law will become Israel's stumbling-block, for this spiritual worship will be strictly conditioned by the vitality of faith.

If souls maintain a personal and intimate relationship of friendship with God, then the Bible shows them completely faithful to the true worship and to the Law. But if these souls enter the path of moral evil, then, even though they may carefully continue their external worship, their faith has faltered. Henceforth the formalism of the priests is attacked by the thundering words of the prophets, who even go so far as to condemn the official worship if the spirit of the Law and the whole Law is not observed in its entirety. Should a Jew forget that God sees him, scrutinizes men's hearts and minds, demands love for love, then the prophets become angry and insist that God be adored in

[211] II Par. 6:19–42.

spirit and in truth. Each of their books could be examined page by page to demonstrate the triple relation of faith, worship and the Law. We need not be surprised that this constituted a long and painful process of education.

Each prophet's mission was determined by the events of his time and concentrated upon the points most in need of defense, the notions which it was most opportune to instil into men's hearts. Sometimes faith had to be saved by opposing idolatry: such was the role of Elias: "If the Lord be God, follow Him; but if Baal, then follow him." [212] Again, there was needed a reminder of the universal and conquering quality of faith, as God declared through Isaias: "I come that I may gather them together with all nations and tongue; and they shall come and shall see My glory." [213] Formalism and the letter of the Law had to be opposed by the demand for purity of heart: "But to whom shall I have respect, but to him that is poor and little, and of a contrite spirit, and that trembleth at My words?" [214]

The special role of Jeremias and of Amos was to strive to develop the practice of brotherly love by unmasking injustice, hardness of heart and hypocrisy. "What is the meaning that My beloved hath wrought much wickedness in My house?" [215] "Hear this, you that crush the poor, and make the needy of the land to fall. . . . The Lord hath sworn against the pride of Jacob: Surely I will never forget all their works." [216]

Finally, it was Osee's great glory to have placed the life of intimate love of God under the auspices of faith and fidelity. "And I will espouse thee to Me forever; and I will

[212] III Kings 18:21.   [213] Isa. 66:18.   [214] Isa. 66:2.
[215] Jer. 11:15.   [216] Amos 8:4, 7.

espouse thee to Me in justice, and judgment, and in mercy, and in commiserations. And I will espouse thee to Me in faith; and thou shalt know that I am the Lord." [217]

If we survey those troubled centuries and consider their general outline, a tragic pattern becomes evident. They consist of a constant struggle against faith, opposed on the one hand by circumstances and on the other by human nature. Indeed, we can find valuable lessons for ourselves by viewing this period of Israel's life. We can first note the banal temptations which arise to trouble a fragile faith which has not yet attained full strength; they are occasioned by contact with the religions of the pagan nations surrounding Israel. A powerful attraction is exercised by the example of their easy life, the enervating luxury of their refined civilization, the seduction of their profane ideas and sciences, as well as their dissipated habits. The Law, which spurns all this, seems austere and although it is quite new, it may already be termed "old-fashioned." The temptations of the flesh and of the spirit corrupt and slowly kill faith.[218]

Opposing this current is the "reactionary" tendency maintained by the prophets: the puritanism of Amos and of that fierce recluse, Elias; the longing for the desert filling the hearts of Osee and Jeremias, who began his book with the Lord's words: "I have remembered thee, pitying thy youth, and the love of thy espousals, when thou followedst Me in the desert, in a land which is not sown." [219] This, of course, was not because the time spent in the desert was a model of moral life, but the covenant between God and His people had been established there. There Israel, in poverty and deprived of all help save Yahweh, lived its most thrilling

[217] Osee 2:19–20.   [218] Cf. I Tim., chap. 6.   [219] Jer. 2:2.

moments. In the desert God had spoken to human hearts. And so Osee recorded this promise: "I that am the Lord thy God . . . will yet cause thee to dwell in tabernacles, as in the days of the feast." [220]

Thus, prophecy reminded men of the necessary discipline of austerity and poverty, temperance and simplicity.[221] How many pungent pages attack women's vanity, their bracelets and their rouge! How many warnings against the "technique" of civilized nations! Israel must rely, not on chariots and ingenious weapons, but on faith in God's help. A decree in the Book of Deuteronomy obliged the king himself to lead a simple and pious life: "And when he is made king, he shall not multiply horses to himself. . . . He shall not have many wives that may allure his mind, nor immense sums of silver and gold. . . . But he shall copy out . . . this Law . . . and he shall read it all the days of his life." [222] But, alas, how many kings of Juda and Israel refused to do what Yahweh wished! Their wealth, their harem, their ambition soon led them to practice idolatry, to lose their faith in Yahweh, the living God, their protector and their guide. What a hard but precious lesson! It is a lesson ever needed to recall to us that faith is a gratuitous gift which must be jealously guarded, defended against seductions, nourished by fraternal charity.

To provide magnificent examples of devout perseverance and heroic fidelity in the life of faith was the purpose of the Books of Ruth and of Tobias. The nobility of those lives passed in poverty and even destitution, the serene joy of

[220] Osee 12:9.
[221] St. Peter teaches the same lesson of sobriety and the same need of a faith that can resist the world (I Pet., chap. 6).
[222] Deut. 17:16–19.

those courageous souls, was derived from their keen and fervent faith, their unalterable trust in God's goodness, their reverence of His sublimity. Faith, fidelity and truth are preserved by means of great simplicity of life and by a constant desire to remain ever in the presence of God, the soul's only treasure.

If faith is preserved in the midst of an existence which is exemplary but lacking great trials, it runs the risk of being somewhat superficial. The examples of Ruth and Tobias are significant in this respect. God, therefore, used events to stimulate, or to try to stimulate, Israel's faith. We have revealing proof of the evolution of faith in Israel, if we observe that God began to treat the nation in a different way. His fidelity had already provided sufficient base and support for the people's faith; henceforth He will require the adherence of their wills without material proof; no longer will He give tangible rewards for constancy. Formerly, sin had provoked immediate punishment; fidelity met with prosperity. The faith of a nation still in infancy was thus spurred and supported. But now the Jews must learn that whatever happens, God cannot deceive them. In the eyes of worldly men events will seem bewildering.

When the Jews mingle with pagan nations and participate in their sins, prosperity comes; foreign alliances, which had been forbidden by the Law, bring wealth, flourishing commerce and internal peace. What a formidable temptation for faith! In vain did the prophets foretell punishment! And even when punishment occurred in the form of a foreign invasion or pillage, how natural it was to believe that the neighbor's god was stronger than Yahweh and should be worshipped. Thus, idolatry became even more widespread.

"They have denied the Lord, and said, It is not He; and the evil shall not come upon us; we shall not see the sword and famine. The prophets have spoken in the wind, and there was no word of God in them." [223]

Even the kings no longer recognize God's hand in the events of the world. That is because few among them are true servants of God. Of Ezechias, however, it is written in the Second Book of Paralipomenon: "But yet in the embassy of the princes of Babylon, that were sent to him to inquire of the wonder that had happened upon the earth, God left him that he might be tempted, and all things might be made known that were in his heart." [224] This shows what spiritual attitude God expected of His people. The prophets alone, or almost alone, saw clearly; their reproaches testify to their amazing lucidity. Their vehement faith and fiery words were in striking contrast with the people's waverings. "Behold I will make My words in thy mouth as fire, and this people as wood, and it shall devour them." [225] Their messages contradict the assurances of the evil shepherds who keep saying: "Peace, peace, when there was no peace." [226] They recall the truth, the truth which the blinded people no longer discern, for apostasy and abandonment of the Law cannot be multiplied with impunity. Let Israel heed the prophets' words and recover the faith; perhaps then the nation may survive. "For behold the Lord will come with fire, and His chariots are like a whirlwind, to render His wrath in indignation, and His rebuke with flames of fire." [227]

We can well understand that such sharp words wounded to the quick those to whom they were addressed, provoking

[223] Jer. 5:12–13.   [224] II Par. 32:31.   [225] Jer. 5:14.
[226] Jer. 8:11.   [227] Isa. 66:15.

each listener to examine, at least furtively, his sins, even those committed in secret. It can be said, therefore, that the prophecy—especially Isaias' vigorous blows against pride, the very root of the sin against faith—accomplished the transition from collective faith to personal faith. Or rather prophecy emphasized the personal structure of faith and fully clarified what had always been taught and should never have been forgotten. Indeed, the prophets in all their teaching urged the people to recover a faith animated by personal contact with God and by a true self-commitment.

Affliction was an opportunity for this awakening of conscience. By unmasking Israel's pride a counter-attack was launched against the strongest element of that original malice which enticed men away from their belief in God's gratuitous gift and proposed that they set themselves up as gods. "If you will not believe, you shall not continue." [228] By these words Isaias meant: "Even if the whole world is united against you, until you are left alone and without weapons, yet if your faith is total and absolute, you shall be strong with the very strength of God present in your hearts. The example of Jeremias, left alone to defend faith and truth at a critical moment in the life and the destiny of Israel, provided a glorious proof of Isaias' words. He showed that the prophets did not hesitate to confirm their preaching by heroic and invincible testimony.

Faced by Israel's sins and with an urgency proportionate to the people's infidelity, the prophets have expressed to them God's invitation to believe. Each prophet shared in the task of implanting this faith more deeply in their hearts. Thanks to the prophets, Israel recovered a sense of truly

[228] Isa. 7:9.

personal faith; many truths formerly uncertain were fully
clarified; many notions of God were developed and deepened. In those cruel times, so disappointing for His love,
God strove as never before to convert His people, to attract
them by the bitter and sweet words of His prophets. By
them He constantly revealed His whole self to Israel. The
whole content of faith is found in the message of the prophetic books which explain the foundation of our dogma
as well as the reasons why we should serve God and love
Him: "I am, I am the Lord; and there is no Savior besides
Me. . . . Thus saith the Lord your Redeemer, the Holy
One of Israel." [229]

Such cries resound constantly, reminding men of God's
sanctity, of His majesty, of His rights as Creator, of His
title of Father and of His nuptial love, of which Osee was
the great herald. No longer could Israel ignore this glory
of God. The world indeed tempts these men, seducing their
senses and their minds. But God, too, tempts them by the
voice of His prophets; He tries to allure them by His beauty,
His goodness and His grace. "Thou hast deceived me, O
Lord, and I am deceived; Thou hast been stronger than I,
and Thou hast prevailed." [230]

This seduction is even effected by the sublime figure of
the Redeemer, whose image gradually became clearer and
closer. God offered this treasure of faith to Israel as an in-
alienable inheritance and possession. The name *rock* was
given to Yahweh in the psalms, but it referred likewise—
and never more aptly than at the time of the prophets—to
the solid and glittering bulk of treasure which God bequeathed to Israel to build the rampart of faith. Israel might

[229] Isa. 43:11–14.   [230] Jer. 20:7.

refuse the offer, but then no excuse could be found. The time was coming when the chosen people, fully informed on the truths of faith, would be ready either for the deliberate sin against the Spirit or for a commitment which would lead them from knowledge to love.

Though Israel had sinned, faith was not dead. As of old, when sin penetrated to the depths of David's heart and brought forth a cry of poignant faith, so the terrible affliction of a double exile gave Israel a deeper insight into the truth and value of the faith. The common folk remained in Palestine as slaves and vassals; for them the problem of suffering was a vital matter. The rich, seeking only to be left undisturbed, went into exile in Egypt, the land of ease. For a long time this "diaspora" was, of course, unfruitful. But the elite of the people—the priests and scribes, the leaders and the educated men—had been brought forcibly to Babylon. While they reacted energetically to the goad of their material difficulties (so that often the conquerors, through sheer opportunism, provided favorable living conditions for them [231]), yet they felt great sorrow in the spiritual ordeal of absence from the holy city. The psalm beginning with the words *Super flumina Babylonis* is a poignant testimony of this sorrow.[232] Only faith and hope helped those exiles to continue living. Their thoughts were absorbed by the hope of a return to Jerusalem and a restoration of the kingdom. To prepare themselves for it, they constructed a theology based on the data of revelation.

Ezechiel received the mission to enrich the faith. The main theme of his prophetic teaching was the necessity of

[231] Cf. the Books of Esther and of Daniel.   [232] Ps. 136.

expiation, proved by his exalting God's holiness and condemning Israel's defilement. These hard lessons, characterized by great severity, were connected with notions of great importance for the full development of faith: the assertion of liberty of conscience, individual responsibility and remuneration for each man according to his deeds. The consequences are incalculable. Henceforth the notion of individual moral and religious conscience is permanently accepted in Israel. The artificial equations between happiness and virtue, unhappiness and sin, survive but a short time. The field of truly religious thought has been ploughed and fertilized by faith until it begins to produce a harvest. Moral life rests on a firm foundation and God's rights are acknowledged. But reflection soon brings up crucial problems, especially those of the just man's suffering and of retribution.

Then appears the Book of Job, a magnificent poem, a monologue of the soul contending with the mystery of God's will. Soon afterward, the author of the Book of Wisdom was to reveal some part of the mystery of redeeming love.

If we seek to discern what spiritual horizons and promises held the gaze of these men of faith, we can find the answer in Ezechiel. Like his predecessors, he preached reform of life. But he also strove with zealous energy to teach Israel to believe in salvation, a boon to be granted as a sheer gift from God, who would ordain it for the glory of His name. Its results would be essentially spiritual and would consist first of all in a total renovation of men's hearts. "And I will give you a new heart and put a new spirit within you; and I will take away the stony heart out of your flesh, and will give you a heart of flesh. And I will put My spirit in the midst of you." [233]

But while this prophet speaks with a kindly voice and elsewhere foretells the coming of a Good Shepherd full of tenderness and mercy ("Behold I myself will seek My sheep, and will visit them. . . . And you My flocks, the flocks of My pasture, are men; and I am the Lord your God." [234]), nevertheless he was not satisfied merely to allow us an intimation of the child-like tenderness that would be the Gospel's special fragrance. He also stared boldly to the end of time and the hereafter, as if he had to seize the divine message on a subject about which faith had hitherto possessed neither certainty nor clarity. In particular, nothing prevents our thinking that the magnificent vision of the bones scattered about on the field and recovering life before the prophet's eyes not only foretells the restoration of Israel but also contains the hope of a more remote and mysterious resurrection.[235] It is also the living image of a faith that does not hesitate to believe in the impossible when all seems lost, and relies steadfastly on God's promises to assert that life overcomes death. Thus, Ezechiel boldly prepares for the future, on the national level, of course, but even more on the religious level. He extended and enriched the frontiers of faith in regions where it had hardly penetrated before his time. The final chapter of his writings evokes the image of the future Temple in the restored kingdom.[236]

Thus, the prophets, and particularly Ezechiel, completed the exploration of faith's domain and prepared the ground for the fullness of revelation, the coming of Christ. Nor

[233] Ezech. 36:26–27.   [234] Ezech. 34:11, 31.
[235] Cf. Ezech., chap. 37.   [236] Cf. Ezech., chap. 48.

were they alone in their work, for the whole nation seems to have cooperated in their efforts. The scribes, or jurists, carried on the same task, though on a more modest scale. Everywhere in the *diaspora* synagogues were multiplied and the scattered people once more received God's word, the source of their faith, and His Law, which is His abiding presence in their midst, revealing His will and enlightening their minds. So it is that the prophets' work, which caused a revival and deepening of Israel's faith, resulted in a return to the Law, but to a Law which had received new life and fertility by the interior action of the Spirit. Thenceforth the prophets could cease to speak and the Temple could remain empty; the Law would be written in men's hearts; it would be studied and explained by the teachers in Israel who would examine its meaning, love it and practice it with strict loyalty.

They take on also the task of preserving the Law from all erroneous interpretation or even deviations in doctrine. It was a time of rapid progress in the formulation of doctrine and in the composition of the definitive versions of the Books in which Israel's oral tradition would be permanently fixed. The priests gave explicit form to the teachings of the Torah, while the scribes did likewise with the lessons of wisdom. Thus, in the course of the cruel affliction of the exile and the dispersal, the flame of faith burned more purely and brightly than ever among the Jews. It was the time of greatest zeal in the task of assembling the various parts of the Bible, that light which was to be the torch of faith until the end of time. It is true that until the time of Christ and afterward as well, God's people continued to experience oppression and slavery, but the testimony of their glorious past which survived was their living faith which they owed, on the one hand, to the martyrs, and on the other hand, to their sacred book which for all future time became the deposit of revelation, the *Book, par excellence.*

We ourselves should see an example and guidance in this return to the sources, this long and patient study of the sacred texts which Israel undertook at that time. To be satisfied with the faith as received, without seeking to deepen and enrich it is to risk sinning against it. Only the man who tirelessly nourishes his heart and mind on God's testament discovers the meaning and the worth of this treasure, as he begins to understand that his faith is the entrance to a mystery that all eternity will not fully explore.

The Temple was rebuilt, though on a modest scale. While the nation was not restored, new proof of the vitality of its faith was manifested. As Judaism was being formed, all the energy and moral strength of the people were devoted to the defense and improvement and widespread propagation of their religious values. Already the last writings of Isaias had departed from Palestine to spread the monotheist and universalist faith of Israel. In Alexandria and on all the shores of the Mediterranean basin the wisdom of the nations is assimilated and united to the ancestral inheritance which was ever faithfully preserved, yet constantly enriched. How far away seems the time when the Jews trembled before every petty king of the vicinity and constantly risked their lives and faith in dangerous battles! Although Israel wore the unbearable yoke of a foreign power that crushed and enslaved the people, although the nation was faced with the temptation of collaborating with the enemy, yet it remained steadfast, and the reason was its faith. Faith or-

ganized the resistance against the enemy; faith provided
strength to stay true to the Law. Heroes gave their lives for
the law: Eleazar, the Machabees, and so many others whose
names are unknown. For the Jew does not accept defeat like
other men. Even when he is conquered and his land is oc-
cupied by the enemy, he is still the uncompromising adorer
of Yahweh, the relentless observer of the Law.

In viewing so many painful events, it is hard to say what
best proves the growth of faith among the Jews. Most likely
it is the whole body of truth that is jealously preserved in
the Bible, the storehouse and the torch of revelation. When
the torch was held up by Christ, the whole world was illuminated. He fulfilled revelation and, in particular, introduced
faith in the resurrection and in eternal life. So were realized
the hopes which, in the last period of Old Testament times,
were obscurely stirring in Israel's soul. Until the coming of
Christ, no word or gesture of God had ratified these hopes
which rose in human hearts and could not be suppressed.
Such hope offers the boldest and most profound evidence
of a faith that could never be destroyed but was constantly
growing. Belief in a future life showed Israel's passionate
trust in God's kindness, mercy and love for man. It antici-
pated Christ's teaching so directly that it seemed to voice
an appeal which He could not resist. Who knows but that
the Messiah's coming was hastened by such ardent faith?
And so it was that the best of the Jews, after expecting and
seeking God in faith, were rewarded by seeing their Savior
in the flesh before contemplating Him forever in heaven.
Old Simeon's prayer proves that the radiance guiding these
men of faith derived its brightness from the eternal light:
"Now Thou dost dismiss Thy servant, O Lord, according to

Thy word in peace; because my eyes have seen Thy salvation." [237]

FAITH DESCRIBED IN THE PSALMS

In Thee, O Lord, have I hoped, let me never be confounded.[238]

The nation which was to welcome Christ in words like those of old Simeon possessed ardent faith which found in Israel an original and spontaneous expression. Other nations expressed their faith in forms of art or worship. As the people of a God of whom no image should be made, Israel followed its own unique bent in expressing faith by the medium of the word. Speech is the essential element in Jewish worship and the foundation of belief. That branch of art flourished in Israel and produced masterpieces, particularly the psalms, which raise an imperishable monument to the nation's faith.

For while each psalm shows the author's heartfelt impulses and deep personal inspiration, the psalms are also the reflection and echo of Israel's soul, the form of its prayer, the poem of its life. This is proved, as the Bible testifies, by the fact that no Jew hesitated to appropriate particular verses or even whole psalms to express his own feelings. The Gospel too shows the same evidence. We need only notice how frequently the psalms are quoted there, and how they are used by Elizabeth and the Blessed Virgin herself. All Israel's children are familiar with the psalms and find their own soul therein. For teaching, for prayer or for praise, the Jews turn to the psalms, which nourish their private meditations and provide the thread from which is woven their collective prayer.

[237] Luke 2:29–30.   [238] Ps. 30:1.

The originality of the psalms stems partly from the circumstances of their composition. Usually a concrete fact or a particular occasion inspired the author and furnished a reason for him to sing of his faith in the omnipotent and merciful God. The whole life of the people is expressed in the psalms with great liberty and variety of inspiration: David's prayers, so closely connected with historical events; psalms for the sons of Core or of Asaph—"to give understanding"; the "gradual" canticles for journeying forth; the songs of homecoming; even the blessing of the priests for evening prayer or for the Feast of the Dedication. All were reminded of the great events in the history of God's people as they heard the account of mighty deeds of past times, the cries of distress uttered in moments of danger and the canticles of praise that followed a victory. The rhythmic, stylized prayers of adoration or thanksgiving, the tones of penance and humble trust so often heard in the psalms became inscribed on Israel's memory. The ardent soul of the nation always continued to find there the authentic expression of its feelings.

Because the psalms are profoundly human and also divinely inspired, they never fail to lead us back to the basic attitudes of the soul. That is the secret of their influence. The humble seed planted in the psalmist's heart sprouted, flourished throughout the nation, conveyed the voice of the multitude, and even today proves its lasting worth as a universal prayer.

Just as life is both simple and complex—simple because from its first dawning it is directed to its end; complex by reason of the events which mark its course—so also the psalms show extreme simplicity of line because of the faith which inspires them, and great complexity because of the varied nuances of sentiments. However, little does it matter how many conditions or situations are treated, provided one basic attitude transcends all else and one truth lends order and unity. This truth is faith. Whatever may be the circumstances, what is uppermost in the psalmist's mind is not to inform God of what God already well knows, nor even to explain a truth of faith or a judicious opinion; his essential purpose is to refresh his soul by repeating to God that He is God and that He is *my* God, by pledging to Him once more absolute faith and trust. Events occur and develop, fortunate or menacing, but one reality alone remains unchanged: the reality of God in whom Israel believes, God who alone *is,* God who has abounded in mercy toward His people, God who is forever faithful and true. Every occasion offers a chance to say it once more, and to say it is essential and sufficient.

Throughout the psalms the most diverse sentiments follow each other without transition. Thus, praise comes directly after a cry of distress. What forms the link is faith, which never finds fault, which is sure of God. Israel prays to God, knowing that the prayer has been granted. Even then faith was what would one day be called "the substance of things to be hoped for" [239] or what St. John Chrysostom called the reality that we have received in substance but have not yet seen.

Faith occupies a central place in the psalms because it is at the center of Israel's life. With all their heart and all their strength the men of this nation turn to God by faith. Their whole life is exposed to His gaze. No wonder, then, that humility wells up in the psalms and that these poems still form a model of all prayer, even for us.

[239] Heb. 11:1.

Faith likewise moved the psalmist to put himself under the control and the complete domination of the Law, which is so often extolled. The psalmist loved this dependence which brought him a more intimate acquaintance with God. In his soul's thirsting for divinity, God was everything. The dominant quality of the psalmist was a "sense of God." The atmosphere of the psalms is, therefore, distinctly theocentric. The primacy of God is emphatically asserted. God stands at the center; all else converges on Him.

So engrossed with God was the psalmist that he was unable to detach his mind and heart from Him even for a moment. It can be said that he lived constantly in His presence. Thence arises the deep rhythm of soul and his dearest desire. "Walk before Me, and be perfect." [240] These words, uttered by God to the father of all believers, became the psalmist's rule and ideal. In turn he begged God: "Quicken me in Thy way. . . . Make Thy face to shine upon Thy servant." [241] The psalmist's belief in God no longer relies primarily upon divine manifestations, as was the case with his forefathers. It has been purified and has gradually become a real life of faith. His one hope and desire is to stand in the sunshine of God's invisible light, to be exposed to its action in order to receive life. "O God, I have declared to Thee my life." [242] With deep joy, then, and in a kind of ecstasy, the psalmist sings out: "I come before Thee, to see Thy power and Thy glory. . . . Thou hast been my helper and I will rejoice under the covert of Thy wings; my soul hath stuck close to Thee; Thy right hand hath received me." [243]

By faith, Israel not only lived in the presence of God, but possessed Him, as the psalms tell us. Formerly the certainty

[240] Gen. 17:1.   [241] Ps. 118:37, 135.   [242] Ps. 55:8.
[243] Ps. 62:3, 8–9.

of possessing God was based on the material presence of the Ark, which belonged to Israel as Israel belonged to God. To lose the Ark was to lose God. God's many interventions in their favor gave His people increased assurance that He was truly *their* God. Their appeal to Him, therefore, displayed both trust and pride. "Thou dwellest in the holy place, the praise of Israel." [244] Later they recognized His presence in the events of history. No one who considered them could doubt that the glory of the Almighty dwelt in the midst of His people and that the divine hand sustained them.

But at length the Jews were asked to possess God by faith alone. They understood that He who is a Spirit cannot be enclosed in earthly dwellings nor possessed in a material way. They remembered the words of Moses, who had directed them not to seek God in heaven or across the seas, but to offer Him the sanctuary of their hearts and to hold Him by love. That could be done by obeying His word, for "the word is very nigh unto thee, in thy mouth and in thy heart, that thou mayst do it." [245] Israel understood that this is the secret of God's presence and this is the way to possess Him. The people who so dearly loved to glorify God "in the highest," to contemplate Him who uses the heavens as His footstool, to proclaim Him higher than the cherubim, hesitate no longer to find and to possess Him by obeying His commandments.[246] By faith and by the Law the Jews found God, who made them His people by His words ac-

---

[244] Ps. 21:4.   [245] Deut. 30:14.

[246] Christ was to develop this teaching fully in the Gospel: "If you keep My commandments, you shall abide in My love" (John 15:10).

cepted and written on their hearts. They were sustained by the divine will and to them God's command was God Himself.

By faith the Jews also possessed Him whom they expected and hoped for: the Redeemer. It is true that they continued to wait for Him, but with eyes of faith they saw Him coming, and with outstretched arms of faith they longed for the Liberator.[247]

"Thou art near, O Lord." [248] "My soul hath relied on His word, . . . with Him is plentiful redemption." [249] The psalmist did not need to wait for this "plentiful redemption" to know that God is eternally and infinitely holy and merciful. Christ had not yet instituted the kingdom of God; the gates of death were bolted and allowed no light to filter through; but already the psalmist exulted in the delights of friendship with God.

> The Lord is the portion of my inheritance and of my cup; it is Thou that wilt restore my inheritance to me. The lines are fallen unto me in goodly places; for my inheritance is goodly to me.[250]
> For Thee my flesh and my heart hath fainted away; Thou art the God of my heart.[251]

In his heart possession increases desire, while desire then calls for possession.

> For Thee my soul hath thirsted; for Thee my flesh, O how many ways! In a desert land, and where there is no way, and

[247] "Abraham your father rejoiced that he might see My day; he saw it, and was glad" (John 8:56).
[248] Ps. 118:151.   [249] Ps. 129:4, 7.   [250] Ps. 15:5-6.
[251] Ps. 72:26.

no water; so in the sanctuary have I come before Thee. . . .
If I have remembered Thee upon my bed, I will meditate on
Thee in the morning.[252]

Such words show well what was the life and the joy of that
soul so strong in faith. It would seem that there were but
few in Israel whose faith gained them entry to the mystical
experience extolled by the psalmist who, after finding God
and being captivated by Him, cried out: "My soul hath stuck
close to Thee; Thy right hand hath received me." [253] But at
least for this people, hoping and believing are not meaning-
less concepts but living and actual realities, infinitely noble,
precious and satisfying experiences. During most of their
history the Israelites, unlike ourselves, did not have the
possibility, and in a sense the temptation, to postpone divine
consolations until the next life. The pious Jew was a man
of the immediate present and felt the need to go the whole
way in his experience of God right here and now. And what
he did not yet possess, he made bold to beg for in fervent
prayer. He lived by faith more than we do and he realized
what it actually is: knowledge and love forthwith. "O taste
and see that the Lord is sweet." [254]

So true is this that in the Bible God never says that He
will give faith, but He says: "I will be known in the eyes of
many nations." [255] "And I will give them a heart to know
Me, that I am the Lord." [256]

To know is the same verb the Bible uses to designate the
relationship of husband and wife,[257] which clearly indicates
that when applied to the relation of God to the soul, the
word conjured up the notion of a reciprocal gift, an ineffable

[252] Ps. 62:2–3, 7.   [253] Ps. 62:9.   [254] Ps. 33:9.
[255] Ezech. 38:23.   [256] Jer. 24:7.   [257] Cf. Gen. 4:1, 17, 25.

intimacy, illimitable ownership, a unique and indescribable reality. To know God, to see Him and to taste Him is the goal of Israel's living faith. It is likewise the goal which Christ assigned to us, both here below and in eternity. The soul, embraced by God, will be admitted to the very life of the Trinity and will be permeated by its warm and dazzling Light. "Now this is eternal life: that they may know Thee, the only true God." [258]

This luminous and fervent life of faith was for God's people a vague aspiration, but for the psalmist, to a certain extent, an actual experience. Therefore faith displays the thrilling qualities of total commitment and matchless intimacy whereby God imparts obscure, sweet knowledge of Himself in a direct and constantly intensified experience. Faith becomes a personal contact. Now this personal quality of faith is particularly stressed in the psalms, where we see it, sometimes serene, sometimes excited and afflicted, then imbued with trust and humility in David's heart. Thus we see the depth it attains and the union it effects between the soul and its God. Every psalm and each verse would have to be reread in this light. The diversity of sentiments expressed reflects the manifold phases of this experience of God whom the soul grasps under the aspect of His transcendence or that of His mercy, but always in His fidelity. The psalms are never a cold account of abstract ideas, but a warm and living reality reflecting a personal and fully experienced event. And if we, in turn, have even the slightest experience of the same kind, then the psalms awaken echoes in our souls and rouse them to new life. Through the psalms we continue our experience of God and know that He is

[258] John 17:3.

love, light and mercy. Thanks to them, the divine light shines by day and by night in the hearts of the believer, just as it did in ancient times. "Light is risen to the just. . . . To the righteous a light is risen up in darkness." [259]

The psalmist's eager enthusiasm in God's service shows how his faith leads him to communion with infinite charity and enrolls him to work for His glory. The true believer does not separate service of neighbor from his aspiration toward God. The faith which enables him to taste God and to find there his whole heart's desire also makes him want to communicate with his fellow-men, to impart his convictions to others. "For the zeal of Thy house has eaten me up." [260] The psalmist, therefore, keeps proclaiming his faith, thinking that to sing its praises is both to profess it and to attract new believers, enthralled by wonderful beauty. For he experiences, even here on earth, a deep spiritual joy, a jubilant delight which no human words can describe.

The light of Thy countenance, O Lord, is signed upon us; Thou hast given gladness in my heart.[261]
The rich have wanted and have suffered hunger; but they that seek the Lord shall not be deprived of any good.[262]

Even the artless simplicity of these last words helps us to understand that the happiness enjoyed by the psalmist in living his faith fully surpasses every promise and every hope.

The soul struggling along the pathways of faith is refreshed and restored by the words of the psalms, which are like a gentle blessing, a welcome dew. They give courage for the ascent and delight in the plains. For a divine voice

[259] Ps. 96:11; 111:4.   [260] Ps. 68:10.   [261] Ps. 4:7.
[262] Ps. 33:11.

is heard there; already it is Christ who speaks. Thus, we approach the secret of this great joy and we understand the value of the divine experience that comes through these inspired prayers. It has been said that every word of the psalms can be referred to Christ. He Himself recited them repeatedly, expressing through them His prayer for men, His love for His Father, His trust. When He suffered the mysterious dereliction of Gethsemane and Calvary, was it not the psalms that He used to call upon His Father? "Oh God, My God, look upon Me; why hast Thou forsaken Me?" [263] He cried out in utter trust: "Father, into Thy hands I commend My spirit." [264]

Keen faith and intimate union with God are proved by trust and total self-surrender of a soul that knows it is loved by God. In the psalms reverberate the first notes of the Gospel's trust, that trust which Christ would soon tell us must be like that of a little child. "As a child that is weaned is toward his mother, so reward in my soul." [265]

The soul's certainty that it can never be overcome if it relies on God is the result of the way of spiritual childhood, that way which Christ would one day tell the world, but which the psalms already foretold. Trust absorbs the obscurity of faith; all agitation gradually subsides; peace enters the soul and prevails.

My heart hath been glad, and my tongue hath rejoiced; moreover my flesh also shall rest in hope.[266]
I will not fear what flesh can do against me.[267]

Nothing can separate the trusting soul from God. It no longer asks questions; it ceases to speak. All its concerns are

[263] Ps. 21:1.   [264] Luke 23:46, quoting Ps. 30:6.
[265] Ps. 130:2.   [266] Ps. 15:9.   [267] Ps. 55:5.

known to Another who looks after its life and leads it where it is good to go.

The Lord ruleth me, and I shall want nothing. . . . He hath led me on the paths of justice, for His own name's sake. For though I should walk in the midst of the shadow of death, I will fear no evils, for Thou art with me.[268]

By trust the soul caresses God in response to His caress. It is the kiss that bestows the substance of things hoped for. Trust obtains all because it already possesses all. By it the soul depends on God, whose merciful love it feels. Trust is likewise an aspect of the purification of love which seeks joy only in Him who is sure to provide. In trustful surrender the soul keeps praising and admiring God, constantly finding new reasons to love and praise Him more and more. "Blessed be the Lord the God of Israel from eternity to eternity. So be it. So be it." [269]

That is why most of the psalms and the psalter itself end with words of praise and blessing. "Praise Him on cymbals of joy; let every spirit praise the Lord. Alleluia." [270]

A PILGRIM OF FAITH

But one thing is necessary.[271]

There is in the psalter one song of praise and love—Psalm 118—which testifies to a life entirely spent in the service of God and His law. It reveals what faith demands of a soul determined to remain faithful. We see there its joys, its struggles, its sufferings, the dangers encountered and the ultimate

[268] Ps. 22:1–4.   [269] Ps. 40:14.   [270] Ps. 150:5.
[271] Luke 10:42.

victory. All this becomes evident only after careful scrutiny, for the psalmist has told his story with discretion and modesty, partly because he reserved first place for praise of God and partly because his whole life had been spent in continuous heart-to-heart communication with God who invited him—and us with him—to pray with a gentle murmur rather than a loud voice.

The author seems to have reached the twilight of life. He has made a long pilgrimage, a pilgrimage of no earthly destination, though he already tastes the peace of God's friendship. One single love has guided him and has overcome all difficulties. This love resonates in every verse and proclaims the trust and hope of a soul attentive to God's word and subject to His will. It sings of perfection in tones of sustained fervor and cadences of exquisite serenity. It describes the support and consolation found in sincere piety, invincible attachment to God's law and absolute trust in divine mercy. It flows along limpidly, with an even, almost monotonous rhythm, like a fountain deep in the forest where the water bubbles slowly in the sunshine.

But let us make no mistake. As the shadow of mighty trees intensifies the light that they encircle and enhances its beauty, so the value of the psalms derives in great part from the underlying experience of pain. The hidden suffering glimpsed through this prayer gives it greater worth and depth, greater beauty too. The author of the psalm has known many vicissitudes. He has tasted the bitterness of earthly things, but now his soul feasts on a happiness that will not be taken away from him. The inspired poet's song already has the accent of the music of eternity. "Blessed are the undefiled in the way, who walk in the Law of the Lord." [272]

A whole lifetime unfolds in the slow psalmody. In his youth the psalmist learned to consider the ways of the just and the wicked and to prize the divine decrees. He made his choice with all the enthusiasm demanded by the first commandment: "Thou shalt love with all thy strength." He accepted the Law and resolved to observe it exactly, with God's help.

I will keep Thy justifications. . . . With my whole heart have I sought after Thee. . . . Thy words have I hidden in my heart. . . . Enliven me, and I shall keep Thy words.[273]

In the verses which at first seem almost similar from the beginning to the end of this long poem, an undercurrent is noticeable; nuances appear which show the soul's evolution and the stages of its development. First the psalm introduces a young pilgrim, his heart burning with desire, but as yet lacking in understanding.[274] With juvenile impatience he laments that he cannot yet fly swiftly along the path on which he has set forth. "My soul hath cleaved to the pavement." [275] Though he moans, he trusts that grace, which has led him to the right road, will help him to stay on it. But he finds it hard to mark time and to remain in the darkness. He yearns to understand, to see God's "wondrous works" [276] spread before his gaze. His soul grieves because of the obstacle that prevents his reaching his heart's desire. "Remove from me the way of iniquity; and out of Thy law have mercy on me." [277] He reminds God that he has "chosen the way of

[272] Ps. 118:1.   [273] Ps. 118:8, 10, 11, 17.   [274] Ps. 118:16–32.
[275] Ps. 118:25.   [276] Ps. 118:27.   [277] Ps. 118:29.

truth." [278] If the Lord sustains him in the heroic adventure he is undertaking, he will dash forward without fear. "I have run the way of Thy commandments, when Thou didst enlarge my heart." [279]

But soon difficulties arise, introducing a new stage on the road.[280] The pilgrim stumbles on the way, discovers his weakness and frailty, realizes how miserable he is. He had overestimated his strength; now he understands that, left to itself, his feeble soul would turn to covetousness and vanity; he still fears reproach and scorn.[281] What he needs most is mercy in order that he may stay on the right road and preserve the treasure of life for which he now humbly begs. It is true that he loves the ways of the Law, but he admits that he "does not the good that he would and does the evil that he would not." He is abashed before those who mock him and cannot answer them. In spite of everything, hope sustains him and binds him to God. "In Thy words I have hoped exceedingly." [282] This fidelity enables the pilgrim to press forward henceforth on the route. "And I walked at large; because I have sought after Thy commandments. And I spoke of Thy testimonies before kings; and I was not ashamed." [283] He is rewarded immediately, as his soul savors the delight of God's friendship and loves to meditate on the divine law.[284] This gentle and virile lesson is needed by all beginners, all apprentices in the spiritual life, who must learn that the more violent the temptation, the quicker they should be to have recourse to prayer.

But again the road becomes more arduous; the day's bur-

---

[278] Ps. 118:30. [279] Ps. 118:32. [280] Ps. 118:33–48.
[281] Ps. 118:36–39. [282] Ps. 118:43. [283] Ps. 118:45–46.
[284] Ps. 118:47.

den is oppressive.[285] To regain strength, the pilgrim looks backward toward the morning's promises, which cannot fail. "Be Thou mindful of Thy word to Thy servant, in which Thou hast given me hope." [286] Now he is in a dreadful predicament; alone in an alien land, surrounded by the wicked. But he remains steadfast, however, and even in his dejection he feels a new strength, for he became absorbed in prayer, taking shelter with God in the midst of the darkness all around. "In the night I have remembered Thy name, O Lord, and have kept Thy law." [287] Consoled and enlightened by meditation, once more he resolves to serve God faithfully, this time with full knowledge and foresight. His "portion" is to keep the Law.[288] "I am ready and am not troubled"; [289] so he declares with the firm and virile voice of one who knows what he is sacrificing and prepares for battle. His cause is just and he feels that he is "a partaker with all them that fear Thee, and that keep Thy commandments." [290] His thought attains a universal scope. "The earth, O Lord, is full of Thy mercy; teach me Thy justifications." [291]

The next section of the psalm [292] gives evidence of a certain spiritual maturity in the psalmist. It has the ring of experience, both of trials and of God's fidelity, by which the soul was enabled to triumph over the trials. He even goes a step further—and this is certainly the most characteristic feature of this stage of his spiritual life—he proclaims three times the benefits of humiliation.

Before I was humbled I offended; therefore have I kept Thy word. . . . It is good for me that Thou hast humbled me . . .

---

[285] Ps. 118:49–64. [286] Ps. 118:49. [287] Ps. 118:55.
[288] Ps. 118:57. [289] Ps. 118:60. [290] Ps. 118:63.
[291] Ps. 118:64. [292] Ps. 118:64–80.

I know, O Lord, that Thy judgments are equity; and in Thy truth Thou hast humbled me.[293]

Through humiliation he has learned to prefer spiritual assets and to value them properly. "The law of Thy mouth is good to me, above thousands of gold and silver." [294] He appeals to divine mercy for continued help. Relying on the tender love of his Creator, he makes bold to ask for the discernment of true good and the gift of wisdom which will keep him steadily on the right path. Then God's justice will be manifested and the psalmist, supported by God's word, "may not be confounded." [295]

The soul indeed needed this renewed contact with God in order to support the frightful trials which strike once more without transition and are now described.[296] Are these external trials? To some extent, since he mentions persecutions, but these are aggravated by interior trials which prove much more painful. Alone with the attacks of enemies, this desolation leaves the soul at bay, on the verge of death. "My soul hath fainted after Thy salvation." [297] This suffering is without any relief, for interior aridity and desolation prevail. "My eyes have failed for Thy word, saying: When wilt Thou comfort me? For I am become like a bottle in the frost." [298] Then the soul speaks to God of its painful surprise at such treatment, considering that it had ever remained true to Him. "I have not forgotten Thy justifications. . . . They have persecuted me unjustly; do Thou help me." [299] But with trustful submission he adds: "Quicken Thou me according to Thy mercy; and I shall keep the testimonies of

[293] Ps. 118:67, 71, 75.   [294] Ps. 118:72.   [295] Ps. 118:80.
[296] Ps. 118:81–102.   [297] Ps. 118:81.   [298] Ps. 118:82–83.
[299] Ps. 118:83, 86.

Thy mouth." [300] The same attitude is found in those whose faith is being purified by God. The same plaintive astonishment is expressed by all who have to suffer, even though they have been faithful. All vow their fidelity to God, but ask the same anguished question when faced with the mystery of the divine plan.

Like all those who are tried and suffer, the psalmist did not seize at the time the meaning of God's treatment of him, but as soon as his suffering is somewhat relieved, he understands. He suddenly receives the strongest possible conviction of his own vileness, ignorance, and pettiness; at the same time he understands as never before how mighty God is and how inscrutable His purposes. This greatly strengthens the attitude of submission. "I am Thine; save Thou me." [301] Affliction also teaches him to adore the secrets of divine wisdom, which transcends all human understanding and experience. This attitude is a source of serene and joyous peace. Thus the soul becomes wise and henceforth is better able to glimpse the meaning of God's law, which is revealed as a law of love. "How sweet are Thy words to my palate; more than honey to my mouth. . . . Thy word is a lamp to my feet, and a light to my paths." [302]

At this stage of the soul's pilgrimage, it has obtained a sweet and illuminating experience of God. But once more trouble strikes: "I have been humbled. . . . My soul is continually in my hands" [in danger].[303] But the treasure of which the bride of the Canticle spoke, "I held Him and I will not let Him go," [304] is possessed likewise by the psalmist and he will not relinquish it. "I have purchased Thy testi-

[300] Ps. 118:88.   [301] Ps. 118:94.   [302] Ps. 118:103, 105.
[303] Ps. 118:103, 105.   [304] Cant 3:4.

monies for an inheritance forever; because they are the joy of my heart." [305] What delicate restraint and modesty are shown in these verses, which let us perceive through the veiled references the ineffable communication received and the exchange of gifts that has taken place. "I have inclined my heart to do Thy justifications forever, for the reward." [306]

St. John of the Cross was to express the same thought: "The loving soul cannot fail to desire the recompense and wages of its love, for the sake of which recompense it serves the Beloved, for otherwise its love would not be true; the which wages and recompense are naught else nor can the soul desire naught else, than greater love, until it attains to being in perfection of love, which confers no payment save of itself." [307]

Is the psalmist's vehement love the reason for his sudden burst of hatred against sinners? [308] He seems to shudder at their approach, less through fear of attack than because of God's horror of sin. Holy fear causes even a physical revulsion at the idea that he might become like them. "Pierce Thou my flesh with Thy fear; for I am afraid of Thy judgments." [309] God grants his prayer and henceforth a wholly divine light enables him to judge evil and to hate it.

This new suffering in the face of sin makes him shed many tears as he sees that the Law is not observed. He is consumed with zeal on noticing that God's words are forgotten. Thus the psalmist's soul, first cowardly, then shaken and depressed, finally becomes an apostle's soul, wholly intent on praising, in strains of exquisite poetry, the beauty and truth of God's decrees. "The declaration of Thy words

[305] Ps. 118:111.   [306] Ps. 118:112.   [307] *Op. cit.,* II, p. 62.
[308] Ps. 118:113–144.   [309] Ps. 118:120.

giveth light and giveth understanding to little ones. I opened my mouth, and panted, because I longed for Thy commandments." [310] Even in times of trouble and anguish, the soul loves to ponder on the divine commandments. "Thy word is exceedingly refined and Thy servant hath loved it. I am very young and despised, but I forget not Thy justifications." [311] Such sentiments cause God great joy, for they are a proof of true love, limited in its deeds, but infinitely strong in itself, for it springs from a purified heart which is pleasing to the Lord.

The soul, therefore, seeks only to please God more and more.[312] Ever increasing fidelity brings union with the Beloved. Hence it is ever rigid in observance of His will, ever watchful at prayer, rising before the dawn. It seems the cry of a soul possessing less and less, turning to a God ever more and more eager to grant mercy. How easy it is to see here the effects of a keen faith far advanced in the knowledge of God and of self! Henceforth the psalmist's only fear is to be separated from God. Better than protestations of fidelity, this humble fear unalterably attached to his love. United to God, he knows a peace that nothing can ever disturb. "Much peace have they that love Thy law, and to them there is no stumblingblock." [313]

At length the time has come for the psalmist to sum up the experience of his long life in a few wonderfully serene verses in which the words are accompanied by a melody of *nunc dimittis* with overtones of happy hope. This prayer God heeds. "I have kept Thy commandments and Thy testimonies, because all my ways are in Thy sight. . . . Let my

[310] Ps. 118:130–131.   [311] Ps. 118:140, 141.
[312] Ps. 118:143–176.   [313] Ps. 118:165.

request come in before Thee; deliver Thou me according to Thy word." [314] Like incense silently rising in the evening air, the psalmist's praise is exhaled. "My lips shall utter a hymn. . . . My tongue shall pronounce Thy word." [315] The hour has come for the good servant to commit his soul into the hands of Him from whom all his gifts have come. Ardently and humbly, he utters his last wish: to be happy at length in the eternal pastures. This explains the final image—at first sight puzzling—of the sheep seeking its shepherd. The soul that has suffered here below, longs to be led into the sheepfold to taste endless peace and joy. "I have gone astray like a sheep that is lost; seek Thy servant, because I have not forgotten Thy commandments." [316] In faith and in fidelity to the Law, the psalmist has completed his earthly pilgrimage. Trustfully he prepares to land on the shores of eternity.

[314] Ps. 118:168, 170.   [315] Ps. 118:171-172.
[316] Ps. 118:176.

Chapter 2

❀ WISDOM

And who shall know Thy thought, except Thou give wisdom? [1]

But if any of you want wisdom, let him ask of God, who giveth to all men abundantly, . . . and it shall be given him. [2]

Faith is not the only pathway to God which the Bible shows us. Wisdom is another which the "Wisdom Books" are especially designated to reveal to men. In certain passages these Books depict wisdom as a woman of mysterious countenance. By her unearthly beauty and by the role assigned to her, she attracts our attention and arouses our love. Whoever has heard her voice can never forget it. Charged with a mission to men, she calls them, converses with them, undertakes to educate and guide them. To those who follow her and vow absolute fidelity to her, she promises many treasures and unequaled happiness. Nor is that all. Coming as God's envoy, she plays the role of mediatrix among men, offers to guide them to Him, to bring them even to His own

[1] Wisd. 9:17.   [2] Jas. 1:5.

home. In this respect, wisdom appears essentially as a gift of God, the fruit of divine initiative toward men, a fully gratuitous mercy.

But elsewhere the wisdom authors seem merely to accomplish a human task. They accumulate advice, proverbs and maxims that testify to a deep knowledge of men and wide experience of life. Some of these sayings are of Hebrew origin; others are borrowed from the wisdom literature of other peoples, such as the Assyrians or the Egyptians. They convey the moral and social atmosphere and ideal of the period; from them can be drawn up a whole code of good living and self-improvement, in which many people fail to detect anything more than practical, down-to-earth common sense. And yet the sages considered that this too deserved the name of "wisdom." The co-existence of these two viewpoints in the Wisdom Books, and sometimes even in a single text, is wholly obvious and the difficulty it causes must be faced. Indeed, the Wisdom Books carefully retained these two aspects in order to teach us clearly that both must be united in true wisdom, the only wisdom that can guide man along the pathway of life's concrete problems to his home in God.

On the one hand, man, by dint of reflection and effort, should fit into the rhythm which the Creator has arranged in the world. Thus he will achieve a state of balance assuring security, peace and happiness. For this purpose he will draw upon the treasure which human wisdom has patiently accumulated throughout the centuries. On the other hand, he should be open to heavenly inspiration, become wholly "teachable" and hearken to the voice that murmurs in his own soul. Human experience had sufficed to form the wisdom of the nations from whom Israel did not hesitate to borrow. But only revelation enabled the Hebrew sages to detect the divine voice and to transmit its accents and its message, which the inspired books have the mission to give us. Now, as of old, men should seek true wisdom there.

But God's teaching by no means cancels human experience. The human lessons which the sages so carefully collected and transmitted in the deposit of revelation truly deserved their place in it. The fact that inspiration guarantees that part of Scripture equally with the rest, suggests that man's contribution and effort are and always will be necessary to the pursuit of wisdom. But however valuable we may find the psychological observations of the Books of Proverbs, Ecclesiasticus or Wisdom, and however much human enrichment we may derive from familiarity with these Books and meditation upon them, their true value goes far beyond all this. It is found in the interior and spiritual attitude that is taught. A careful reading of these Books shows that this attitude is posited as the essential condition of all initiation into the mystery of wisdom and all approach to God. The inspired authors, therefore, particularly strive to develop this attitude in all those who come seeking wisdom from them.

A question that spontaneously arises is: "Who were these sages?" The answer is becoming ever clearer and we can now fill in the portraits of these inspired scribes who wrote the Wisdom Books.[3] The fact that they were intent on trans-

---

[3] It seems useful to give a few succinct notes on the Wisdom Books and their authors. This type of literature is clearly enough characterized to constitute a distinct section of the inspired writings, including Proverbs, Ecclesiastes, Ecclesiasticus and Wisdom.

mitting the divine gift revealed to them, the gift which first
was their own treasure and then made them heralds of the
truth, shows that they were first of all men of deep faith,
believers ever scrutinizing the Torah, religious souls whose
entire lives depended utterly upon God, whom they asked
for guidance in their thinking and in their lives. On the

Other biblical Books, however, such as Job and Baruch, are more
or less closely related to the same class of writing. It must be
admitted also that many of the psalmists were also true "wisdom
writers." There is still much uncertainty among biblical scholars
regarding the personalities of the writers of these books.

The Book of Proverbs was not written by one author but by a
number of the king's attendants, mostly scribes, that is, connected
with the court, the civil service, the management of the kingdom.
They were therefore immersed in business and every-day matters,
intent upon practical ability, which they defined in various maxims
that they bequeathed to their successors as a breviary of wisdom.

The problem of Ecclesiastes (*Qoheleth*) is not yet solved. This
Book, which for a long time was erroneously attributed to Solomon,
reflects the thoughts of a man of noble birth who has experienced
all the pleasures of life and is eager to warn people against vanity.
He does not forbid the use of life's advantages and comforts within
the framework of the divine commandments, but he knows that
man's thirst for happiness cannot be quenched by pleasure.

Ecclesiasticus (*Ben Sirach*) is the type of ordinary man, satisfied
with life, the society of his day, and the gifts he has received from
God, especially the Torah's guiding light. He has no material worries and he avoids extreme opinions, devoting his serene leisure
to extolling the glories of creation and to forming disciples according to his own heart.

The author of the Book of Wisdom undoubtedly lived at the
time of the *diaspora*. As an exile in Alexandria, he was in contact
with Greek wisdom and acquainted with scientific progress, but
at the same time deeply imbued with Jewish theology, then in the
process of formation. He treats life's problems with the broad-
mindedness of a universal mentality and he invites his readers to

other hand, their evident experience, their lavish imparting of advice, and even the type of problems that they seek to solve, prove them to be men of action, closely involved in business, dedicated to public service. Indeed, some of them belong to the category of royal officials.

Their zeal in opening "schools of wisdom," where nu-

---

proceed from the most humble realities to the highest metaphysical concepts.

In spite of much important investigation devoted to the Book of Job, it is not yet possible to say exactly when the author lived or what influences entered into the writing of the poem. The actual story of Job, as of Tobias, belonged to a very ancient patrimony common to various peoples. The biblical version is the work of a metaphysical and literary genius, appearing at a period of Israel's history when the whole tale embodied the problems of the time. This auspicious moment was probably after the exile and the persecutions. Various influences, particularly Ezechiel, brought about the formation of independent religious conscience; this led to the consideration of the problem of suffering, which, in turn, prepared the way for the crucified Messiah.

Baruch seems to have been Jeremias' scribe or secretary. He was an educated man and showed intelligence and skill in delivering his message. As a prophet he deviates but little from his master's teaching, but as a man he displays a delightful sense of humor, as in the last part of his message about idols. While his marvellously well-written poem on wisdom does not introduce any new ideas, it ranks him as one of the truest representatives of Israel's wisdom. He was well-versed in the Law and maintained boundless confidence in the destiny of his people, in spite of the terrible affliction that had struck them down at that time.

As to the psalmists, it is even more difficult to portray their personalities. We can at least note that those among them who belong to the "wisdom" group of writers were men of activity, anxious to solve practical problems and to provide men with a code of spiritual life which would set them free from all forms of slavery, either material or moral.

merous disciples could be trained, shows their apostolic
tendency. What they long to convey to their pupils is less
any didactic teaching or technique than a spiritual attitude
made up of humility, trust, frankness and religious atten-
tiveness. For they know by experience that nothing is more
decisive for progress along the path of wisdom than the
humble fear of God which Christ was to praise when He
prayed: "I confess to Thee, O Father, Lord of heaven and
earth, because Thou hast hid these things from the wise and
prudent, and hast revealed them to little ones." [4] He confirmed that "where humility is, there also is wisdom." [5]

To overcome difficulties and to advance step by step in
their journey to God, the sages relied on holy fear rather
than worldly wisdom. Whether they deal with the problem
of knowledge, the search for happiness or the development
of wisdom, they always keep emphasizing fear of God and
they depend upon it to keep them in the way of the commandments, which is the way to wisdom and to union with
God. They consider fear of God as the efficacious and proxi-
mate condition for meeting God, the soil where His potent
grace can thrive, the place for union with wisdom.

The sages were not satisfied merely to prepare their disciples' souls; they felt an urgent mission to spread the knowledge and love of that wisdom which was their goal. With
bountiful generosity, or rather, with true charity, they pour
into our souls the treasures entrusted to them and they
pass on to us the secrets of love which nourish and sustain
them. "This wisdom went before me, . . . which I have
learned without guile, and communicate without envy, and
her riches I hide not." [6] They also describe the one who is

[4] Matt. 11:25.   [5] Prov. 11:2.   [6] Wisd. 7:13.

coming to meet us. For they themselves have met wisdom, whom they know and love as a mother and as a bride. That is why they speak so eloquently of her and display her beauty in the rays of such warm, pure and ardent light. Those to whom they reveal this beauty cannot help but yearn for wisdom and join in the quest of "the brightness of eternal light, . . . [who] maketh the friends of God." [7]

THE PROBLEM OF KNOWLEDGE

Be not wise in your own conceits.[8]

At the base of the sages' search for wisdom was there a problem of knowledge that forced them to take the preliminary step of setting limits on their investigations in religion as well as in philosophy and metaphysics? Did they feel qualms lest they trespass into realms that seemed prohibited to human knowledge? None of the texts indicate it. On the contrary, the ease and simplicity with which they undertake incidental discussion of very deep problems prove that in this respect their minds are free of all worry. As men of faith they are deliberately and firmly determined not to break even the least of the commandments of the Law, but they do not think that God forbids them to use their minds. They do not fear that their search for knowledge in any way offends the divine majesty. But on the other hand, they do not intend to ask God any rash questions. They do not challenge Him or claim to become at all "like Him" by their knowledge. Doubtless Satan tempted them, as he tempts all men, but he was not admitted to their hearts.

The quest and the anxiety of the sages was of an entirely

[7] Wisd. 7:26–27.   [8] Rom. 12:16.

different nature. Their meditations bear upon a twofold subject: the complexity of the world and the simplicity of God. Man, who stands halfway between these two realities, has to find out how the world fits into God's plan. He has to discover the principle of unity that may enable him to settle the difficulties of this world. Therein lies the sages' problem of knowledge.

They are not concerned with increasing their store of information by constant addition of new fragments. While most of the sages by no means disdained to investigate the various branches of learning that were cultivated in the society of their time—sciences, medicine, arts, skills and crafts—and while a few of them had partial acquaintance with ancient philosophies, they did not expect to find *their* problem solved by these diverse intellectual achievements. Moreover, they see the world as a single entity to which, in a way, nothing can be added, any more than anything can be added to God. There exists, however, a divine purpose; to discover it was the task to which the sages devoted their energies. The harmony and order apparent in the world are the result of its submission to God's wishes. Man, too, must enter into this order if he is to participate in the harmony. The sages know the necessary truths. What is good and what is useful has been revealed to them and whether they know little or much in the realm of human learning does not matter at all.

On the other hand, they must take great precautions against pride, the chief obstacle on wisdom's path. "Seek not the things that are too high for thee, and search not into things above thy ability. . . . For many things are shown to thee above the understanding of men. And the suspicion of them hath deceived many, and hath detained their minds in vanity." [9] Should we, then, go so far as to say with one of them: "Because I have not known learning, I will enter into the powers of the Lord"? [10] Yes, but only if we grasp the writer's meaning. He does not refer here to books of learning or to the great book of nature, but to casuistry with its barren quibbling. True learning is not condemned. On the contrary, if it is directed to a purpose higher than the immediate profit of the individual or of society, if it is an unselfish search for wisdom, then it offers strong testimony to man's dignity. It shows him how to use his faculties in complete liberty, free of all servile constraint and utilitarianism. It proves that he is capable of devoting himself to a spiritual world which is in opposition with the flesh and its instincts. Viewed and understood in this way, learning is good and we may say that it gives a first glimpse of man's eternal destiny.

But even so, the sage does not expect his final answer from the world, but from God. He questions God and converses with Him. True, God does not speak, but He has spoken in former days and His words are recorded in the sacred books and in the Law. Those who study the inspired writings (especially Genesis) humbly, respectfully, attentively, receive the answer to the problem of knowledge that the sages discuss. They seem to have preferred the fall of man to all other biblical episodes as the subject of their meditations; they saw it as an enlightening pattern. Adam and Eve were punished for eating the fruit of the tree of knowledge. Their sin was not solely one of disobedience, but

[9] Ecclus. 3:22, 25–26.   [10] Ps. 70:15–16.

a failure to inquire of God Himself regarding whatever they wished to know. They considered themselves independent and then they were led astray by an outside voice. The sages profited by this lesson and maintained an attitude of humble dependence on God's law, using it as the starting-point and the destination of all their intellectual quests. The vast, practically unlimited field of knowledge could yield its treasures only if explored by the light of divine revelation. The wisdom authors did not doubt that this field was theirs to clear and to cultivate. They did not think that their deep-seated, insatiable thirst for understanding and knowledge was bad, for God gave it, in giving them their minds. Did He not likewise give them the ability to discern good and evil? It was, then, man's responsibility to make good or bad use of his desire for knowledge. The Wisdom Books, therefore, are more concerned with the way man used his mind than with actual principles of knowledge. This teaching should be helpful for us too, because "the spirit indeed is willing, but the flesh weak." [11] Men may believe that they are heeding God's voice when in reality they are being seduced by other attractions.

In dealing with the enigma of order in the world and the existence of a scale of values, the sages often referred back to the origins, perceiving therein an outline of both duties and rights. Thus, the author of the Book of Wisdom, after asserting that man was created to dominate and to govern the world, invokes God as follows: "God of my fathers, and Lord of mercy, who hast made all things with Thy word, and by Thy wisdom hast appointed man, that he should

[11] Matt. 26:41.

have dominion over the creature that was made by Thee, that he should order the world according to equity and justice." [12]

Even after the fall this right remained, though henceforth associated with trouble, suffering and tears. But God in nowise withdrew from man the power conferred on Adam: to "name" all creatures and to govern them. God appointed man to this position and keeps him there for time and for eternity. Many texts of Scripture speak of man's future participation in the kingship of God's Son for eternity. "For God created man incorruptible, and to the image of His own likeness He made him." [13] On this account, God also gave man the ability to know, to understand, to love, to judge and to rule. His particular task and mission involve reflection and love, but must be directed toward God. As he should contribute in some way to the order and the beauty of the kingdom committed to his care, he needs and should develop whatever knowledge and insight are appropriate to his task. "Give an occasion to a wise man, and wisdom shall be added to him. Teach a just man, and he shall make haste to receive it." [14]

Does this mean that the sage can find the object of his desire entirely in the fruits of his own hard work? No. His efforts lose all meaning if detached from their cause and unrelated to the divine order. In any case it is impossible to find in the world an explanation of the world, or in man an explanation of man.

And I applied my heart to know wisdom, and to understand the distraction that is upon earth; for there are some that day and night take no sleep with their eyes. And I understood that

[12] Wisd. 9:1–3.   [13] Wisd. 2:23.   [14] Prov. 9:9.

man can find no reason of all those works of God that are done under the sun; and the more he shall labor to seek, so much the less shall he find; yea, though the wise man shall say that he knoweth it, he shall not be able to find it.[15]

It was but normal and human that a vehement desire should have led him first to an apprenticeship of curiosity, as he examined the whole visible world and bent every effort to know it. From this ardent quest he returned in disappointment. However much he may have seen and learned, the essential object of his search still eluded him. But the search was not useless, if, on the way, he succeeded in reading God's own signature on the world, and if his faith in the Creator thus became more deeply rooted.

But all men are vain, in whom there is not the knowledge of God; and who by these good things that are seen, could not understand Him, that is, neither by attending to the works have acknowledged who are the workman, but have imagined either the fire, or the wind, or the swift air, or the circle of the stars, or the great water, or the sun and moon to be the gods that rule the world. With whole beauty, if they being delighted, took them to be gods, let them know how much the Lord of them is more beautiful than they; for the first Author of all beauty made all those things. Or if they admired their power and their effects, let them understand by them, that He that made them is mightier than they; for by the greatness of the beauty, and of the creature, the Creator of them may be seen, so as to be known thereby.[16]

But the power that directs the world, the ultimate explanation of the many problems which the sage's search showed him as even more numerous and arduous than he has sup-

[15] Eccles. 8:16–17.   [16] Wisd. 13:1–5.

posed, was not encountered in his associations with men or with nature, nor at the conclusion of the many experiments he conducted. Thus, his search for the so-called wisdom contained in things and to be found in the world ended in failure, and on realizing, perhaps more keenly than others, the utter uselessness of his effort, he felt hurt and worried.

I Ecclesiastes was king over Israel in Jerusalem. . . . Behold I am become great, and have gone beyond all in wisdom, that were before me in Jerusalem; and my mind hath contemplated many things wisely, and I have learned. And I have given my heart to know prudence, and learning, and errors, and folly; and I have perceived that in these also there was labor and vexation of spirit, because in much wisdom there is much indignation; and he that addeth knowledge, addeth also labor.[17]

Like him, most of the sages acknowledge that they have not found wisdom at the end of their arduous search. The world does not reveal the divine plan, nor does it transmit a distinct statement in God's voice. It is true that God's image appears in the world, but it is like a pattern hollowed out; His presence is perceived as an absence. We must remember the central place given to divine transcendence in Old Testament faith in order to understand why the sages thought it necessary to turn to the world to seek the principles of a kind of wisdom that would be accessible. They had to attempt the experiment of a stubborn effort to discover in the created world the secret of its creative Principle, but creation refused to tell its secret. "But where is

[17] Eccles. 1:12–18.

wisdom to be found, and where is the place of understanding? . . . It is hid from the eyes of all living." [18] Is it then inevitable that such an experiment should give wholly negative results? Indeed not. Those who attempt it in all sincerity and armed with indomitable faith derive from it the proper disposition to enter upon the paths of true wisdom at long last. The search and the effort teach them the dimensions of their minds, their own limitations and the importance of relying utterly upon divine light to lead them to their destination. "All is vanity," the wise man kept repeating. But he did not condemn on that account all intellectual or scientific activity, all questioning of the world which refuses to divulge its secret. It is lawful, and even urgent, for each man to busy himself at his proper task, to exploit all his talents and potentialities, to accomplish the humble yet immense mission of building a better society. [19]

But what the sage emphasizes in his gemlike maxim, "All is vanity," is the nothingness of all things by comparison with the one desired reality which cannot be attained here below. He means that all human wisdom is finite and incomplete; all glory that men think they can achieve by their own efforts is a delusion. "The eye is not filled with seeing, neither is the ear filled with hearing." [20] Man is

[18] Job 28:12, 21.

[19] We may well ask if the author of the Book of Wisdom in particular had not already foreseen the new dispensation which St. Paul was to announce to the Ephesians when he spoke of the restoration of God's kingdom, which was "to re-establish all things in Christ, that are in heaven and on the earth" (Eph. 1:10). All true progress and every human conquest of the material world contributes to this submission of all things to the Son of God as universal King (cf. I Cor. 15:28).

[20] Eccles. 1:8.

always inferior to his aspirations. His carnal nature imposes not only limitations, but numberless restraints.

For the thoughts of mortal men are fearful, and our counsels uncertain. For the corruptible body is a load upon the soul, and the earthly habitation presseth down the mind that museth upon many things. And hardly do we guess aright at things that are upon earth; and with labor do we find the things that are before us. But the things that are in heaven, who shall search out? [21]

That painful test was required to convince the sages of man's fundamental insufficiency and his absolute need for divine help. One of them who had attempted, in spite of everything, to look at God with his blind eyes, admitted that at least he was given proof of his own strange weakness and foolishness. From that time on, every echo set him listening for the divine name.

I am the most foolish of men, and the wisdom of men is not with me. I have not learned wisdom and have not known the science of saints. Who hath ascended up into heaven, and descended? Who hath held the wind in his hands? Who hath bound up the waters together as in a garment? Who hath raised up all the borders of the earth? What is his name, and what is the name of his son, if thou knowest? [22]

These men of God offer us wonderful lessons which are the fruit of their tears and weary efforts. Before teaching their austere maxims, they have lived them. For instance, who can doubt that the author of the Book of Job is retracing a deeply felt personal experience when he evokes the voice of God confuting his rash complaints?

[21] Wisd. 9:14–16.   [22] Prov. 30:1–4.

Who is this that wrappeth up sentences in unskillful words?
. . . Where wast thou when I laid the foundations of the
earth? . . . Upon what are its bases grounded? . . . Dost
thou know the order of heaven? . . . Gird up thy loins like
a man; I will ask thee, and do thou tell Me.[23]

Faced with such reproaches, what could Job do but
repent humbly of his bold presumption. "I know that Thou
canst do all things, and no thought is hid from Thee. . . .
Therefore I have spoken unwisely, and things that above
measure exceeded my knowledge. . . . Therefore I repre-
hend myself, and do penance in dust and ashes." [24] And yet
it was not God that Job meant to attack, but only God's
works. But the sages consider that even creation is beyond
the limits and grasp of our intelligence. Men have to renounce the attempt to uncover nature's secrets by their own
unaided efforts. Confronted with mysteries far surpassing
those of the material universe around them, what can they
perceive of the spiritual world? Who can even know his own
heart and judge his own actions? "All the ways of a man
are open to His eyes; the Lord is the weigher of spirits.
. . . Who is the man that can understand his own way?" [25]
A great lesson and an authoritative example of humility are
derived from contact with the experience of the sages.
Humility is the essence of their message and it is displayed
like a treasure dearly bought but well worth the price. This
experience, which produces saints and sages, begins with
counsels of common sense and moderation.

Seek not the things that are too high for thee, and search
not into things above thy ability; but the things that God hath

[23] Job 38, *passim*, 40:2.   [24] Job 42:2–3, 6.
[25] Prov. 16:2; 20:24.

commanded thee, think on them always, and in many of His works be not curious. . . . In unnecessary matters be not over-curious, and in many of His works thou shalt not be inquisitive. For many things are shown to thee above the understanding of men. And the suspicion of them hath deceived many, and hath detained their minds in vanity.[26]

While Qoheleth's thought follows a somewhat different direction, his conclusions are substantially the same:

He hath made all things good in their time and hath delivered the world to their consideration, so that man cannot find out the work which God hath made from the beginning to the end. . . . I have tried all things in wisdom . . . and it departed farther from me. Much more than it was; it is a great depth, who shall find it out? . . . I have surveyed all things with my mind, to know, and consider, and seek out wisdom and reason. . . . Which yet my soul seeketh, and I have not found it.[27]

But while the sages compared themselves to what was greater than they, and became more humble by acquiring a deep sense of their own fundamental insufficiency, this by no means eradicated their desire for wisdom. It would be a mistake to judge them merely by the apparent modesty of some of their ambitions. They were enlightened in their sense of value. On the one hand, the object of their search became defined and fixed; on the other hand, the value and relativity of intellectual achievements became apparent and took on proper proportions and order.

It is indeed noteworthy that in the history of Israel the quest for wisdom was ever accompanied by constant participation in human activities and even public affairs. The

[26] Ecclus. 3:22–26.   [27] Eccles. 3:11; 7:24–25, 26, 29.

sages were aware of and concerned in all the problems of their contemporaries. While Joseph excelled in secular and sacred knowledge, that did not prevent his being a great man of action and the savior of his people. Moses, who was "instructed in all the wisdom of the Egyptians," [28] built a new society. The early Jewish kings gave the world the paragon of wisdom: Solomon. Daniel, the sage and the visionary, was also an active ambassador on behalf of his dispersed nation. We need only read the wisdom writings to guess that their authors were men immersed in public affairs. But however attracted they were by manifold intellectual delights—Egyptian and Assyrian science, the arts and learning of foreign courts, and (for the author of the Book of Wisdom) Greek genius—however much they extolled this secular knowledge and acquired it for themselves according to their opportunities, they assigned essential value and prime importance to one form of knowledge only. To it they devoted the best of their powers: the knowledge of God, model of all wisdom.

This does not mean that the sages underestimated the value of study and research or the benefits therein for individuals and for society. But it must be admitted that the sages' tremendous activity in every field of life seemed a duty to them only so far as their activity was subordinated to wisdom, which alone was worthy of complete devotion and effort. Israel let other nations glory in scientists, artists, scholars. God's people had a better message to bring to the world. The Jews did not scatter their energies, but gave mankind geniuses who were wise according to God's standard. Thus they declared the superiority of divine reality

[28] Acts 7:22.

over all human achievement, the singular value of the single thing that is truly necessary.

All the sages, at some time in their careers, encountered the problem of knowledge which gave them pause to reflect, but it did not stop them on their quest. Modest, but full of determination, they would set out once more on their journey, more humble in heart, less lofty in their ambitions. Pascal has said that true Christianity demands submission and proper use of the mind. The biblical sages had already judged that these were the conditions necessary for the pursuit of wisdom. They practiced total submission to the spirit of God, His teachings and His law, about which they never had the slightest misgivings. At the same time they maintained that reason, reflection and intellect, though inadequate, were not given by God to be disdained, but to be directed toward the one true light that could confer all knowledge, all understanding and all real wisdom.

THE QUEST FOR HAPPINESS

The sages sought in wisdom an explanation of the world and the proper attitude toward it. They likewise inquired about the road to happiness.

Keep His precepts and commandments, which I command thee, that it may be well with thee, and thy children after thee, and thou mayest remain a long time upon the land, which the Lord thy God will give thee. . . . Hear, O Israel, and observe to do the things which the Lord hath commanded thee, that it may be well with thee.[29]

This text, which makes the problem depend upon fidelity, affirms that happiness is possible and that the just man has

[29] Deut. 4:40; 6:3.

a right to it. This is the clear doctrine of the Old Testament, to be prolonged and raised to a higher level in the New Testament.[30] It is opposed to the notions of pagan antiquity.

We need only think of the characters of classical tragedies who feared that any lasting happiness would arouse the jealousy of the gods. The gods, moreover, ruthlessly strike down all who are tempted by any form of excess. The heroes and wise men of antiquity are resigned to unhappiness and injustice as a dark and mysterious fate. The same is not true of biblical characters, who do not show such submission as to an inevitable necessity, bearing down upon them with blind cruelty. Thus, if Job complains so bitterly and Ecclesiastes expresses so much indignation, is it not because they refuse to bow down before what seems to them unjust, abnormal and unacceptable?

For the inspired authors, then, happiness is not a matter of unexpected good luck in the drawing of lots. It is a goal toward which man should strive, on which he even has a certain claim. Nor has God left him deprived of help in

[30] St. Paul's preaching, the supreme development of Old Testament wisdom, revolves upon the mystery of suffering, the annihilation of the cross (cf. I Cor.). But, as St. Peter proclaimed, the mystery is inevitably accompanied by joy (I Pet. 4:12, 19). The Christian sage cannot harvest joy by fleeing from the things of this world, but he attains it by reaching the crucified Christ by means of things. That is the happiness which Christ promised for "this day" to His companion on Calvary. Profound realism and a true sense of God's ways inspired Old Testament men to seek happiness in the direct experience of everyday life. Unlike other oriental peoples, the Jews did not postulate indifference and repression of feeling as conditions of happiness, but believed that suffering had a purpose and could be spiritualized. They required renunciation also. The same current of thought runs through the whole Bible.

attaining his destination. Israel's belief in happiness rests on a solid foundation, supported by revelation, particularly the account of man's creation. There man appears as the personal product, the masterpiece of God's hands. Therefore his nature bears an ineffaceable divine imprint and an indestructible link with God. This sign of God's merciful goodness is the source of man's hope. The story of the earthly paradise proves that God had prepared both material and spiritual happiness for man and intended to make him an intimate and familiar friend. All creation was planned and fashioned for this purpose.

It may seem that the fall ruined man's happiness and even cancelled his right to happiness, but a careful reading of the inspired text reveals that while the original purpose was seriously jeopardized by the fall, it was not changed.[31] It is true that man, in punishment of his sin, is condemned to suffering, hard work, sickness and death: heavy mortgages on his happiness. But on the other hand, he still remains king of creation. The psalmist exclaimed: "What is man that Thou art mindful of him? . . . Thou hast made him a little less than the angels." [32] Moreover, the friendship between God and man, the deepest and surest source of human happiness, was soon resumed. God renewed it and officially ratified it by the covenant. The whole Pentateuch was a proof that God remained faithful to His covenant. In this respect, as in so many other ways, the covenant was a pivotal idea in the Bible; it explains Israel's

[31] God wants happiness, not misfortune, for man. Christ often gave proof of this divine benevolence (Luke, chap. 12; Matt., chap. 6).

[32] Ps. 8:5–6.

conviction that happiness can be attained here on earth. By that contract God requires of man fidelity to His commandments. He promises happiness in return. The whole history of Israel supports these promises, for it is a constant succession of wonders and marvels, proving that God kept His promise to grant protection and the possibility of happiness to those who were faithful to Him. The entire Old Testament expresses this theme of happiness as the fruit of the covenant and the response of God's fidelity to man's fidelity. Deuteronomy solemnly affirms it, as do the psalms, which proclaim a future happiness which was then envisaged as a purely material affair: "But the meek shall inherit the land, and shall delight in abundance of peace." [33]

Ben Sirah follows the same idea, although he emphasizes that the rewards given to the just are entirely gratuitous. "The gift of God abideth with the just, and his advancement shall have success forever." [34] Countless texts express this attitude and throughout her history Israel remained certain that prosperity and happiness, as well as success in battle, were the reward of fidelity. Even the enemies of Israel knew this so well that they dared not attack the nation except in periods when the people were notoriously unfaithful.

And there was no one that triumphs over this people, but when they departed from the worship of the Lord their God. . . . And as often as they were penitent for having revolted from the worship of their God, the God of heaven gave them power to resist. . . . And as long as they sinned not in the sight of their God, it was well with them; for their God hateth iniquity.[35]

[33] Ps. 36:11.   [34] Ecclus. 11:17.   [35] Judith 5:17, 19, 21.

So spoke Achior to Holophernes. Thus, we see that for the nation as for the individual, happiness was the reward for observance of the covenant, the reward of the just. The Old Testament constantly affirms, in God's name, that the happiness which is man's deepest desire, is indeed possible for him. But it was not enough merely to declare, even in God's name, that happiness was possible. The road leading to it had to be clearly marked and the sages devoted their best efforts to that task.

At the beginning of Israel's history a kind of opposition seemed to exist between the conditions required for happiness and the nature of that happiness. The gift of happiness depended upon obedience to a wholly spiritual law: "Who shall give them to have such a mind, to fear Me, and to keep all My commandments at all times, that it may be well with them and with their children forever?"[36] But the happiness promised was depicted in a wholly material form, practically identified with good harvests and fertility:

If after thou hast heard these judgments, thou keep and do them, the Lord thy God will also keep His covenant to thee, and the mercy which He swore to thy fathers; and He will love thee and multiply thee, and will bless the fruit of thy womb, and the fruit of thy land, thy corn and thy vintage, thy oil and thy herds, and the flocks of thy sheep upon the land, for which He swore to thy fathers that He would give it thee. Blessed shalt thou be among all people. No one shall be barren among you of either sex, neither of men nor cattle. The Lord will take away from thee all sickness. . . . If then you obey my commandments, which I command you this day, . . . He will give to your land the early rain and the latter rain.[37]

[36] Deut. 5:29.
[37] Deut. 7:12–15; 11:13–14. We may question whether the world

Long centuries and hard effort were needed before men
would glimpse the notion that the true reward of fidelity
to God's law was happiness of a spiritual kind. Only the
authority of God's own Son finally convinced man that
true happiness did not consist in material ease and comfort,
but in faithful service of God, even at the cost of struggle,
sacrifice and renunciation. It is an error to suppose that in
this matter the Gospel merely confirms an intellectual evolution already completed. It is true that the Old Testament
glimmers with the first presentiments of the Gospel light,
like the dawn announcing the day. We can trace a real
evolution of thought. But to make the transition from the
Old Testament's highest concepts of happiness to the doctrine of the beatitudes required Christ Himself. He alone
had the authority to promulgate a new chart of happiness:
"Blessed are the poor in spirit. . . . Blessed are they that
suffer persecution for justice' sake, for theirs is the kingdom
of heaven." [38]

Does this mean that previous efforts were ineffectual? Not
at all; and we should be lacking in gratitude to the sages
if we failed to appreciate the value of their work in this
field. By raising the notion of happiness to the level of a

---

has made much progress in this regard. On the other hand, we
must not forget that while material conditions do not produce
happiness, they greatly contribute to it. St. Thomas Aquinas, and
the Church with him, recognized that a minimum of material well-
being is required before man can desire spiritual goods and strive
to obtain them. This principle is the foundation of Christian eco-
nomics.

[38] Matt. 5:3, 10. Cf. also: "I exceedingly abound with joy in all
our tribulation" (II Cor. 7:4). "And they indeed went from the
presence of the council, rejoicing that they were accounted worthy
to suffer reproach for the name of Jesus" (Acts 5:41).

well-balanced, moderate ideal of life, and even a moral life of very lofty standards, the sages proved great benefactors of mankind and precursors of the Gospel.

The authors of the wisdom literature base their ideas of happiness upon the lessons of human experience. Certain life principles and circumstances have successfully stood the test of time; these they try to clarify. They have looked about as men who know how to observe and understand. As experienced psychologists and moralists, they are not deceived by appearances and their books are full of shrewd observations. A treasury of natural wisdom is to be found in the advice and recommendations that these teachers shower upon their disciples.

First of all, whoever wishes to be wise must sort out the tangled skeins of appearances and realities, seeking out what is safe and sure. "Praise not a man for his beauty, neither despise a man for his look. The bee is small among flying things, but her fruit hath the chiefest sweetness." [39]

The first requirement for happiness is to be independent of others, for "it is a miserable life to go as a guest from house to house." [40]

Each man should provide for himself, and only work assures the personal independence which is the first condition of dignity. Idleness, on the other hand, always causes discontent. "Because of the cold the sluggard would not plough; he shall beg therefore in the summer, and it shall not be given him." [41] Idleness entails bondage, while diligence leads to happiness. "The hand of the valiant shall bear rule; but that which is slothful, shall be under tribute." [42]

[39] Ecclus. 11:2–3.   [40] Ecclus. 29:30.   [41] Prov. 20:4.
[42] Prov. 12:24.

Moreover, for a man with a family and home, careful management of property is necessary. "Be diligent to know the countenance of thy cattle, and consider thy own flocks." [43] A wife will be a joy to her husband if she is an active and astute housekeeper, if she is wise in assigning the tasks and providing the meals for the servants.

She hath sought wool and flax, and hath wrought by the counsel of her hands. . . . And she hath risen in the night, and given a prey to her household, and victuals to her maidens. . . . She hath looked well to the paths of her house, and hath not eaten her bread idle.[44]

But hard work and good management do not suffice of themselves to insure happiness. As man lives in society, he needs profound wisdom in his dealings with his neighbors. To lack this kind of discernment is to invite disaster. The tact required is a delicate blending of friendliness and prudence. In dealing with others, the wise man knows how to weigh his words and often to keep silence. He never becomes involved in imprudent affairs nor acts rashly. "Before judgment prepare thee justice, and learn before thou speak." [45] He avoids quarrelling and is ever modest and humble, however great his knowledge may be. "It is an honor for a man to separate himself from quarrels; but all fools are meddling with reproaches. . . . Where pride is, there also shall be reproach; but where humility is, there also is wisdom." [46]

It would be erroneous to imagine that such an attitude springs from extreme egoism, excessive mistrust or misanthropy. It is not a matter of selfish tactics, but a way of

[43] Prov. 27:23.   [44] Prov. 31:13, 15, 27.   [45] Ecclus. 18:19.
[46] Prov. 20:3; 11:2.

gaining self-control and self-discipline that are essential to all real wisdom.[47] While these counsels of wisdom seem merely utilitarian, actually they form part of a very high ideal; this becomes more apparent when we examine the attitude to justice as expressed in the wisdom writings.

One could hardly expect a wise man to be utterly unconcerned about his own personal profit, but it would be unworthy of him to fail to practice justice. It would be a direct infringement of a divine commandment, for God has a horror of all injustice and He opposes all cruel oppression.

Diverse weights and diverse measures, both are abominable before God. . . . Do no violence to the poor, because he is poor; and do not oppress the needy in the gate; because the Lord will judge his cause and will afflict them that have afflicted his soul.[48]

It is clear that justice is something more than the best way of avoiding all sorts of personal difficulties and annoyances. It requires the practice of a real social sense which far transcends distributive justice and could be called "a sense of solidarity." The just man must be generous: "He that is just, will give, and will not cease." [49] What is even more difficult, he must be able to pardon injuries. "The learning of a man is known by patience; and his glory is to pass over wrongs." [50] Justice likewise requires constancy and kindliness, as well as loving and intelligent understand-

[47] We may recall here the brilliant passage of St. James' Epistle on the sins of the tongue. It follows the same lines as the teaching of the wisdom writers. St. James, moreover, takes care to point out that he is referring to true wisdom (Jas. 3:13–18).
[48] Prov. 20:10; 22:22–23.   [49] Prov. 21:26.   [50] Prov. 19:11.

ing of other people's sufferings. "Blessed is he that understandeth concerning the needy and the poor." [51] In short, we can say that this Old Testament justice already has an undercurrent of mercy and charity, along with all the gentleness, patience and tact associated with these virtues.[52]

Let not mercy and truth leave thee. . . . And thou shalt find grace and good understanding before God and men. . . . Say not to thy friend: Go, and come again, and to-morrow I will give to thee, when thou canst give at present.[53]

Turn not away thy eyes from the poor. Despise not the hungry soul, and provoke not the poor in his want. . . . Help the poor because of the commandment. . . . Lose thy money for thy brother and thy friend, and hide it not under a stone to be lost.[54]

Thus we see that only the most superficial acquaintance can view this wisdom as merely utilitarian. Its requirements in the matter of personal morality are similarly lofty. Only those who from early youth and throughout their lives avoid misbehavior, debauchery and dissipation can hope to find happiness. The teachers were constantly warning, instructing and guiding their young disciples whom they wished to protect.

The commandment is a lamp, and the law a light, and reproofs of instruction are the way of life; that they may keep

[51] Ps. 40:1.

[52] St. Paul shows how wisdom and justice are linked together: "For the grace of God our Savior hath appeared to all men; instructing us, that, denying ungodliness and wordly desires, we should live soberly, and justly, and godly in this world" (Tit. 2:11–12).

[53] Prov. 3:3–4, 28.   [54] Ecclus. 4:1–2; 29:12–13.

thee from the evil woman and from the flattering tongue of the stranger. . . . For the price of a harlot is scarce one loaf. . . . He that is an adulterer, for the folly of his heart shall destroy his own soul. . . . Say to wisdom: Thou art my sister; and call prudence thy friend, that she may keep thee from the woman that is not thine, and from the stranger who sweeteneth her words.[55]

On the other hand, happiness is the lot of the man who in early youth finds a wife according to his heart and remains faithful to her. "Let thy vein be blessed, and rejoice with the wife of thy youth; let her be thy dearest hind and most agreeable fawn; let her breasts inebriate thee at all times; be thou delighted continually with her love." [56]

Nevertheless, although "the beauty of a woman cheereth the countenance of her husband," [57] she needs more than beauty to make him happy. She must be virtuous, modest, silent, well-mannered.

If she have a tongue that can cure, and likewise mitigate and show mercy, her husband is not like other men. He that possesseth a good wife, beginneth a possession; she is a help like to himself, and a pillar of rest.[58]

If a child is to reach true maturity, his education must be gentle but firm, painstaking and persevering.

Give thy son his way, and he shall make thee afraid. . . . Give him not liberty in his youth, and wink not at his devices. . . . Instruct thy son, and labor about him, lest his lewd behavior be an offence to thee.[59]

[55] Prov. 6:23–24, 26, 32; 7:4–5.   [56] Prov. 5:18–19.
[57] Ecclus. 36:24.   [58] Prov. 36:25–26.   [59] Ecclus. 30:11, 13.

He that spareth the rod hateth his son; but he that loveth him, correcteth him betimes.[60]

A proper education will help the child to find happiness in wisdom and to be a source of happiness to his family. "He that honoreth his father shall have joy in his own children, and in the day of his prayer he shall be heard. He that honoreth his father shall enjoy a long life; and he that obeyeth the father, shall be a comfort to his mother." [61]

The entire treasury of world wisdom as well as personal experience provided the sages with their store of sound principles and excellent advice for individuals and for society. But their chief merit is that they are in complete agreement with revelation. This gives them their right to a place in the inspired writings and it marks a definite step forward in the history of morality. Because these principles represent a translation of revealed commandments into the circumstances of everyday life, they effectively prepare the souls obeying them for the infusion of divine wisdom. Even when the expression and aims of the biblical writers are kept on a purely human level, we must not forget that the ultimate object of their quest is neither worldly success nor human wisdom, but a specifically religious ideal. In their eyes every little detail and every piece of practical advice is constantly related to God. No particle of the visible world, no human activity or faculty should be considered from a wholly "secular" viewpoint. Each element has its place in a pattern that is religious. If the sages stoop to practical details and give advice in many fields, showing that nothing human is alien to them, it is because nothing in the world or in man is alien to God. All things must converge

[60] Prov. 13:24.   [61] Ecclus. 3:6–7.

toward a spiritual and religious center. A single example can prove this. The Book of Proverbs requests: "Give me neither beggary nor riches; give me only the necessaries of life." [62]

We may well think that this prayer was inspired only by a desire to avoid trouble and worry by seeking refuge in the mediocrity of a kind of bourgeois tranquillity. But as we read on, we see that the true motive is a religious one: "Lest perhaps being filled, I should be tempted to deny, and say: Who is the Lord? Or being compelled by poverty, I should steal, and forswear the name of my God." [63] This orientation toward a spiritual purpose reveals the sages' whole tendency in treating the problem of happiness which otherwise would have remained merely a search for balance and moderation. We can thus measure how much their notion of happiness enabled souls to make progress on the journey to divine wisdom.

But an enormous distance was still to be covered. While the sages were especially illuminated by divine wisdom and therefore capable of discerning spiritual reality, for the most part they shared the notions of their time. Some of them had not even advanced beyond the ideas expressed in the Book of Deuteronomy. "Ruin draweth nigh to the evil man, but the just shall escape out of distress. . . . The just eateth and filleth his soul, but the belly of the wicked is never to be filled." [64]

Many who applied these maxims risked a real danger of moral stagnation, unless, like the authors, they could invigorate such ideas with the influence of a more spiritual viewpoint. The sages themselves had to take care not to

[62] Prov. 30:8.   [63] Prov. 30:9.   [64] Prov. 12:13; 13:25.

stop halfway, not to be satisfied with the light of personal experience alone, not to settle the problem of happiness too cheaply. It would seem, indeed, that some of them owed their optimistic view of life to the fact that their own lives were spent in peace and happiness, well sheltered from misfortune and material difficulties.

However, the experience of history as well as the testimony of the sages prove that in actual fact men persevere in the quest for wisdom and are ready to grasp the proffered gift only if they are conscious of a lack and a desire. "Open thy mouth wide, and I will fill it," said God to the psalmist.[65] And the Lord praises another wise man, Daniel, as "a man of desires." [66] That is why God raised up wise men who, as a result of their own experience, were able to declare with emphatic eloquence that to obtain true happiness one must consent to pay a high price.

APPROACH TO WISDOM BY DISAPPOINTMENT

To determine the conditions of happiness, the sages thought they could supplement the content of revelation by the lessons of experience. This showed wisdom, at least on the natural plane. But a time came when men had to yield to the evidence and admit that observance of the law, whether God's laws or those of experience, did not inevitably insure the happiness that the men of wisdom had promised. The admission was all the more bewildering in that those who made it were also wise men.

The author of the Book of Proverbs affirms that the just man will attain happiness. To him, fidelity, wisdom and happiness all seem closely linked and interdependent. Doubt-

[65] Ps. 80:11.   [66] Dan. 9:23.

less, he could hardly fail to have met good men who were unhappy or bad men who enjoyed untroubled happiness. But so absolute was his trust in divine revelation that it permitted him to close his eyes to these flagrant contradictions raised by experience. Thus, his faith was in nowise troubled by them. When faced with the sufferings of just men, he would call them "the self-styled just men"—those who merely appear so—for he could not believe that suffering and trials would have afflicted them if they were truly just and had always been so. Doubt could not touch the lessons of experience, still less the divine pledges.

Then with Job, scandal burst upon the scene! He was a just man, a genuine just man, and yet he was overwhelmed by sufferings. How can a God who Himself is just, tolerate such flagrant injustice? Job's soul is even more grievously tormented by this problem than his body was by pain. His friends tried to make him admit that the suffering was the result of his sins, but this he would not do. He knew that he was innocent; he was as sure of his innocence as he was of his suffering. He who venerated God so profoundly and obeyed Him so faithfully and lovingly was utterly bewildered by the situation. At any price he had to have an explanation. If he could not find it for himself, he would demand it of God Himself, whom he would summon for the purpose. Such boldness was unheard-of, yet pathetic, because marked by intense pain joined to absolute sincerity. He practically howled with grief, manifesting his exalted concept of God and divine justice, as well as his utter certainty of his own just deserts.

Although I should be simple, even this my soul shall be ignorant of, and I shall be weary of my life. One thing there is

that I have spoken, both the innocent and the wicked He consumeth. If He scourge, let Him kill at once, and not laugh at the
pains of the innocent. The earth is given into the hand of the
wicked, He covereth the face of the judges thereof; and if it
be not He, who is it then? . . . I will say to God: Do not condemn me; tell me why Thou judgest me so. Doth it seem good
to Thee that Thou shouldst calumniate me, and oppress me, the
work of Thy own hands? . . . that Thou shouldst inquire after
my iniquity, and search after my sin? And shouldst know that
I have done no wicked thing. . . . Hold your peace a little
while, that I may speak whatsoever my mind shall suggest to
me. . . . Although He should kill me, I will trust in Him; but
yet I will reprove my ways in His sight.[67]

The problem was fully stated; the obstacle was not mini-
mized. What answer could the author give? How could he
safeguard both the principles of his faith in God's justice
and the value of experience? First he took up and developed
more deeply a theme at which the Book of Proverbs had
hinted: the sufferings of the just man are only an apparent
injustice, for they are a test. The test is even a mark of
divine favor, for God tests those whom He loves. God
deserves to be served for Himself alone and in an unselfish way, not in the manner of mercenaries. If men were
faithful to Him only through hope of reward, would not
this reduce fidelity to the level of a bargain? *Quid pro quo.*

On the contrary, what glory may be offered to God by
a completely unselfish fidelity like Job's! What progress and
high moral standard are shown by such an attitude! Satan

[67] Job 9:21–24; 10:2–7; 13:13–15. Christ's sufferings were likewise a scandal in the eyes of His apostles. While the reason for
them was God's tremendous love for men, they remain His secret
and a mystery for us.

himself emphasizes this point by maintaining that man is incapable of such abnegation. Is it difficult or meritorious to remain true to God when all goes well, and complete, uninterrupted happiness is ours? "Doth Job fear God in vain?" [68] Satan insinuates that the answer to his question is in the negative because Job receives so many benefits as a reward of his fidelity. Then comes the challenge: "But put forth Thy hand, and touch his bone and his flesh, and then Thou shalt see that he will bless Thee to Thy face." [69] God's honor is involved. Without knowing it, Job is the champion of God's cause against Satan.

Satan is a new and by no means negligible element in the drama of suffering. The encounter is not only between man and God; Satan, "the adversary," also plays a role. It is true that this adversary is restrained by God and dependent upon Him, but Satan's conduct introduces a complication into the problem and lets us glimpse a significance that far surpasses any personal drama.

The least we can say of all these answers is that they do not fully satisfy our minds. The suffering of the good remains a deep mystery, even when we elude it by adoring God's impenetrable designs which infinitely transcend man's understanding. That is what the author asks us to do in the case of Job. It is true that men should not seek to solve the enigma, but considering their nature, with their need for knowledge and their innate sense of justice, can they possibly restrain their questioning? The difficulty remains even for a man who continues to believe, in spite of all appearances, in spite of the worst sufferings that strike him, that God is a just and compassionate God. The difficulty

[68] Job 1:9.   [69] Job 2:5.

remains, even in the face of invincible trust, such as Job's: "Although He should kill me, I will trust in Him." [70] We can admire Job, admit that he has the proper attitude, credit the author with having described this attitude, and note what a great step forward it represents in the development of faith; but the fact remains that the problem is not solved.

We may even say that the difficulty has increased. First of all, Job, as a result of his own experience, utters a scathing contradiction of the short-sighted optimism of the author of the Book of Proverbs and of Ben Sirah. Then the problem gains in scope and gravity from the fact that Job is not a historical character but the personification of just men in general, whose cause the author supports in the name of an experience that has been verified in countless episodes. His hero dared to say aloud what many others were probably thinking in silence. He let loose the irrepressible craving for justice that is in man's heart. Henceforth all good men who fall beneath an almost insupportable burden of suffering and are bewildered by it, will join their cries to his or will borrow his. Once the wound in their hearts had been opened, it bled more often and more abundantly. To stop this bleeding, more was required than the too simple remedies of the ancient sages. Only the Savior, by coming Himself, could succeed.

Job had introduced a difficulty in the quest for happiness. Qoheleth, the author of the Book of Ecclesiastes, introduces another, equally formidable and widespread. If we wish to simplify it, we may summarize Job's problem as follows: It is not true that the just man is happy, for God allows His best servants to suffer and even seems to overwhelm them.

[70] Job 13:15 (Vulgate).

Qoheleth's position is: God has promised happiness, but this is a mere enticement, for what is called happiness is vanity of vanities. The first words of the book are known to all:

The words of Ecclesiastes, the son of David, the king of Jerusalem. Vanity of vanities, said Ecclesiastes; vanity of vanities, and all is vanity. What hath a man more of all his labor, that he taketh under the sun? [71]

What profitable lesson of wisdom is hidden in the heart of this bitter and disappointed view of the world? It is evident that the author proposes to speak only from personal experience and to state nothing without proof in hand. His testimony, therefore, is particularly cogent. Qoheleth, the "doubting Thomas" of the Old Testament, believes only what he has seen and touched. Having desired happiness, he set out to try everything that is supposed to procure it. He omits nothing. And everywhere he found only uncertainty, limitations, illusions, falsehood. His testimony is the balance-sheet of his own experience of disappointment. A single phrase expresses it: "All is vanity," that is, all earthly things pass away and disappoint us sooner or later. But in coming to his conclusion, he first catalogues all the things from which men usually expect happiness. He looks at men's toil and worry.

I have seen all things that are done under the sun, and behold all is vanity, and vexation of spirit. . . . What hath man more of his labor? I have seen the trouble, which God hath given the sons of man to be exercised in it. . . . And I have known that there was no better thing than to rejoice, and to do well in this life.[72]

[71] Eccles. 1:1–3.   [72] Eccles. 1:14; 3:9–10, 12.

Men toil and work like slaves for such a paltry result!
One generation destroys what the preceding one erected.
One man's experience is useless to others; it all falls into
oblivion; the same cycle begins over and over again.

One generation passeth away, and another generation
cometh. . . . What is it that hath been? The same thing that
shall be. What is it that hath been done? The same that shall be
done. Nothing under the sun is new.[73]

If we raise the objection that progress is a reality, Ecclesiastes does not deny it, for it is a fact of experience. But
he shows that progress is almost entirely on the material
plane. On the deeper, spiritual plane who could prove that
progress exists? Indeed mankind hardly seems to advance
at all in this realm; it is ever going back to start all over
again.

Work and activity bring nothing but disappointment. Yes,
but perhaps power and ambition can bring happiness. But
once more Qoheleth answers in the name of experience:

And I surpassed in riches all that were before me in Jerusalem;
my wisdom also remained with me. And whatsoever my eyes
desired, I refused them not; and I withheld not my heart from
enjoying every pleasure. . . . And when I turned myself to
all the works which my hands had wrought, and to the labors
wherein I had labored in vain, I saw in all things vanity and
vexation of mind, and that nothing was lasting under the sun.[74]

Is pleasure the answer? But Qoheleth tasted every pleasure and luxury that his immense fortune could afford.

I said in my heart: I will go, and abound with delights, and
enjoy good things. . . . I heaped together for myself silver and

[73] Eccles. 1:4–10.   [74] Eccles. 2:9–11.

gold, and the wealth of kings, and provinces; I made me singing men and singing women, and the delights of the sons of men, cups and vessels to serve to pour out wine. . . . And I withheld not my heart from enjoying every pleasure.[75]

What benefit did he receive from it all? Nothing. Vanity of vanities. But is the quest of wisdom at least exempt from the universal vanity? Here is the answer of this wisest of all wise men:

I passed further to behold wisdom and errors and folly. . . . And I saw that wisdom excelled folly, as much as light differeth from darkness. . . . And I said in my heart: If the death of the fool and mine shall be one, what doth it avail me, that I have applied myself more to the study of wisdom? And speaking with my own mind, I perceived that this also was vanity.[76]

Qoheleth's experience, being complete, forces men to admit that absolutely nothing is free of vanity, that is, disappointment. Happiness seems to be inexorably banished. Qoheleth then attempts a last-minute rescue by admitting voluntary limitations. Like the ancient philosophers, he forces himself to aspire to nothing higher than a haughty or a humble mediocrity. Perhaps it is easier to taste some happiness in a state of modest simplicity? But this surrender fails to disguise the thirst of a soul in its unsuccessful attempt at self-deception. Moreover, as if wishing to cut off the last way of escape, Qoheleth hastens to add that nothing can insure even this mediocre happiness, neither wisdom nor the fear of God. One has only to open his eyes and see!

A just man perisheth in his justice, and a wicked man liveth a long time in his wickedness. . . . There are just men to whom

[75] Eccles. 2:1–10.   [76] Eccles. 2:11–15.

evils happen, as though they had done the works of the wicked; and there are wicked men who are as secure as though they had the deeds of the just; but this also I judge most vain. . . . All things equally happen to the just and to the wicked, to the good and to the evil, to the clean and to the unclean.[77]

That being so, why not enjoy oneself and gather whatever roses are within reach, since they wither so quickly? In saying this, Qoheleth hardly claims to have reached total wisdom. Beyond the vanity that is man's lot, beyond all the new beginnings and the vicious circles, at least God is pursuing a purpose. But the purpose so far transcends human intelligence that man can never hope to glimpse it. What consolation, therefore, can man derive, when it is revealed to him that a divine plan exists, if this plan is so transcendent that it crushes him?

So it is that on the level of experience, where Qoheleth stands and intends to remain (and this makes his testimony all the stronger and more disappointing), no solution can be found to the problem of happiness. The reader feels discouraged as he closes the Book.[78] He understands that there is an infinite distance between man's labor and its fruits, between desires and reality. He realizes that the feeling of emptiness that he experiences originates in the disproportion between what he desires and what he receives. Man's heart is indeed insatiable and his desires are never realized. "The eye is not filled with seeing, neither is the ear filled with hearing." [79] If he chances to obtain what he

[77] Eccles. 7:16; 8:14; 9:2.
[78] But even the bitterness contains a lesson. Man's efforts are in vain. He cannot by himself obtain what he yearns for. His last resort is to bow down and open his heart to grace.
[79] Eccles. 1:8.

wants, he learns, in bitter distress, that things do not contain what they seemed to promise. Not only do they escape his grasp by passing away, but they leave behind nothing but disillusion, a void, a taste of ashes. All is vanity. But that is not all; the drama of happiness is even more tragic, for it involves our whole nature. It is not just the relativity of all things that tortures us, but the fact that we have the sense of the absolute but cannot attain it. Man's misery is all the worse because he remembers the noble estate from which he has fallen. Only the infinite can fulfill and content man, but he is a prisoner of his own limitations.

"Where can wisdom be found?" Such was the cry of Job in his distress. "All is vanity." This was Ecclesiastes' refrain, like a tolling bell. On seeing the failure of these two sages in their quest, should we judge that the pursuit of happiness and the wisdom that is directed to the attainment of happiness are futile? Is there no result of these efforts, except that we become aware that we know nothing and can do nothing? Things are not quite that bleak. The balance-sheet of the sages' experience does not show a complete loss. It is a real credit for a soul to maintain faith and trust in God in the midst of complete abandonment, and to bear such suffering without rebellion. It is a real credit that a man who has been given no certainty about life after death should cry out from the depths of his pain: "For I know that my Redeemer liveth, and in the last day I shall rise out of the earth. And I shall be clothed again with my skin, and in my flesh I shall see my God." [80] Even taking it in its literal sense, this cry, while not unveiling the mystery of the future life, nevertheless turns us in the

[80] Job 19:25–26.

direction of the light and forces the darkness to recede a
little. It is a credit that the author of the Book of Job should
have taught man his need for justice, such a deep-seated
craving that God Himself, who has put it in man, does
not refuse to allow its claims.

A credit it is, likewise, that Qoheleth, proving as never
before the vanity of all things, should have hollowed out
an immense void in the soul, then deepened the void until
the soul was truly unfathomable. It is true that Qoheleth
comes to no conclusion; he leaves the soul to its emptiness
and its obscurity; but the soul is certain that the universe
can never give what it seeks. Far from having discouraged
man, he has increased beyond all limits his thirst for happiness. He has truly revealed the human soul and its capacity
for the infinite.[81]

Thus, even at the horizon's blackest point, all is not dark;
a few rays of light filter through the obscurity. Contrary
to appearances, Job and Qoheleth really helped to build the
edifice of wisdom. They did useful work themselves and
they also cleared the way for their successors and prepared
for the coming of Eternal Wisdom. The difficulties, however serious they may have been, did not invalidate the
principles that the sages had always held regarding the
pursuit of happiness and wisdom. On the contrary, they
provided more ample and solid foundations for these principles. It remains true that happiness is possible for man

[81] St. Paul's message was to complete and bring an answer to
that of Qoheleth: "And if I should have prophecy and should
know all mysteries and all knowledge, and if I should have all
faith, so that I could remove mountains, and have not charity, I
am nothing" (I Cor. 13:2).

and that the just man has a right to happiness. It remains true also that wisdom is a positive reality and its tenets are valid and are based upon a profound experience of life.

But the secret of the fertility of wisdom lies in its dependence upon faith and revelation. By steadfast faith the sages overcome all the difficulties and contradictions they encounter. When experience strikes them down with disappointment, they do not begin to raise questions about everything, nor do they doubt the divine promises. The difficulties become an opportunity to deepen both their notion of wisdom and their faith in God. Since He could not fail to be true and since experience cannot be called into question either, there remains but one solution: to revise their ideas of happiness, to turn to God, who will give them a more interior and more spiritual notion of happiness, to learn from Him the wisdom that infinitely surpasses that of this world. This they do. This is the exact point to which God wished to lead them.

THE SCHOOL OF WISDOM

And the Child grew, and waxed strong, full of wisdom; and the grace of God was in Him.[82]

Had the sages been merely solitary thinkers, philosophers whose judgments of life were lucid but detached, men living apart from the world, the development of their thought would have been relatively unimportant. But we know that most of them were deeply involved in the affairs of life. They held high offices and influenced their environment. Moreover, these educated, experienced leaders were men of

[82] Luke 2:40.

faith and good morals. They were, therefore, universally heeded and respected. A constantly increasing number of people came to consult them. The sages wanted to give these disciples not only advice, but an education. Soon this *musar* or training was given in real schools. The *musar* reflects the mentality, the interests and, to some extent, the thought-processes of the sages. An examination of it, as it is revealed in the wisdom books, shows us a map of the route followed by the teachers and their disciples in their quest for wisdom.

The school of wisdom strove first to inculcate attention, reflection, discipline and the practice of virtue. But, contrary to appearances, the sage did not seek primarily to lead his disciple to knowledge or to happiness as such, but rather to wisdom itself. We may even say that they aspired to meet wisdom "in person." How could the pupil understand all this on entering the master's school? He believes, and perhaps for a long time, that wisdom is acquired by the laborious learning and loyal practice of the lessons taught. But a day comes when a supernatural intervention completes the master's teaching and enlightens the soul. Then indeed he sees clearly that wisdom is something more than teaching, discipline, knowledge or even moral conduct. He discovers wisdom for himself; he lives the life of wisdom, which is an interior attitude, a wholly spiritual state of soul, as well as a living presence and an infinitely lovable reality, flooding the soul with light and love. In the school of wisdom the disciple prepares for the coming of this presence, as step by step he throws open his doors in welcome.

However, though the school of wisdom is something more than teaching and discipline, yet at least in the beginning it must take on that form, all the more so as the master's ideal is higher and more spiritual.[83] Such a method protects the disciple from illusion. He understands that wisdom is not found along easy paths free of obstacles.[84] As a child he had often been admonished and corrected by his parents. Now also a firm hand should guide him and, if necessary, beat him, on his way up the steep path of wisdom. This education, like God's method, is energetic but always paternal. "My son, reject not the correction of the Lord; and do not faint when thou art chastised by Him; for whom the Lord loveth, He chastiseth; and as a father in the son He pleaseth Himself." [85]

The youth is warned that he will find but little pleasure in the life of discipline, but he must prepare for trials, be diligent and generous, not only bear a heavy yoke but even reach the point of loving it.

My son, from thy youth up receive instruction, and even to thy gray hairs thou shalt find wisdom. . . . Give ear, my son, and take wise counsel, and cast not away my advice. Put thy feet into her fetters, and thy neck into her chains. Bow down thy shoulder, and bear her, and be not grieved with her bands. Come to her with all thy mind, and keep her ways with all thy power.[86]

---

[83] The rich young man of the Gospel is a typical example of the young disciple of the Old Testament, who has practiced the commandments since childhood and who, eager for perfection, goes in search of one who appears to him as a master of wisdom (Matt. 19:17–23; Mark 10:17–31; Luke 18:18–30).

[84] Later Christ, too, would teach this. His first directions to those who wish to be His disciples were to leave everything, to take up their cross and to follow Him.

[85] Prov. 3:11–12.   [86] Ecclus. 6:18, 24–27.

He will find scarcely any consolation along the way. On the contrary, a strange obscurity may oppress his soul, causing him terror and anxiety. Yet he should not be discouraged.

For she [wisdom] walketh with him in temptation, and at the first she chooseth him. She will bring upon him fear and dread and trial; and she will scourge him with the affliction of her discipline, till she try him by her laws and trust his soul. Then she will strengthen him, and make a straight way to him, and give him joy. . . . Come to her as one that plougheth and soweth, and wait for her good fruits; for in working about her thou shalt labor a little and shalt quickly eat of her fruits. How very unpleasant is wisdom to the unlearned, and the unwise will not continue with her.[87]

The master alternates severe warnings with helpful encouragement. His words stimulate his disciple to generous effort, eagerness to learn, patient, persevering investigation. The pupil is advised to associate with old and experienced men: his father and trustworthy friends, while all dissipation, flighty conversations and vain curiosity are forbidden. The test may seem very hard to a young man, yet he feels that the maxims of deeply-experienced, prudent men are not vain words, but the fruit of genuine knowledge which he himself should acquire for his own benefit. What rich meaning is contained in this emphatic promise:

My son, if thou wilt receive my words and wilt hide my commandments with thee, that thy ear may hearken to wisdom, incline thy heart to know prudence; for if thou shalt call for wisdom, and incline thy heart to prudence; if thou shalt seek her as money, and shalt dig for her as for a treasure; then shalt thou

[87] Ecclus. 4:18–20; 6:19–21.

understand the fear of the Lord, and shalt find the knowledge of God.[88]

Thus, the pupil must strive to be attentive and observant as well as practice the active virtues which are frequently discussed. But what is most important is the heart's attitude of attention, the inclination to love what is good and to preserve personal integrity.

With all watchfulness keep thy heart, because life issueth out from it. Remove from thee a forward mouth, and let detracting lips be far from thee. Let thy eyes look straight on, and let thy eyelids go before thy steps. Make straight the path for thy feet, and all thy ways shall be established. Decline not to the right hand, nor to the left; turn away thy foot from evil.[89]

Only when the young man has acquired wisdom will he safe from the seductions that debar him from the path of life.

If wisdom shall enter into thy heart, and knowledge please thy soul, counsel shall keep thee and prudence shall preserve thee, that thou mayest be delivered from the evil way, . . . that thou mayest be delivered from the strange women, and from the stranger, who softeneth her words.[90]

The disciple must know that he cannot reap until he has laboriously ploughed. Effort is the price of wisdom.

[88] Prov. 2:1–5.

[89] Prov. 4:23–27. The same note is heard in St. Paul's advice to Titus and to Timothy: "Flee thou youthful desires, . . . and avoid foolish and unlearned questions" (II Tim. 2:22–23). "For he also that striveth for the mastery is not crowned, except he strive lawfully. . . . Understand what I say, for the Lord will give thee in all things understanding" (II Tim. 2:5–7).

[90] Prov. 2:10–16.

"My heart delighted in her, my foot walked in the right way, from my youth up I sought after her." [91]

But the master, knowing the eager spontaneity and wild passions of young hearts, will be lenient to his disciples in their first faults. He will encourage them, rally their forces and, if need be, remind them of the Lord's great mercy. "To the penitent He hath given the way of justice, and He hath strengthened them that were fainting in patience, and hath appointed to them the lot of truth. . . . How great is the mercy of the Lord, and His forgiveness to them that turn to Him." [92] The master does not conceal how hard a combat must be undertaken for wisdom's sake, but at the same time he shows the way by the example of his own experience:

When I was yet young, before I wandered about, I sought for wisdom openly in my prayer. I prayed for her before the Temple, and unto the very end I will seek after her, and she flourished as a grape soon ripe. My heart delighted in her, my foot walked in the right way, from my youth up I sought after her. I bowed down my ear a little, and received her. I found much wisdom in myself, and I profited much therein. . . . I stretched forth my hands on high, and I bewailed my ignorance of her. I directed my soul to her, and in knowledge I found her. I possessed my heart with her from the beginning; therefore I shall not be forsaken. My entrails were troubled in seeking her; therefore shall I possess a good possession.[93]

These words of the master, full of fervor and ardent zeal, along with his affectionate and understanding manner, fill the disciple's heart with hope. The latter is, therefore, will-

[91] Ecclus. 51:20.   [92] Ecclus. 17:20, 28.
[93] Ecclus. 51:18–22, 26–29.

ing to remain in the dark for the time being and to struggle without immediate results. This acceptance opens his heart, frees him of all fraud and hypocrisy, enables him to make a free choice which is a true dedication of his whole soul and all his strength. "The Holy Spirit of discipline will flee from the deceitful." [94] The disciple will not deceive God nor will he deceive himself; therefore he will not be thwarted in his quest. "Think of the Lord in goodness, and seek Him in simplicity of heart. For He is found by them that tempt Him not, and He showeth Himself to them that have faith in Him." [95]

For a long period, then, the young man must be trained in the discipline of wisdom: custody of the senses and custody of the heart. During this time he learns to look inward and to appraise, among a thousand proffered possibilities, the best choice and the most direct route to happiness. It is a disagreeable time when the field of his rebellious nature must be cleared of underbrush to allow the good seed to sprout.

In our day this ascesis, this training in good habits, would be termed the practice of virtues. These virtues are but little respected by persons who are not attracted to the ideal of perfection, but are lovingly and energetically pursued by others as the only way of salvation. But the Old Testament notion is somewhat different. It is true that in some of the biblical maxims we can discern one or another of the virtues which centuries later would be queens of Christendom and stand in our cathedrals sculptured in stone: justice, prudence, fortitude and temperance. We see also that in the

[94] Wisd. 1:5.   [95] Wisd. 1:1–2.

Bible the role of these virtues is to smooth the way and trace a path to spiritual realities, so that grace may more readily enter the soul. But to understand the role of the virtues in the attainment of wisdom, we must know their exact relation to the theological virtues, to the infused virtues and gifts, and to charity.[96] This is a difficult task, for in the Bible the same term can designate different realities.

Fortitude, for instance, refers to the acquired virtue or to the cardinal virtue or to the gift of the Holy Ghost. It is difficult at times to know which meaning is intended. But a careful scrutiny is sure to make it clear. The following passage, for instance, unquestionably refers to the fortitude obtained by long perseverance and great effort. "A frame of wood bound together in the foundation of a building shall not be loosed; so neither shall the heart that is established by advised counsel." [97] But when the master exhorts his disciple in these terms: "Put thy feet into her fetters, . . . bow down thy shoulder, . . . come to her with all thy mind, . . . and when thou hast gotten her, let her not go," [98] he refers to a mobilization of all the soul's forces, attracted and sustained by supernatural grace which animates them and confers the strength to seize what is so ardently desired. Finally, when Abraham's triumphant fortitude is praised in the Book of Wisdom, the author refers to the wholly gratuitous gift from God which compensates for natural insufficiency and weakness, provided that the

[96] In the apostles' teaching of the early Church the virtues were presented as a form of charity. This followed the Old Testament tradition.

[97] Ecclus. 22:19.   [98] Ecclus. 6:25–28.

will be directed entirely toward the task in hand: "[Wisdom] . . . preserved him without blame to God, and kept him strong against the compassion for his son." [99]

In the Book of Proverbs the passage in praise of the strong woman demonstrates very well this scale of moral values. There is first the judicious use of property and authority, then the wholly interior fortitude derived from the practice of charity, and finally the crowning of these virtues by the divine gift which satisfied the soul. "Strength and beauty are her clothing." [100]

Thus there is limitless scope for the disciple's efforts, but he may often encounter many maxims without realizing their meaning. Only the sage knows that even the slightest effort is of some use and that the greatest gifts are for the hearts that are fully prepared to receive them. Like the wise virgins of the Gospel, who prepare their lamps as they go out to meet the Bridegroom, the disciples dispose their hearts for the coming of a more profound knowledge, pregnant with truths already half glimpsed.

Of all the virtues which rise to the summons of diverse circumstances, there seems to be one which the disciple must practice continuously and which the master ranks very high, close to wisdom itself: "Forsake childishness, and live and walk by the ways of prudence." [101] The sage's first counsel to men is to be prudent. Prudence is one of the least respected virtues of our day. Indeed, if we equate it with an attitude of petty and distrustful scheming with regard to the world, our neighbor and ourselves, then we would be right to prefer to lack foresight, to take risks, to be daring. But prudence is something quite different and,

[99] Wisd. 10:5.   [100] Prov. 31:25.   [101] Prov. 9:6.

despite appearances, we should not let the Wisdom Books put us on the wrong scent. It is true that the master often urges his disciples to practice that human prudence which avoids dangerous enterprises, seeks protection against exterior peril, maintains an attitude of discreet reserve toward strangers, that is, unknown persons who might bring trouble. But cowardice is certainly not a virtue in Israel. The Jews are not intended to practice a form of prudence in which shrewd maneuvers compensate for weakness.

But the learning of wickedness is not wisdom; and the device of sinners is not prudence. . . . Woe to them that are of a double heart and to wicked lips and to the hands that do evil, and to the sinner that goeth on the earth two ways. Woe to them that are fainthearted, who believe not God.[102]

It is apparent, too, that the sage has also experienced risks: the serious risks of expending all his energies and denying himself even licit pleasures, without perhaps receiving anything in return. His time and his youth seem to have been devoted to an uncertain ideal. Moreover, he has abstained from amassing a fortune, as that task would have monopolized the energy that he was saving for a better purpose. "Gold and silver make the feet stand sure; but wise counsel is above them both." [103] He ran a risk. He sacrificed everything to the pursuit of wisdom and that was true prudence, wearing the mask of folly. That is the wisdom for which Solomon prayed.

Wherefore I wished, and understanding was given me; and I called upon God, and the spirit of wisdom came upon me. . . .

[102] Ecclus. 19:19; 2:14–15.   [103] Ecclus. 40:25.

For she knoweth and understandeth all things, and shall lead me soberly in all my works, and shall preserve me by her power.[104]

Far from being a maneuver, prudence is a mobilization of forces in well-balanced order that makes them effective. Its positive aspects are discretion, reflection and foresight.

Reduced to its human elements alone, prudence is powerless to guide us. For by ourselves what can we accomplish? The sage, therefore, turns his irony against himself and admits that if we measure ourselves by God, "in His hand are both we and our words and all wisdom and the knowledge and skill of works." [105] But when prudence attains its point of perfection, that is, when it receives supernatural light and guidance, it is a communication with wisdom, as well as a protection against the mortal dangers that threaten.

To think therefore upon her, is perfect understanding; and he that watcheth for her, shall quickly be secure. . . . A man that shall wander out of the way of the doctrine, shall abide in the company of the giants.[106]

Thus, prudence plays a leading role in the wisdom literature. Even considered in its simplest aspect as practical common sense, it requires attention and reflection, which themselves are of great educational value. It trains the soul, not to withdraw from experience, but to pause first, to discover its true nature and to weigh its real value. Time is its ally; well-ordered and creative activity is its normal fruit. "Strive not in a matter which doth not concern thee. . . . My son, meddle not with many matters. . . . The wisdom of a scribe cometh by his time of leisure; and he that is less in action, shall receive wisdom." [107]

[104] Wisd. 7:7; 9:11.   [105] Wisd. 7:16.
[106] Wisd. 6:16; Prov. 21:16.   [107] Ecclus. 11:9–10; 38:24.

Does this mean that wisdom flourishes in idleness? Of course not; all the sages condemn this vice. Work confers nobility and dignity upon man, as countless texts affirm. But man's purpose is not to possess material things. He is created for a spiritual end and he should be the master, not the slave, of those things that could become obstacles on his path. Once he has assured his independence by honest work, he should then devote himself to unselfish pursuits which carry their own reward. All cold egoism should be banished from the quest of wisdom. "Establish within thyself a heart of good counsel; for there is no other thing of more worth to thee than it. . . . A skillful man hath taught many, and is sweet to his own soul. . . . A wise man instructeth his own people, and the fruits of his understanding are faithful." [108]

Prudence likewise requires fortitude, for it is hard for a man to suppress his desires, to dominate his rash impulses and reflexes. Prudence also leads to temperance, because a man who reflects and controls himself refrains from every excess and every abuse. He takes care not to use the things around him in an improper way.[109] By the path of prudence, finally, the wise man attains justice, the exact compliance with both rights and duties in dealing with all things. So it was that Christ's advice to be prudent as serpents and simple as doves had already been practiced in the Old Testament.

The simplicity that is a part of prudence is not naïvete or artificial candor, but a clear-eyed innocence that is free of

[108] Ecclus. 37:17–26.
[109] "See therefore, brethren, how you walk circumspectly; not as unwise" (Eph. 5:15). "Be prudent, therefore, and watch in prayers" (I Pet. 4:7).

devious, hypocritical ways.[110] It expresses a state of inner unity, the true self of a man who has become sincere in his deeds. The prudent man, once he knows that something is good and should be done, does it immediately and without reservation. Far from being contrary to prudence, simplicity is its choicest fruit. Man loses his simplicity, the treasure of childhood; to recover it he must not fear the "folly" of prudence. By prudence he withdraws from evil and dwells in silence, not to find himself, but to find unadulterated simplicity—humble, gentle simplicity that opens wide the doors of his prison. The man who dedicates his whole being to the quest of simplicity soon sees the inner meaning of Christ's words: "If thy eye be single, thy whole body will be lightsome." [111] Prudence and simplicity will help and guide him in the ways of wisdom.

We have been able to see the sage in a different light as we watched him training his disciples. Without ceasing to be the experienced man of faith, he has shown us a new side of himself, more intimate, more profound, more attractive; in short, he has revealed his soul. By giving his pupils a glimpse of the ultimate goal sought, he can demand of them the conditions required for its attainment. How, indeed, could they appreciate the value of the rules imposed unless

---

[110] St. Paul's simplicity seems to proceed from humility. The realization that everything comes from God leads to spontaneous performance of duty: "For I say, by the grace that is given me, to all that are among you, not to be more wise than it behoveth to be wise, but to be wise unto sobriety, and according as God hath divided to every one the measure of faith. . . . Having different gifts, . . . he that exhorteth, in exhorting; he that giveth, with simplicity" (Rom. 12:3, 8).

[111] Luke 11:34 (Vulgate).

they knew something about the prize to be awarded? Once wisdom had revealed her true features, the disciples understood that what was demanded of them was neither a sumtotal of information nor a proper notion of happiness nor a severe ascesis nor the practice of virtues. It was, rather, a spiritual attitude of open-heartedness and receptivity, a kind of state of grace, a readiness to welcome a friend whom they daily learn to know and love, whose coming fills them with holy, reverent joy.

Such a quick glance can give but a hint of the immense treasures contained in the sages' doctrine. May it at least encourage us to join their school. To profit from their teaching, we must put aside, to some extent, our modern ways of thought. Only if we strive to be attentive and receptive can we become acclimatized to and feel at home in their utterly God-centered atmosphere. Often people are upset by Israel's anthropomorphisms and by the turbulent passion of Jewish life. Sometimes the Old Testament itself disappoints those who expect to find in it a kind of "treatise of spirituality." But it can be taken for granted that those who pass by God's word without heeding it, run the risk of never drinking from the font of true spirituality.

The sage of Israel, who is encountered at the heart of the Old Testament, is the soul that hears the word and keeps it. He is not, on that account, separated from his people, who indeed re-echo the message which he receives and transmits. For this supremely theocentric nation views all problems in the light of faith. Seeking only God, the Jews relate all else to Him, particularly "the spiritual life." The phrase did not have even the same meaning for them as it has for us. We cannot be at all sure that it had *any* meaning. Pious Jews concentrated their attention upon God's glory and did not feel the need to dwell upon or to define the action of God in the soul. Their interior life is revealed only accidentally by the phrasing of a prayer or when they utter cries of joy or bitterness. On the other hand, they attached great importance to the duty of praising the beauty which they had glimpsed and of explaining true and immutable values. In addition, the sage wished to call other souls to the feast where he had already been summoned, for he wanted to help them to share it with him. "Blessed is the man that shall continue in wisdom, and that shall meditate in his justice, and in his mind shall think of the all-seeing eye of God." [112]

These few words summarize the doctrine of the ancient masters and convey a hint of the happiness in store for those who enroll in their school.

Blessed is the man that shall continue in wisdom. He is separated from appearances and from vanity. He tastes the substantial joy of truth, as his heart becomes more and more silent and the word is decanted with its aroma of God's light.

Blessed is the man . . . that shall meditate in his justice. So often have we encountered such men in both the Old and the New Testaments that their image is associated with the landscape of Palestine. Even in the earliest times Isaac "was gone forth to meditate in the field, the day being now well spent." [113] The days of nomadic life may have passed away, but not the eternal truths proposed for man's meditation. Only in the silence of meditation—a meditation that is prayer and life—can the soul discover the reality that transports it into the true and eternal kingdom. He meditates *in justice,* for with true judgment and proper estimation of human values, he is assured of a just appreciation of divine

[112] Ecclus. 14:22.   [113] Gen. 24:63.

things too. The sage does not seek to take refuge in the realm of the miraculous and the sublime, but he chooses to live in the fullness of reality, the fullness of truth.

In his mind he shall think of the all-seeing eye of God. This thoughtfulness is characteristic of the judicious man whose heart is tender, but has control of his soul and his mind. He knows what he wants and neglects nothing to attain his goal, for his will is very strong. Prudently and in the fear of God he decides on the most effective means; then, like one determined to win the race, he dashes along the road.

He shall think. Understanding is the indispensable ally of a zealous will. Can a man be satisfied with imperfect knowledge of the one he loves? He thinks, because the object of his love deserves total striving toward greater knowledge and deeper love. But the author adds that the sage's thought will dwell on *the all-seeing eye of God.* A threshold has been crossed; man has already been admitted to the kingdom; he has already found what he continues to seek.

But if the discipline imposed upon himself has borne fruit, it is not entirely because of his efforts, but because of the general atmosphere of study, meditation, reflection and—most important of all—prayer, in which he has lived day after day. Any harvest he has gathered can be attributed to the spiritual and religious attitude which has led him step by step to the heart of the mystery of wisdom, the attitude that is known as "the fear of God."

FEAR OF GOD

The problem of knowledge and the quest for happiness were matters occupying the boundaries of wisdom. The disappointments occasioned by experience had the merit of presenting the problem in its proper terms. The school of wisdom allowed us to glimpse the solution by showing the sages' preoccupations and demonstrating their methods. But the key of the riddle is found only in the fear of God. The itinerary drawn up by wisdom for a soul in search of God should not be imagined as a journey with its successive halting-places. It is more like a progressive discovery of inner depths within the soul, or the exploration of a town where the innermost dwellings are the finest.

At the very center lies the fear of God. There the soul must settle if it is to find wisdom. Only the souls dwelling in the fear of God are visited and possessed by wisdom. This state of fear of God, so similar to the "state of grace" in its meaning and in the substance of the reality experienced, develops in proportion to the soul's consciousness of its vocation to divine life and in proportion to its being invaded and possessed by wisdom. Of course, from the very beginning a spark of that fear burned in the wise man's heart and the effects which he felt were the reason for his starting off on his quest. But only after great effort and struggle, when he has a presentiment that wisdom is approaching, only then does he see the fear of God in its proper light and in its true nature: as the fertile soil where wisdom can push up its roots, spread out its branches and finally bear fruits of grace and glory. Fear indeed plays a primary role in the minds of the sages who keep stressing and praising it. "The fear of God hath set itself above all things; blessed is the man to whom it is given to have the fear of God." [114]

A passage from the prophet Baruch describes how mercifully and how courteously God bestowed it on men in order

[114] Ecclus. 25:14–15.

that they might love and develop it. "Because for this end Thou hast put Thy fear in our hearts, to the intent that we should call upon Thy name and praise Thee." [115] This passage echoes Ben Sirah's words: "The fear of the Lord is honor and glory and gladness and a crown of joy." [116] A crown of joy; fear is precious particularly because it is indeed a gift, an endowment. It is true that considered from a human viewpoint it appears as the object and final fruit of the master's training or *musar* ("The fear of the Lord is the lesson of wisdom" [117]), but from God's viewpoint it is both the beginning of His gifts and the sign of their perfection. "The fear of the Lord is the beginning of wisdom." [118] "To fear God is the fullness of wisdom." [119]

Though it may seem to occupy the frontier between the human and the divine realms, or between the acquired and the infused virtues, it cannot at all be considered as a human conquest, a fruit of man's effort. It belongs to the category of divine gifts, the category of grace. A threshold must be crossed and a door opened before we meet fear of the Lord. The sages would readily say of fear what we say of charity: *Ubi caritas et amor, Deus ibi est.* They believe that the presence of fear of God in the soul is a sure sign of the divine presence and influence.

What, then, is this fear? In vain would we seek an exhaustive definition in the wisdom literature. But by the inclinations it arouses and develops, by its effect on the sage's attitude as he scrutinizes the world around him, by the fruits it bears and the perfection it confers, by all this we can form an idea of what it is.

[115] Bar. 3:7. [116] Ecclus. 1:11. [117] Prov. 15:33.
[118] Prov. 1:7. [119] Ecclus. 1:20.

It is evident that the sages thirsted for knowledge and depended upon experience to acquire it. But no personal advantage could attract them to the kind of intellectual progress that either attacks or simply ignores God's teaching. They cannot even conceive of the knowledge that demands an account from God. What keeps them humbly dependent upon divine doctrine and therefore brings them enlightenment is the fear of God. Truly, it is a bridge built between human knowledge and divine intelligence. "The fear of the Lord is the religiousness of knowledge." [120] The sages adopt a humbly dependent attitude; they refuse to confine themselves to purely human knowledge which is unconcerned with the relations of knowledge to revelation. For this reason they are admitted to God's friendship, which they cherish and preserve as the path to the delights of wisdom. They know that fear of God is the solid food of their souls, more profitable than all other learning.[121]

There is something wonderfully beautiful and touching in the sages' attitude: an attitude of unconditional trust, of submission, of acceptance, of total dependence. For them, happiness consists in pleasing God and being docile to His directions. We recall the cry of Job, who was so famous for his fear of God: "This may be my comfort, that afflicting me with sorrow, He spare not, nor I contradict the words of the Holy One." [122] While the wisdom they all seek may evade their eager grasp, yet they know that in a way it has already been given to them and dwells with them, preserving

[120] Ecclus. 1:17.

[121] In the New Testament, too, the man who best pleases God is the one who fears Him (cf. Acts 10:2).

[122] Job. 6:10.

them from the loss of God and His friendship. "The fear of the Lord, that is wisdom; and to depart from evil, is understanding." [123]

The fear of God strongly affects the sage's understanding of the world around him. As cantor of the divine transcendence, he takes care not to view creatures as separated from their Creator. Perhaps the most beautiful pages of the Wisdom Books deal with the Creator's relation to His creatures and with the sanctity of all creation. Not only does the wise man strive to know God's works as they are, in their intrinsic beauty, but he also considers them in their essence and in their relation to their Maker, so that he sees them clothed in dazzling light. He studies and questions them, restraining his examination only when the mystery of love in them fills him with such respect that he falls to his knees. Then he ceases to question and remains silent. While he would probably like to seize, if not God, at least His reflection inherent in His works, as he knows that this is the key to all things and the secret of wisdom, yet his fear of God, which is his love of the mystery in which God Himself has willed to conceal Himself, forbids his forcing the divine will.

We can recall the violent diatribe in which Job's four friends all accuse him of lacking this reverential fear. They keep repeating in various ways the question: "Who are you to dare to question the Almighty?" But Job is not to be frustrated in a hope which God Himself has put in his heart. His fear of God will obtain for him something more than a mere technical knowledge of the world's secrets. He is granted a view of the divine proportions and value of all things. This value expresses neither measurable quantities

[123] Job 28:28.

nor numbers, but rather the unique and necessary place of each item in the created universe. That is how the author of the Book of Job views the diffusion of wisdom throughout the earth. "[God] . . . made a weight for the winds, and weighed the waters by measure, when He gave a law for the rain and a way for the sounding storms." [124] Whether it be wind or rain, social virtues or moral virtues, everything can be verified; everything fits into the pattern, in spite of appearances. By the fear of God infused into his heart, the sage glimpses the relations among things and, on a higher level, their relation to God. Of course, he is not the architect who planned the edifice and determined the functions and proportions of each part, but he is able to discern them in order that whatever degree of collaboration God expects of man may follow the same golden rules and may bring the structure to its completion. "Thou hast ordained all things in measure, and number, and weight." [125] "All the works of the Lord are good, and He will furnish every work in due time. It is not to be said: This is worse than that." [126]

The good which God wills and the evil which He permits combine in a plan that the sage can discover and recognize, provided the fear of God be with him. And if indeed he discovers these values, proportions, and this divine rhythm, if he understands the hidden springs of each creature's functioning under God's direction, it is because he ventures forth guided by God's authoritative word and clothed in the cloak of respectful fear. "He that sendeth forth light, and it goeth; and hath called it, and it obeyeth Him with trembling." [127]

Without neglecting any of the lessons he has received, the wise man advances, full of fear. He fears indeed, but this fear

[124] Job 28:25-26.   [125] Wisd. 11:21.   [126] Ecclus. 39:39.
[127] Bar. 3:33.

is not the terror Adam and Eve felt in the Garden of Eden. It is rather the awe which makes the angels themselves tremble in the Lord's presence, the fear experienced by all who draw near to Him.[128]

God's presence is so living and so evident to the wise man that the world can never seem non-religious to him, can never be viewed apart from divine holiness. He knows that he is always in God's presence and whenever he speaks, his words are, in a way, addressed to Him and to Him alone. "God is witness of his reins, and He is a true searcher of his heart, and a hearer of his tongue. . . . That which containeth all things, hath knowledge of the voice." [129]

The sages view God's presence not only as the exercise of authority but as a source of spiritual life. They are always referring to this contact which regenerates and sanctifies every human activity. Their fear of God enables them to experience this presence and to live by it. As a result, they are utterly and constantly dependent upon God, who not only supports their lives but leads them to wisdom and initiates them in the divine mysteries. "For if thou shalt call for wisdom and incline thy heart to prudence, . . . then shalt thou understand the fear of the Lord, and shalt find the knowledge of God." [130]

Thus, the fear of God is not a reaction to coercion nor a slave's attitude. It requires a lofty gaze toward the light emanating from God's sanctity. The sage meditates quietly until the dark night slowly vanishes, pierced by the rising light.

The fear which kept the sage in God's presence with faith

[128] Fear seized the apostles at the time of Christ's transfiguration, and St. Paul on the road to Damascus.

[129] Wisd. 1:6-7.   [130] Prov. 2:3-5.

and with reverence likewise provides the foundation of humility in his heart.[131] No fault is more feared and assailed by the wise man than pride, which in its very roots is an error, a sin against the truth. Far from posing as a god, the wise man acknowledges his weakness. On many occasions he impresses upon his pupils the lesson that every man is defective in virtue: "The beginning of the pride of man, is to fall off from God; because his heart is departed from Him that made him." [132]

What undertones of sadness in these words! Fear, on the other hand, banishes pride by giving man a deep consciousness of his dependence upon God. He then lives in humility, which is truth; in gentleness, which is justice; and, finally, in love. "Perfect charity casteth out fear." [133] But he refers to the fear that is terror or fright; of these the wise man is free. He is not terrified of God. He speaks to Him familiarly, though always respectfully. Job's attitude is a good example. It is true that he fears the divine judgments and there are frequent references to the "dread of Yahweh," but this indicates the resonance set up in a finite and limited soul that is touched and possessed by the divinity. This tremendous experience causes a certain overstrain. Moreover, the entire Old Testament is dominated by Yahweh's glory that is manifested in disquieting ways.[134]

[131] "Be not highminded, but fear" (Rom. 11:20).
[132] Ecclus. 10:14–15.   [133] I John 4:18.
[134] With regard to this transition from fright to fear, an episode from the Gospel of St. Mark is very enlightening: "Master, doth it not concern Thee that we perish? And rising up, He rebuked the wind, and said to the sea: Peace, be still. And the wind ceased; and there was made a great calm. And He said to them: Why are you fearful? Have you not faith yet? And they feared ex-

But habitually the fear of Yahweh enables the wise man to live in a relationship of filial trust and love toward God. It is as Father and Creator, not as a tyrant, that God has willed that man should be subject to Him. "With all thy soul fear the Lord, and . . . with all thy strength love Him that made thee." [135]

The fear of God is combined with love, even permeated with love. Because the wise man fears God, he also believes in the divine goodness, tenderness and mercy. "Because thou art Lord of all, Thou makest Thyself gracious to all. . . . Thou being master of power, judgest with tranquillity; and with great favor disposest of us; for Thy power is at hand when Thou wilt." [136] Even greater proof of the excellence of fear lies in the fact that Ben Sirah sees it as the pathway to divine charity, as a form of love itself, since it seeks only to please God.

With him that feareth the Lord, it shall go well in the latter end. . . . They that fear the Lord, will seek after the things that are well pleasing to Him; and they that love Him, shall be filled with His law. . . . Blessed is the man to whom it is given to have the fear of God: . . . The fear of God is the beginning of His love.[137]

Frequently, therefore, the sage identifies fear and wisdom. Since fear causes men to conform to God's plan, it disposes them for the action of grace. Small wonder, then, that wisdom and fear should appear as inseparable companions. "To fear God is the fullness of wisdom. . . . The fear of God

---

ceedingly; and they said one to another: Who is this (thinkest thou) that both wind and sea obey Him?" (Mark 4:38–40.)

[135] Ecclus. 7:31–32.   [136] Wisd. 12:16, 18.
[137] Ecclus. 1:13; 2:19; 25:15–16.

is all wisdom." [138] This should not surprise us if we remember that the greatest homage we can pay God is to do His will, not ours, and to be poor and dependent in order that He may enrich us and bind us closer to Himself. That explains the apparent severity of wisdom in declaring: "They shall call upon me, and I will not hear; they shall rise in the morning and shall not find me; because they have hated instruction and received not the fear of the Lord." [139]

There is no likelihood of the fear of God becoming less necessary as the soul advances toward God. On the contrary, it becomes all the more so in proportion as the soul seeks more intimate union with Him.[140] And just as truly great noblemen are accustomed to defer graciously to the merits of poor and simple men, so wisdom in all her glory and purity defers to her humble sister and delights in the companionship of this hidden and diligent worker. "The fear of the Lord is a crown of wisdom." [141] Thereupon fear, eager to render due homage to God, declines the ultimate tribute and humbly replies: "The perfection of the fear of God is wisdom and understanding." [142]

GOD'S WISDOM

Send her out of Thy holy heaven.[143]

Men have not only sought wisdom, they have called out for it. This revealing fact opens new horizons of the vast mystery. While wisdom, even on the natural level, is certainly so precious that it justifies all the patient and diligent

---

[138] Ecclus. 1:20; 19:18.   [139] Prov. 1:28–29.

[140] "Let us cleanse ourselves . . . perfecting sanctification in the fear of God" (II Cor. 7:1).

[141] Ecclus. 1:22.   [142] Ecclus. 21:13.   [143] Wisd. 9:10.

efforts of those seeking it, it is most enlightening to note how, without ceasing their own strivings, they lifted their eyes to the mountains in search of help,[144] so that what began as a study is completed in an appeal and a prayer. These appeals are something more than prayers; their diverse shades of meaning reveal all the aspirations of the sages. Spiritual impulses are found side by side with material concerns. There sometimes appears a rather down-to-earth common sense together with a philosophy of life by no means exempt of greed or the desire for worldly honor. How could it be otherwise? For they have not yet experienced the wisdom which they are requesting; they ignore the joy of her friendship; they have at most only a hint of it. Just as they are they turn to her, and her precise role is to bring them what they lack, to purify their desires of the selfish and carnal elements still in them. She is to initiate and educate them in divine things.

The contrasts found in the wisdom literature should not, then, surprise us. Let us rather admire the dawning of sublime aspirations and the discernment of the sages, who realize how much wisdom can give to those who seek it and ask for it. Some passages of the Book of Wisdom are typical examples of this double trend.

Wisdom is glorious. . . . The beginning of her is the most true desire of discipline. And the care of discipline is love; and love is the keeping of her laws; and the keeping of her laws is the firm foundation of incorruption; and incorruption bringeth near to God. Therefore the desire of wisdom bringeth to the everlasting kingdom. If then your delight be in thrones and sceptres, O ye kings of the people, love wisdom.[145]

[144] Cf. Ps. 120:1.   [145] Wisd. 6:13–25.

How beautiful and yet how disappointing is this text. The inspired writer leads us to the heights in his sublime song, but then brings us back to the level of mere human ambition, for it seems to be an earthly kingship to which he refers. Equally revealing is the prayer formerly attributed to Solomon:

I myself also am a mortal man, like all others, and of the race of him that was first made of the earth. . . . Wherefore I wished, and understanding was given me; and I called upon God, and the spirit of wisdom came upon me; and I preferred her before kingdoms and thrones, and esteemed riches nothing in comparison of her. Neither did I compare unto her any precious stone; for all gold in comparison of her is as a little sand, and silver in respect to her shall be counted as clay. I loved her above health and beauty, and chose to have her instead of light; for her light cannot be put out. . . . Her have I loved, and have sought her out from my youth, and have desired to take her for my spouse, and I became a lover of her beauty. . . . I purposed therefore to take her to me to live with me, knowing that she will communicate to me of her good things, and will be a comfort in my cares and grief. For her sake I shall have glory among the multitude, and honor with the ancients, though I be young; and I shall be found of a quick conceit in judgment, and shall be admired in the sight of the mighty. . . . Moreover, by the means of her I shall have immortality, and shall leave behind me an everlasting memory to them that come after me.[146]

The text presents an almost painful contrast as the young man turns from his sublimely beautiful dream to confess his craving for human renown. In old age he would probably have repudiated these words uttered in the days of ardent

[146] Wisd. 7:1-10; 8:2-13.

desire and uncontrolled ambition. The same ambition is expressed by Ben Sirah, who concludes an admirable chant in praise of wisdom by saying: "She shall exalt him among his neighbors, and in the midst of the church she shall open his mouth." [147] We may wish that the sages had been less concerned with the material profits and personal advantages which they meant to derive from the gift bestowed upon them. But was this possible in their situation?

At any rate, the remnants of earthly appetite subsisting in them do not suppress the other desire, the supra-terrestrial longing that stirs their hearts. It little matters what tribute they pay to human nature, provided only that they are docile in welcoming the divine gift. After all, how well did they know this mysterious wisdom that demanded that they cease their reasoning and submit their minds? We should admire their docility and their fidelity in retaining divine grace and aspiring toward a goal which for them was still wrapped in mystery. The essential matter is that the sages perceived wisdom as a grace far surpassing any merit of theirs and they turned humbly to the only one who could communicate it.

And as I knew that I could not otherwise be continent, except God gave it, and this also was a point of wisdom, to know whose gift it was, I went to the Lord, and besought Him, and said with my whole heart: . . . Send her out of Thy holy heaven, and from the throne of Thy majesty.[148]

Imbued with the fear of God, the wise man feels an urgent divine invitation to welcome wholeheartedly the entrance of this totally gratuitous gift. An infinitely sweet foretaste of the hidden presence overwhelms him with joy. "She will strengthen him, . . . and give him joy, and will disclose

[147] Ecclus. 15:4–5.   [148] Wisd. 8:21; 9:10.

her secrets to him." [149] We hear this note of anticipation in the author of the Book of Wisdom: "Her have I loved, and have sought her out from my youth," [150] and in Ben Sirah: "Blessed is the man . . . that lodgeth near her house, and fastening a pin in her walls shall set up his tent nigh unto her." [151]

The yearning which springs forth from the depths of men's being is evoked, though they may not realize it, by wisdom; the response is brought by wisdom and it, too, is a yearning: "O ye men, to you I call, and my voice is to the sons of men." [152] "Come over to me, all ye that desire me, and be filled with my fruits." [153]

It is a yearning and a persistent invitation, very urgent and yet wholly respecting liberty, as if wisdom, in response to her gratuitous love, sought nothing less than a spontaneous love, not summoned by command, but rising, like her own, from an impulse of the heart. As these appeals are an expression of love and expect a response of love, we should not be surprised to find them both infinitely satisfying and infinitely demanding: infinitely satisfying, for love's only desire is to satisfy her lover and give herself to him; infinitely demanding, because such a gift requires, in return, a no less generous total gift. So wisdom acts. But the more a man experiences the bountiful perfection of this spontaneous love, the poorer and weaker and meaner appears his own love. He therefore strives to increase and develop it. Thus, the sages who convey wisdom's invitation to their pupils also teach them to respond. In short, the school of wisdom is a school of divine love.

The author of the Book of Proverbs has uttered wisdom's

---

[149] Ecclus. 4:20–21.   [150] Wisd. 8:2.   [151] Ecclus. 14:22–25.
[152] Prov. 8:4.   [153] Ecclus. 24:26.

summons, which resounds in three passages with ever increasing urgency. In the first, wisdom sees to it that the multitude will hear her voice: "Wisdom preacheth abroad, she
uttereth her voice in the streets; at the head of multitudes
she crieth out, in the entrance of the gates of the city she
uttereth her words." [154] But her message is a reproach to
men for not heeding her. Thus, it is not the first time that
she has spoken to them; she had already appealed to them,
probably in a more intimate way, but all in vain. Now she
announces their punishment. "Because I called, and you refused; I stretched out my hand, and there was none that
regarded. You have despised all my counsel and have neg-
lected my reprehensions." [155] But in her love for them
she hastens to set a marvellous promise alongside the reproaches: "Turn ye at my reproof: behold I will utter my
spirit to you and will show you my words." [156] But the rebellious people do not listen to wisdom's invitation, just as
later they failed to hear Christ's call. The prophet Isaias
had predicted it: "I said: Behold me, behold me, to a nation
that did not call upon my name. I have spread forth my
hands all the day to an unbelieving people." [157]

But still wisdom tirelessly renews her appeal, now speaking particularly to fools, mockers and dullards, that is, to all
who are unwise.

Doth not wisdom cry aloud, and prudence put forth her
voice? Standing in the top of the highest places by the way, in
the midst of the paths. Beside the gates of the city, in the very

---

[154] Prov. 1:20–21.   [155] Prov. 1:24–25.   [156] Prov. 1:23.

[157] Isa. 65:1–2. "Then he said to his servants: The marriage
indeed is ready; but they that were invited were not worthy. Go
ye therefore into the highways; and as many as you shall find,
call to the marriage" (Matt. 22:8–9).

doors she speaketh, saying: O ye men, to you I call, and my voice is to the sons of men. O little ones, understand subtility, and ye unwise, take notice.[158]

To convince and win men, she silences her tones of reproach and then utters promises and displays her attractions:

Hear, for I will speak of great things; and my lips shall be opened to preach right things. . . . Receive my instruction, and not money; choose knowledge rather than gold. For wisdom is better than all the most precious things; and whatsoever may be desired cannot be compared to it.[159]

Then, praising her beauty and declaring her divine origin, she reveals, with exquisite tact, her tender love for men: "I was set up from eternity, and of old before the earth was made. . . . I was with him forming all things, and was delighted every day, playing before him at all times, playing in the world; and my delights were to be with the children of men." [160] All her motherly love shows in this eager invitation:

Now therefore, ye children, hear me: Blessed are they that keep my ways. Hear instruction and be wise, and refuse it not. Blessed is the man that heareth me, and that watcheth daily at my gates, and waiteth at the posts of my doors. He that shall find me, shall find life, and shall have salvation from the Lord.[161]

This second appeal, expressed with such urgency, was intended to instruct men, to enlighten and allure their minds. The third, which is different in character, goes a step beyond the promise of treasures, benefits and even spiritual advan-

---

[158] Prov. 8:1–5.   [159] Prov. 8:6, 10–11.
[160] Prov. 8:23, 30–31.   [161] Prov. 8:32–35.

tages. What wisdom now offers to men is intimate friendship with her. Using the typical image of the banquet, to
which Christ also frequently returned, and which always
symbolizes union with God, wisdom invites men to partake
of the supernatural favors she has set forth for them. The
first of these is her love.

Wisdom hath built herself a house, she hath hewn her out
seven pillars. She hath slain her victims, mingled her wine, and
set forth her table. She hath sent her maids to invite to the
tower and to the walls of the city; whosoever is a little one, let
him come to me.[162]

The sacred banquet is carefully prepared, from the room
with its mysterious columns to the choice fare that wisdom
sets forth for the guests; symbols of the wonderful gifts she
wishes to bestow on her friends.[163]

The author of the Book of Proverbs is not the only writer
to express wisdom's yearning. Ben Sirah likewise voices a
particularly tender and moving invitation.

Come over to me, all ye that desire me, and be filled with my
fruits. For my spirit is sweet above honey and my inheritance
above honey and the honeycomb. My memory is unto everlasting generations. They that eat me, shall yet hunger; and they
that drink me, shall yet thirst. He that hearkeneth to me shall
not be confounded; and they that work by me, shall not sin.[164]

If the appeals in the Book of Proverbs gave a hint of the
message which Incarnate Wisdom would one day utter, this

[162] Prov. 9:1–4.
[163] "Behold, I stand at the gate and knock. If any man shall
hear My voice and open to Me the door, I will come in to him,
and will sup with him, and he with Me (Apoc. 3:20).
[164] Ecclus. 24:26–30.

last text of Ecclesiasticus inevitably reminds us of a passage in St. John's Gospel: "And on the last, and great day of the festivity, Jesus stood and cried, saying: If any man thirst, let him come to Me and drink. He that believeth in Me, as the Scripture saith, out of his belly shall flow rivers of living water." [165] The same yearning is echoed in St. Matthew: "Come to Me, all you that labor and are burdened, and I will refresh you. . . . You shall find rest to your souls." [166]

These gentle appeals are also sternly exacting, for wisdom is offered to all but is communicated only to those who are already attuned to her touch. "Whoever is a little one, let him come to me." [167] Christ was to speak similarly to His apostles: "Suffer the little children, and forbid them not to come to Me; for the kingdom of heaven is for such." [168] Thus, a secret harmony and an ineffable interior union pervades the meeting of wisdom with her disciples: "I love them that love me; and they that in the morning early watch for me, shall find me." [169]

But she who hastens so eagerly to men remains aloof from them until their yearning and their response mature. She waits uneasily. But when she sees their hearts' assent, when she sees them possessed by the one desire for simplicity and purity, then she lavishes upon them her promises of happiness, assuring them of complete contentment, of participation in her inexhaustible treasures. "Come over to me, all ye that desire me, and be filled with my fruits." [170]

REVELATION OF GOD'S WISDOM

What deep emotion and amazement must have seized the sages' souls when wisdom revealed her true self to them! And

[165] John 7:37–38.   [166] Matt. 11:28–29.   [167] Prov. 9:4.
[168] Matt. 19:14.   [169] Prov. 8:17.   [170] Ecclus. 24:26.

how vivid and thrilling are the pages in which they tried to transcribe for us this exciting experience.[171] First, they emphasize the matchless price of wisdom: "For if one be perfect among the children of men, yet if Thy wisdom be not with him, he shall be nothing regarded." [172] *Thy* wisdom; the divine origin of wisdom is the dazzling truth which impressed them most. "Now what wisdom is, and what was her origin, I will declare, and I will not hide from you the mysteries of God, but will seek her out from the beginning of her birth, and bring the knowledge of her birth, and will not pass over the truth." [173] Wisdom comes from God; it derives from Him all its beauty, intelligence, and perfection. It comes from Him; He alone possesses it fully; He alone can confer it on others.

The word of God on high is the fountain of wisdom. . . . There is one most high Creator Almighty, and a powerful King, and greatly to be feared. . . . All wisdom is from the Lord God, and hath been always with Him, and is before all time.[174]

Wisdom dwells with God as His intimate companion, the confidant of His secrets, known to Him alone.

Thy wisdom with Thee, which knoweth Thy works, which then also was present when Thou madest the world, and knew what was aggreeable to Thy eyes, and what was right in Thy commandments.[175]

Who hath gone up into heaven, and taken [wisdom] and brought her down from the clouds? . . . There is none that is

---

[171] "What lovely gems!" was the exclamation of St. John of the Cross when he asked to have the Canticle of Canticles read to him as he lay dying. The same can be said of the beauties found in all the Wisdom Books.

[172] Wisd. 9:6.   [173] Wisd. 6:24.   [174] Ecclus. 1:5, 8, 1.

[175] Wisd. 9:9.

able to know her ways, nor that can search out her paths; but He that knoweth all things, knoweth her and hath found her out with His understanding.[176]

Wisdom is a mystery unfathomable to man, a part of the mystery of God Himself. Its roots reach back into the very depths of eternity. "Wisdom hath been created before all things, and the understanding of prudence from everlasting. . . . He created her in the Holy Ghost, and saw her, and numbered her, and measured her." [177]

Wisdom was with God from the very beginning and is eternal like Him. "From the beginning and before the world, was I created, and unto the world to come I shall not cease to be, and in the holy dwelling place I have ministered before Him." [178]

A wonderful page, which has never been surpassed in poetic beauty, though it belongs to Proverbs, the oldest of the Wisdom Books, tells of wisdom's ineffable intimacy with God in the fullness of divine liberty and joy:

The Lord possessed me in the beginning of His ways, before He made anything from the beginning. I was set up from eternity, and of old before the earth was made. The depths were not as yet, and I was already conceived; neither had the fountains of waters as yet sprung out. The mountains with their huge bulk had not as yet been established; before the hills I was brought forth. He had not yet made the earth, nor the rivers, nor the poles of the world. When He prepared the heavens, I was present; when with a certain law and compass He enclosed the depths; when He established the sky above and poised the fountains of waters; when He compassed the sea with its bounds

[176] Bar. 3:29, 31–32.   [177] Ecclus. 1:4, 9.   [178] Wisd. 24:14.

and set a law to the waters that they should not pass their limits; when He balanced the foundations of the earth.[179]

None of the sages ever deviated from this splendid text. Its light may enable us to discern the reason for the reverent and loving fear in which men arrayed themselves to approach wisdom, whose divine origin had been revealed to them.

The wisdom that dwells with God is eternal, as He is, and it also possesses, like Him, a purely spiritual nature. This spirit is endowed with amazing attributes:

For in her is the spirit of understanding: holy, one, manifold, subtile, eloquent, active, undefiled, sure, sweet, loving that which is good, quick, which nothing hindereth, beneficent, gentle, kind, steadfast, assured, secure, having all power, overseeing all things, and containing all spirits, intelligible, pure, subtile. For wisdom is more active than all active things, and reacheth everywhere by reason of her purity.[180]

This admirable description almost overwhelms the reader by the precision and opulent luxury of expression. Even the reading of the text leads the soul to a state of recollection.[181] The presence of so many ineffable and transcendental qualities persuades the sage that wisdom is far more than a "reflection" of God.

For she is the brightness of eternal light, and the unspotted mirror of God's majesty, and the image of His goodness. And being but one, she can do all things; and remaining in herself the

[179] Prov. 8:22–29.   [180] Wisd. 7:22–24.
[181] Like the recollection of St. Paul's soul before the immensity and perfection of divine wisdom: "O the depth of the riches of the wisdom and of the knowledge of God! How incomprehensible are His judgments, and how unsearchable His ways!" (Rom. 11:33.)

same, she reneweth all things. . . . For she is more beautiful than the sun and above all the order of the stars; being compared with the light, she is found before it. For after this cometh night, but no evil can overcome wisdom. She reacheth therefore from end to end mightily, and ordereth all things sweetly.[182]

How daring it was to affirm the real existence of an emanation from God, an emanation so closely linked to divine mystery! How daring it was to declare that "being but one, she can do all things"! If we consider the sages' jealous faith in the unity of a God whose attributes are not really distinct from His living and ineffable existence, we can see how bold was this description of wisdom. And yet the author of the Book of Wisdom is not alone in his assertions. Ben Sirah had also declared that wisdom enjoys equality with God, shares his beatitude and exercises power similar to His: "I came out of the mouth of the Most High, the firstborn before all creatures. . . . I dwelt in the highest places, and my throne is in a pillar of a cloud." [183]

But wisdom possessed additional divine qualities. Israel never saw any opposition between God's transcendence and His nearness and mercy. The same is true of divine wisdom. However transcendent it is, its relations with men were never cut off. On the contrary, mercy seems to be one of the favorite words traced by the pens of the sages. If mercy is treated in the Bible, and especially in the wisdom literature, as God's privilege, it likewise belongs to wisdom, ever kind and gentle to men, for whom she is a savior. "According to His greatness, so also is His mercy with Him. . . . Therefore God is patient in [men] and poureth forth His mercy upon them. . . . The compassion of man is toward his

[182] Wisd. 7:25–30; 8:1.   [183] Ecclus. 24:5, 7.

neighbor, but the mercy of God is upon all flesh." [184] However, the sages view mercy as much in those who receive it as in the one who grants it. "Grace and peace is to His elect." [185] This concept causes them to stress the means whereby God practices mercy, the means which in these texts of the Book of Wisdom was for the first designated by the Greek word *charis,* a word destined for a unique role, since it was to indicate the supreme grace or remission bestowed upon men by Incarnate Wisdom.[186] Men truly need this remission, this gift of mercy. Human weakness, misery and sins require grace. This the sages know well and they emphasize wisdom's enlightening, forgiving and saving function.

The sages' deep conviction that wisdom's nature is purely spiritual and that it acts as mediator for men led them to study other concepts in seeking to define the nature of God's activity. We can note particularly the concepts of God's *spirit* and God's *word.* Like wisdom, God's incorruptible spirit is sent from above to the men whom He loves. Like wisdom, too, the spirit has universal effects, but is incompatible with evil.

[184] Ecclus. 2:23; 18:9, 12.   [185] Wisd. 3:9.
[186] In speaking of wisdom, St. Paul particularly stresses its importance as an initiation into the divine mysteries. For him that is its essential role. By wisdom men learn of God's tremendous love for them; they are converted and saved. "In whom we have redemption . . . according to the riches of His grace, which hath superabounded in us in all wisdom and prudence, that He might make known to us the mystery of His will" (Eph. 1:7–9). "But we preach Christ crucified, unto the Jews indeed a stumblingblock and unto the Gentiles foolishness; but unto them that are called, both Jews and Greeks, Christ the power of God and the wisdom of God" (I Cor. 1:23–24).

For wisdom will not enter into a malicious soul nor dwell in a body subject to sins. For the Holy Spirit of discipline will flee from the deceitful. . . . For the spirit of wisdom is benevolent, and will not acquit the evil speaker from his lips; for God is witness of his reins and He is a true searcher of his heart and a hearer of his tongue. For the spirit of the Lord hath filled the whole world; and that which containeth all things hath knowledge of the voice.[187]

Wisdom and the spirit make God's will known to men. "And who shall know Thy thought, except Thou give wisdom and send Thy Holy Spirit from above?" [188]

The gifts claimed by wisdom are the same that the Spirit of Yahweh would one day bestow upon the Messiah.

Doth not wisdom cry aloud. . . . Counsel and equity is mine, prudence is mine, strength is mine. By me princes rule and the mighty decree justice. I love them that love me.[189]

And the spirit of the Lord shall rest upon him; the spirit of wisdom, and of understanding, the spirit of counsel, and of fortitude, the spirit of knowledge, and of godliness. And he shall be filled with the spirit of the fear of the Lord.[190]

The spirit of God and wisdom are the source of inspiration, for wisdom "conveyeth herself into holy souls; she maketh the friends of God and prophets." [191] The spirit of wisdom was granted to Solomon when he prayed for it.[192] Israel has likewise received the revelation of the divine

[187] Wisd. 1:4–7.

[188] Wisd. 9:17. "And the manifestation of the Spirit is given to every man unto profit. To one is given the word of wisdom, and to another, the word of knowledge" (I Cor. 12:7).

[189] Prov. 8:1, 14–17.   [190] Isa. 2:2–3.   [191] Wisd. 7:27.

[192] Cf. Wisd. chap. 9.

"word," the *memrah*. God's word, first preserved in the form of writing on the tablets of stone, little by little showed its spiritual nature and worth. The sages often associate the word with wisdom: both carry out the divine will; both have the same origin. Like the word, wisdom, too, "came out of the mouth of the Most High." [193] Both share God's throne. "Thy almighty word leapt down from heaven from Thy royal throne. . . . Give me wisdom, that sitteth by Thy throne. . . . Send her out of Thy holy heaven, and from the throne of Thy majesty." [194] Wisdom "knoweth Thy works, . . . was present when Thou madest the world." [195] It is likewise by the word that all creation was brought forth and is maintained in existence. "God of my fathers and Lord of mercy, who hast made all things with Thy word, and by Thy wisdom hast appointed man, that he should have dominion over the creature that was made by Thee." [196] "By the words of the Lord are His works. . . . By His word all things are regulated." [197]

Finally, like wisdom,[198] the word too is the benefactor and savior of the people of Israel, as it will become for all mankind in the future. "For it was neither herb, nor mollifying plaster that healed them, but thy word, O Lord, which healeth all things." [199] It is not surprising, therefore, to hear wisdom promise to send both God's spirit and God's words down to men. "Wisdom preacheth abroad, she uttereth her voice in the streets. . . . Behold I will utter my spirit to you, and will show you my words." [200]

---

[193] Ecclus. 24:5.   [194] Wisd. 18:15; 9:4, 10.   [195] Wisd. 9:9.
[196] Wisd. 9:1–2.   [197] Ecclus. 42:15; 43:28.
[198] Cf. Wisd. chap. 10.   [199] Wisd. 16:12.
[200] Prov. 1:20, 23.

God's activity, formerly designated by the inspired authors as His *word* or His *spirit,* later became assimilated to the concept *wisdom,* which, therefore, takes on greater importance and plays a leading role as God's instrument *par excellence.* Thus, when God decides to show His mercy, He sends wisdom as messenger of redemption to act as His mediator with men. God had His reasons to reveal first the divine origin and nature of wisdom and then later to display her work of mercy and mediation. He did so because He intended to reveal progressively His perfect plan, which was so marvellous that men could never sufficiently admire it. Not that there is any question of comparing the wisdom of Old Testament writings to a divine personality; the whole Old Testament mission and monotheistic trend emphatically deny such an interpretation. The most we can find in this wisdom that is so closely united to the highest spiritual concepts of the times is an obscure presentiment of what Christ was to reveal later. But though it be rash to seek any sort of hypostasis in biblical wisdom, it is not rash to view its role of mediator as an efficacious preparation for the action of Christ's saving grace. In this light all becomes clear and God's plan becomes evident. Since Christ was to appear as divine wisdom, men had to be prepared to receive Him as such.

The entire Old Testament expresses the expectation of a redeeming and saving Messiah. But this notion, however true and important it may be, is incomplete and shows only one aspect of the situation. Mankind's sin postulates a Redeemer, but the salvation He was to bring was not limited to a mere cleansing from sin. Salvation is truly effective only through a positive grace which regenerates and brings new life. Man must be grafted into a new life by receiving divine life itself. "I have said: You are gods and all of you the sons of the Most High." [201] Liberation and purification are but the first effects of the positive grace communicated by the Redeemer. The Old Testament prepared men to recognize the Messiah as a Savior, but it also has to teach them to see Him as the Author of grace and the Light of the world.[202]

It was not enough to consider Christ only as divine mercy, tenderly relieving the world's misery by gestures of infinite pity. He also had to appear as the Benefactor whose free gift of grace communicated His light, His spirit, His very life. "I am come that they may have life. . . . I am the light of the world. . . . I am the way, and the truth, and the life." [203] These words of Christ, which have become familiar to us, required a preparation of the minds and hearts of Old Testament men. For grace is not a gift extrinsic to Himself, which God confers, but it is the actual gift *of* Himself to His creature; therein lies its value and beauty. "If thou didst know the gift of God," Jesus was to say to the Samaritan woman.[204] While such a revelation as that was not possible at the time of the sages, mankind had to be led to the road leading to that destination. The Old Testament, therefore, emphasized the divine nature of wisdom, which shared the privileges and prerogatives of God.

This intellectual preparation was accomplished so skill-

[201] Ps. 81:6.

[202] St. Paul, indeed, identified grace and supernatural wisdom: "For our glory is this, the testimony of our conscience, that in simplicity of heart and sincerity of God, and not in carnal wisdom, but in the grace of God, we have conversed in this world" (II Cor. 1:12). "For the grace of God our Savior hath appeared to all men, instructing us that . . . we should live soberly, and justly, and godly in this world" (Tit. 1:11–12).

[203] John 10:10; 8:12; 14:6.   [204] John 4:10.

fully that, while Old Testament wisdom could never be considered as a divine hypostasis, when the time came it was easy to recognize in Christ, the Incarnate Word and Incarnate Wisdom, the same divine wisdom whose veiled figure had been traced in the Scriptures. Christ called Himself "a greater than Solomon," [205] and St. Paul preached "Christ crucified . . . the power of God and the wisdom of God." [206] We are, therefore, justified in viewing wisdom's mission to men as a prototype of the mission of the Author of grace. There is ample proof, moreover, that the sages themselves view wisdom in this way. The wisdom which they seek and commend to their disciples assumes in their minds the form of grace. This means that they were prepared to see it as the supreme mediator between God and men. Such, indeed, is the portrait that they show us.

GOD'S WISDOM AS MEDIATOR

Wisdom's role as mediator for men is clearly shown in the Old Testament. In fact, with the exception of the predicted Messiah, there is no more definite personification in the Bible. This is hardly surprising, since Christ was to appear as Incarnate Wisdom. It is an undeniable fact that wisdom is depicted in the Old Testament with the features of a person, a woman who is at one and the same time a mother, a teacher and a bride. She speaks to men, educates them, instructs them, confers wonderful gifts upon them and strengthens them. Her tireless activity takes on countless forms.[207]

[205] Matt. 12:42.   [206] I Cor. 1:24.

[207] St. Paul was to show these manifold activities of divine wisdom when he spoke of his mission "to enlighten all men, that they may see

Wisdom leaves heaven and descends to earth, charged with a mission to men, a mission which is universal.

I came out of the mouth of the Most High, . . . and as a cloud I covered all the earth. . . . I alone have compassed the circuit of heaven and have penetrated into the bottom of the deep and have walked in the waves of the sea and have stood in all the earth and in every people. And in every nation I have had the chief rule.[208]

But she decides to settle in Israel. In this, as in so many other ways, she resembles the Messiah.

In all these I sought rest, and I shall abide in the inheritance of the Lord. Then the Creator of all things commanded and said to me, and He that made me rested in my tabernacle. And He said to me: Let thy dwelling be in Jacob, and thy inheritance in Israel, and take root in My elect.[209]

This temporary limitation in no way impairs the universality of wisdom's mission. This divine seed, as later also the Messiah, was to be preserved for a while in Israel, not in a spirit of jealous and exclusive pride, but as a protection and a safeguard while awaiting the time to widen her field of influence and scatter her fruits to the whole world. The sages found no paradox in this notion of a hidden treasure, a mysterious presence destined in the future for a marvellous manifestation and fertility. Proof is furnished by Ben Sirah who, in the same chapter in which he seems to claim wisdom

---

what is the dispensation of the mystery which hath been hidden from eternity in God . . . that the manifold wisdom of God may be made known . . . according to the eternal purpose, which He made, in Christ Jesus our Lord" (Eph. 3:9–11).

[208] Ecclus. 24:5–10. [209] Ecclus. 24:11–13.

as Israel's property, shows how her influence and her fruits reach progressively to the very ends of the earth:

In the holy dwelling-place I have ministered before Him. And so was I established in Sion, and in the holy city likewise I rested, and my power was in Jerusalem. And I took root in an honorable people, and in the portion of my God His inheritance, and my abode is in the full assembly of saints. I was exalted like a cedar in Libanus, and as a cypress tree on Mount Sion. I was exalted like a palm tree in the plains, and as a plane tree by the water in the streets, was I exalted. I gave a sweet smell like cinnamon, and aromatical balm; I yielded a sweet odor like the best myrrh; and I perfumed my dwelling as storax, and galbanum, and onyx, and aloes, and as the frankincense not cut, and my odor is as the purest balm. I have stretched out my branches as the turpentine tree, and my branches are of honor and grace. As the vine I have brought forth a pleasant odor; and my flowers are the fruit of honor and riches. . . . I wisdom have poured out rivers. I, like a brook out of a river of a mighty water; I, like a channel of a river, and like an aqueduct, came out of paradise. I said: I will water my garden of plants, and I will water abundantly the fruits of my meadow. And behold my brook became a great river, and my river came near to a sea.[210]

Like the mediating role of Christ at a later time, that of wisdom also had a double function: creation and redemption. In the order of creation wisdom "is more active than all active things. . . . She can do all things, . . . reneweth all things. . . . She reacheth therefore from end to end mightily, and ordereth all things sweetly." [211] She has limitless power to create and to regulate the universe. "The Lord by wisdom hath founded the earth, hath established

[210] Ecclus. 24:14–23, 40–43.   [211] Wisd. 7:24–30; 8:1.

the heavens by prudence." [212] She accompanied the Almighty when He created the universe. "I was with him forming all things." [213] "And Thy wisdom with Thee, which knoweth Thy works, which then also was present when Thou madest the world." [214]

But wisdom's task is even vaster. Not only does creation owe its existence to her; it is constantly visited, inhabited and, as it were, irrigated by her influence. This means that she makes creatures good, just and lovable; she clothes all creation in beauty. Ben Sirah never tires of extolling the marvellous works which the Lord has made by means of His wisdom, and in which He has left an image of His countenance.[215]

Hath not the Lord made the saints to declare all His wonderful works? . . . He hath beautified the glorious works of His wisdom. . . . O how desirable are all His works, and what we can know is but as a spark. . . . And who shall be filled with beholding His glory? [216]

Wisdom's creative and regulating influence is not limited to the material world, but is even more effective in the spiritual realm. This spirit of understanding "overseeing all things and containing all spirits, intelligible, pure, subtle," confers increased vigor and amazing discernment.[217] The

[212] Prov. 3:19.   [213] Prov. 8:30.   [214] Wisd. 9:9.

[215] Cf. St. John of the Cross, op. cit., II, Spiritual Canticle, stanza 5: "He passed through these groves in haste, and, looking upon them as He went, left them, by His glance alone, clothed with beauty."

[216] Ecclus. 42:17–26.

[217] Wisd. 7:23. "That the God of our Lord Jesus Christ, the Father of glory, may give unto you the spirit of wisdom and of revelation, in the knowledge of Him; the eyes of your heart enlight-

sages, as men of intelligence, could not fail to note this aspect of wisdom's activity; very often they praise her for helping to develop man's chief faculties. "If wisdom shall enter into thy heart, . . . counsel shall keep thee." [218] At times wisdom's effect seems to resemble the gift of understanding. "Blessed is the man that findeth wisdom and is rich in prudence." [219] For the sages, wisdom was characterized primarily as an intelligent spirit. She invites men to a banquet of understanding. "Come, eat my bread, and drink the wine which I have mingled for you. . . . And walk by the ways of prudence." [220]

Besides opening men's minds, wisdom also creates life. In this wonderful function she resembles the life-giving sap, uniting all beings to their source. She is likewise a spiritual bond and therein lies her particular claim as mediator of creation. She controls the spiritual life of creatures much more than their physical life. As creator of men, she strives to defend and immunize their souls against death. In the wisdom literature she appears in constant opposition to death and to evil viewed as a destructive power. The man who trusts her protection is ever safe.

Her ways are beautiful ways, and all her paths are peaceable.[221]

He that shall find me, shall find life, and shall have salvation from the Lord; but he that shall sin against me, shall hurt his own soul. All that hate me love death.[222]

---

ened, that you may know what the hope is of His calling" (Eph. 1:17–18).

[218] Prov. 2:10–11.   [219] Prov. 3:13.   [220] Prov. 9:5–6.
[221] Prov. 3:17.   [222] Prov. 8:35–36.

For those who welcome her, she performs a truly creative work by producing the cardinal virtues.

And if a man love justice, her labors have great virtues; for she teacheth temperance, and prudence, and justice, and fortitude, which are such things as men can have nothing more profitable in life.[223]

He that loveth her, loveth life; and they that watch for her, shall embrace sweetness.[224]

Wisdom is a tree bearing delicious fruits; she is a return to the original light, to the life of paradise, where the first man in his fear of God had nothing else to fear, neither scarcity, nor disorder, nor death.

She is a tree of life to them that lay hold on her: and he that shall retain her is blessed.[225]

To fear God is the fullness of wisdom, and fullness is from the fruits thereof. She shall fill all her house with her increase, and the storehouses with her treasures. The fear of the Lord is a crown of wisdom, filling up peace and the fruit of salvation; and it hath seen and numbered her; but both are the gifts of God. Wisdom shall distribute knowledge and understanding of prudence; and exalteth the glory of them that hold her. The root of wisdom is to fear the Lord, and the branches thereof are long-lived.[226]

Both the sages and psalmists often described the happiness of men who found wisdom, comparing them to trees planted beside the waters, spreading out their branches loaded with fruit.[227] Wisdom is the strong and vigorous vinestock, sending out its sap to circulate in all the branches; it

[223] Wisd. 8:7.   [224] Ecclus. 4:13.   [225] Prov. 3:18.
[226] Ecclus. 1:20–25.   [227] Cf. Ps. 1.

is the table ever offering abundance of food; it is the treasure which the disciples can never exhaust. Everything belongs to her and she alone distributes the wealth.

Counsel and equity is mine, prudence is mine, strength is mine. By me kings reign, and lawgivers decree just things. By me princes rule, and the mighty decree justice. . . . With me are riches and glory, glorious riches and justice. For my fruit is better than gold and the precious stone, and my blossoms than choice silver. I walk in the way of justice, in the midst of the paths of judgment, that I may enrich them that love me, and may fill their treasures.[228]

Wisdom, the mediator of creation and of life, is also, and perhaps even more truly, if that be possible, the mediator of salvation and of redemption. Without her, man is poor, hungry, unhappy and a fool. Without her he can do nothing but wander about, never finding the door which, even here on earth, admits him to the kingdom of God. In this kingdom man is released from sin and protected from harm, so that he experiences the free and blissful life of the spirit. "He that hearkeneth to me, shall not be confounded; and they that work by me, shall not sin." [229] Wisdom had already saved men by giving them life; she continues to save them by detaching them from vanity and nothingness. She attacks folly as often as she attacks death. Folly is a noisy and vain woman inviting senseless men to a banquet of vanity. "And he did not know that giants are there, and that her guests are in the depths of hell." [230] On the contrary, he who is guided by wisdom knows "the wickedness of the fool, and the error of the imprudent." [231] He understands well that

[228] Prov. 8:14–21.   [229] Ecclus. 24:30.   [230] Prov. 9:18.
[231] Eccles. 7:26.

"wisdom excelled folly, as much as light differeth from darkness." [232] Folly reigns in the land of obscurity because she feeds only on illusions and mirages. First she blinds men; then she leads them to their death.[233]

Wisdom is of the realm of realities which never pass away, the realm of *what is,* as opposed to the realm of *what is not.* As all that comes from her is true, it brings life and salvation. "My mouth shall meditate truth. . . . All my words are just, there is nothing wicked nor perverse in them. They are right to them that understand, and just to them that find knowledge." [234] The Book of Wisdom clearly declares that the mystery of wisdom is a redeeming mystery:

And who shall know Thy thought, except Thou give wisdom, and send Thy Holy Spirit from above; and so the ways of them that are upon earth may be corrected, and men may learn the things that please Thee? For by wisdom they were healed.[235]

In the Old Testament, wisdom contains a mystery of salvation and it manifests redeeming love. "She conveyeth herself into holy souls, she maketh the friends of God and prophets. For God loveth none but him that dwelleth with wisdom." [236] Chapters 10 to 13 of the Book of Wisdom help us to understand how wisdom carried out this role of savior in the epoch of primitive humanity:

She preserved him, that was first formed by God . . . and brought him out of his sin. . . . For whose [Cain's] cause,

[232] Eccles. 2:13.

[233] "For professing themselves to be wise, they became fools" (Rom. 1:22). In the Epistles human wisdom is constantly opposed to spiritual wisdom. "Hath not God made foolish the wisdom of this world? . . . For the foolishness of God is wiser than men" (I Cor. 1:20, 25).

[234] Prov. 8:7-9.   [235] Wisd. 9:17-19.   [236] Wisd. 7:27-28.

when water destroyed the earth, wisdom healed it again, directing the course of the just [Noe] by contemptible wood. . . . She knew the just [Abraham] and preserved him without blame to God, and kept him strong against the compassion for his son. She delivered the just man [Lot] who fled from the wicked that were perishing, when the fire came down upon the Pentapolis. . . . She conducted the just [Jacob] when he fled from his brother's wrath, through the right ways, and showed him the kingdom of God, and gave him the knowledge of the holy things. . . . She kept him safe from his enemies, . . . and gave him a strong conflict, that he might overcome, and know that wisdom is mightier than all. . . . She forsook not the just [Joseph] when he was sold, but delivered him from sinners . . . and gave him everlasting glory.[237]

The salvation granted to individuals was then extended to the whole nation of God's chosen people. "She delivered the just people, and blameless seed from the nations that oppressed them. . . . And she rendered to the just the wages of their labors, and conducted them in a wonderful way; and she was to them for a covert by day, and for the light of stars by night." [238]

By His wisdom, God protects the good; by His wisdom, too, He strikes the wicked. "But their enemies she drowned in the sea, and from the depth of hell she brought them out." [239] Thus does God prove His strength "when men will not believe Thee to be absolute in power." [240] But an even more important role of wisdom is that of mediator of divine mercy, "the image of [God's] goodness." [241] "Therefore thou chastisest them that err, by little and little; and ad-

---

[237] Wisd., chap. 10, *passim.*   [238] Wisd. 10:15, 17.
[239] Wisd. 10:19.   [240] Wisd. 12:17.   [241] Wisd. 7:26.

monishest them, and speakest to them concerning the things wherein they offend; that leaving their wickedness, they may believe in Thee, O Lord." [242] "But executing Thy judgments by degrees, Thou gavest them place of repentance." [243]

This divine mercy comprises infinite goodness and power, infinite justice and compassion:

Thou hast ordered all things in measure, and number, and weight. For great power always belonged to Thee alone; and who shall resist the strength of Thy arm? For the whole world before Thee is as the least grain of the balance, and as a drop of the morning dew, that falleth down upon the earth. But Thou hast mercy upon all, because Thou canst do all things, and overlookest the sins of men for the sake of repentance. For Thou lovest all things that are, and hatest none of the things which Thou hast made; for Thou didst not appoint or make any thing hating it. And how could any thing endure, if Thou wouldst not? Or be preserved, if not called by Thee? But Thou sparest all because they are Thine, O Lord, who lovest souls.[244]

But in spite of such kind and thoughtful care, in spite of wisdom's choice of Israel for her visit and her dwelling, she was betrayed and abandoned by the nation she had loved above all others. This alone explains the afflictions that struck the people:

Hear, O Israel, the commandments of life; give ear, that thou mayest learn wisdom. How happeneth it, O Israel, that thou art in thy enemies' land? Thou art grown old in a strange country. . . . Thou hast forsaken the fountain of wisdom, for if thou hadst walked in the way of God, thou hadst surely dwelt in peace forever. . . . This is the book of the com-

[242] Wisd. 12:2.   [243] Wisd. 12:10.   [244] Wisd. 11:21–27.

mandments of God, and the Law, that is forever; all they that
keep it, shall come to life; but they that have forsaken it, to
death.[245]

How urgently then, does the prophet implore the faithless
people to return to God and to the life-giving font of
wisdom:

Return, O Jacob, and take hold of it; walk in the way by its
brightness, in the presence of the light thereof. Give not thy
honor to another, nor thy dignity to a strange nation. We are
happy, O Israel, because the things that are pleasing to God are
made known to us.[246]

The prophet mysteriously hints that this return for which
he longs and hopes will be rewarded by a coming of God
to His people in the form of a visitation of divine wisdom.
"This is our God, and there shall no other be accounted of
in comparison of Him. He found out all the way of knowledge, and gave it to Jacob His servant and to Israel His beloved. Afterward He was seen upon earth, and conversed
with men." [247]

But wisdom's role as mediator, so vividly described in
the biblical texts, was not understood by the rabbis who
persisted in seeing in them nothing beyond the Torah. While
it is not right to do violence to the Old Testament texts, and
while it was reserved to the New Testament to determine
how the ancient events were to reach ultimate fulfillment,

[245] Bar. 3:9–13; 4:1.   [246] Bar. 4:2–4.

[247] Bar. 3:36–38. Some scholars prefer here the pronoun *she*
[wisdom], instead of *He* [God]. But even so, the meaning of the text
is not weakened.

we cannot fail to discern there mysterious foreglimpses of some features of the life and mission of Christ, the Savior who is Eternal Wisdom. He too was to appear on earth and converse with men; He too was a Creator and a Giver of life ("All things were made by Him; and without Him was made nothing that was made" [248]); He too came "to save that which was lost." [249] Surely the Holy Spirit, in view of the redeeming role of Incarnate Wisdom, must have inspired the prophets and sages to display and glorify wisdom as a mediator and a savior. They provide a prelude to Christ's universal mediation. But in spite of this preparation, in spite of the sages' appeals and the voice of wisdom herself, men neither heard nor heeded her when she became incarnate and lived among them to carry out her mission of mercy and salvation. After rejecting and deserting wisdom, Israel also rejected Christ. "He came into His own, and His own received Him not." [250]

Not only in the general history of Israel does wisdom act as mediator; it affects men's hearts in an intimate and hidden way. This is without doubt the most excellent sphere of its influence. More than anyone else, the sages were clearly and intensely aware of this influence, as they knew that the just man can hope to find God only by means of wisdom which, in an ineffable way, is the messenger of His will. "And who shall know Thy thought, except Thou give wisdom?" [251] It is she who makes God's hidden mysteries accessible to men,

[248] John 1:3. [249] Matt. 18:11. [250] John 1:11.
[251] Wisd. 9:17. "We also . . . cease not to pray for you, and to beg that you may be filled with the knowledge of His will, in all wisdom and spiritual understanding" (Col. 1:9).

for she is the mirror reflecting God's mind, the medium of the soul's communication with God's goodness and of other perfections.

For she is a vapor of the power of God, and a certain pure emanation of the glory of the almighty God; and therefore no defiled thing cometh into her. For she is the brightness of eternal light, and the unspotted mirror of God's majesty, and the image of His goodness.[252]

The sages who are attracted by wisdom's beauty and, after a long wait, are admitted to her friendship, attain by the light of her presence a wholly new lucidity that is infinitely serene and pure. They no longer judge in a merely human and natural way, but depend upon another order of values, in accord with the completely holy and beautiful harmony that belongs only to God in His goodness, His justice and the prefection of His counsels and His desires. They know that all benefits and graces are conferred by wisdom because she is near to God and lives in intimate friendship with Him. "The Lord of all things hath loved her. For it is she that teacheth the knowledge of God and is the chooser of His works." [253]

The sage, therefore, seeks the answers to his questions by listening to the echoes of this clear and lovely voice within his own soul. Underlying the message confided to him, which he strives to transmit faithfully, the sage glimpses a deeper and more mysterious message. He hears an inner call, receives great secrets in his inmost heart, feels the uniquely sweet allurement emanating from the very Person of divine wisdom. All this he strives to explain. For his own consola-

[252] Wisd. 7:25–26.   [253] Wisd. 8:3–4.

tion and for the sake of his disciples, he would like to chant
the poem of wisdom's friendship with men, showing how she
loves them and gives herself to them. Perhaps they too would
then thrill with awareness of the divinity, thrill as he does
when he sees the mysterious face of the wisdom whose voice
echoes in his soul. To express this is a difficult, a humanly
impossible task. The sage realizes it and therefore he hesi-
tates. Song after song could be composed without ever con-
veying the nobility and charm of the queen for whom he has
sacrificed all things, who reigns in his heart, whose goodness equals her beauty, whom he loves and by whom he
knows that he too is loved more dearly still. He is so moved
by veneration and chaste fear that he begins to tremble before this beloved wisdom who shares God's throne and
leads him toward the mystery of God Himself.

We shall say much, and yet shall want words; but the sum of
our words is: He is all. What shall we be able to do to glorify Him?
For the Almighty Himself is above all His works. The Lord is
terrible and exceedingly great, and His power is admirable.
Glorify the Lord as much as ever you can, for He will yet far
exceed, and His magnificence is wonderful. Blessing the Lord,
exalt Him as much as you can, for He is above all praise. When
you exalt Him, put forth all your strength and be not weary;
for you can never go far enough. Who shall see Him and declare
Him? And who shall magnify Him as He is from the beginning?
There are many things hidden from us that are greater than
these, for we have seen but a few of His works. But the Lord
hath made all things, and to the godly He hath given wisdom.[254]

Since, "the Lord hath given wisdom to the godly," they
have only to allow this divine gift, this grace diffused in

[254] Ecclus. 43:29–37.

their hearts, this wisdom, to speak henceforth herself and reveal her love for men.

WISDOM AS LOVE

Dearly beloved, . . . let us therefore love God, because God first hath loved us.[255]

The subject that we approach now—the personal relationship of the sage to wisdom—belongs to the realm of love. We shall not depart from it again. Love is God's only pathway to men, "for God so loved the world, as to give His only-begotten Son," [256] His Son who is incarnate Wisdom. Love is likewise man's only pathway to God. "If any one love Me, he will keep My word, and My Father will love him, and We will come to him, and will make Our abode with him." [257]

Even in the Old Testament, by the voice of divine wisdom, God expressed to men His longing for love. His appeal was infinitely sweet and infinitely demanding: love calls for love. By divine law man has been commanded to love his God with his whole heart, his whole mind and his whole strength. However, what is perhaps most striking about divine wisdom is the particular atmosphere in which she flourishes throughout the Old Testament, an atmosphere of complete liberty and wholly gratuitous choice. In a gesture of loving preference, God keeps her beside Him, lets her share His life and His activities, admits her to intimate friendship. Wisdom herself speaks but one language, that of love. She whom many texts reveal as God's beloved daughter, speaks ever of love, whether she describes the divine privileges that she

[255] I John 4:1, 19.   [256] John 3:16.   [257] John 14:23.

enjoys or whether she addresses men. She by whom all things are measured, is loved immeasurably. Her whole relationship to God is one of love.

How could she help but be infinitely lovable in His eyes, since she is divine understanding, the ineffable beauty of the spirit which possesses a simplicity and purity which to us are inconceivable? Her attributes are truth, honesty, justice. Wisdom appears as an intelligence that loves, a loving brightness, a wholly understanding love. God's light envelops her and she is diffused by Him. From all eternity she was in His mind; for her and through her He established the universe. She ever played before Him in divine liberty, rejoicing with God's own joy. Her life depends upon Him and she obeys His orders. But what sweet delight she shows in carrying out His wishes! "Then the Creator of all things commanded, . . . and He that made me, rested in my tabernacle." [258] The author of the Book of Wisdom could truly say: "The Lord of all things hath loved her." [259] But he could not fully appreciate the infinite reality to which he referred.

We can glimpse how greatly wisdom is loved by God and what privileges and favors His preference confers on her if we notice how God cherishes the souls that love wisdom. Incarnate Wisdom was to say one day: "He that loveth shall be loved of My Father." [260] The Old Testament expresses a similar thought: "For God loveth none but him that dwelleth with wisdom. . . . And God loveth them that love her. . . . For she is an infinite treasure to men, which they that use, become the friends of God." [261]

[258] Ecclus. 24:12.   [259] Wisd. 8:3.   [260] John 14:21.
[261] Wisd. 7:28; Ecclus. 4:15; Wisd. 7:14.

It is certainly not surprising that God should love as His favorite children those who are born of wisdom and shaped to the divine image by her hands. Such is wisdom's role among men, a role inspired by her love for them. Is she not a spirit that loves men and dwells eternally with them? [262] With a love that is attentive, wholly gratuitous and unbelievably generous, wisdom has wished to dwell among us and has found her joy and sweetest hopes in this intimate intercourse. "My delights were to be with the children of men." [263]

Wisdom's love of man resembles the protecting and benevolent love that God was to reveal in its fullness by sending us His Son. We likewise find in wisdom's lessons to men the same ardor that inspired Christ's heart when, in addition to the commandments that keep men on the narrow path of salvation, He gave the counsels that enable them to *run* along the path.[264] Men then experience the delights of intimacy and the outpourings of love.

If we consider wisdom's role as mediator between God and men, if we realize that her entreaty demands a response, then it is not rash to maintain that she asks the Jews not just to observe the Law, but to surpass it, to attain a higher perfection, in the same way that the Gospel counsels exceed the precepts. While it is true that here and there the man who keeps the commandments is called "just," there ever arises the desire to do more than that. The ancient masters of wisdom spoke like Christ: "If thou wouldst be perfect. . . ." At times the same renunciation is required for the sake of closer friendship with God. The world is scandalized by

[262] Cf. Wisd. 1:6; Ecclus. 1:15.   [263] Prov. 8:31.
[264] Cf. Ps. 118:32.

the path chosen, the narrow path, the path of crucifixion; God's wisdom is always folly in the eyes of the world. The same fidelity is demanded in little actions inspired by love. Finally, the same happiness is promised. "Blessed are the poor. . . ." *Beati immaculati in via.*

It is true that there is only one commandment which leads men to eternal life, and yet we cannot deny that there is also a higher perfection in keeping the commandment, a fullness of love which even the Old Testament presents and eagerly proposes. In the past as in the present, God ever longs to communicate His all to souls, to lead them to the mystery of His exceeding great love. It would seem that the mission which Christ was to perform perfectly had already been entrusted to wisdom.[265] Her task was to prepare friends and children of God, souls open to the supernatural life because they are truly simple and childlike. Thus, the demands wisdom makes upon her disciples stem from her desire to help them to discover and follow the way of perfect love. Another reason is that wisdom's very nature, as well as her mission, was to seek love from her followers and constantly to show her own love for them. Long before St. John declared that God is love, the sages had the intuition that wisdom, which is of divine origin and nature, was total love. They also glimpsed some of the beauty and the delicate nuances of her love.

But how were they to express in earthly language a love that could be neither identified with nor even compared to any love of this world? They realized this difficulty and

---

[265] "But the foolish things of the world hath God chosen, that He may confound the wise; and the weak things of the world hath God chosen, that He may confound the strong" (I Cor. 1:27).

yet the message entrusted to them had to be translated into human terms. Without hesitation, therefore, they sought their bases of comparison in the strength and unselfishness of mother love, along with the ardor of bridal love. So admirable was their portrait of wisdom and her love for men that it aroused souls to a corresponding love without which the divine yearning would have been fruitless. "I am the mother of fair love." [266] "Wisdom inspireth life into her children." [267]

Since God willed to bring men to Himself by means of His own love for them, He had to make this love known to them in order that they might accept it. How could men learn of it, if no one came to reveal it to them? They needed a teacher to train them in love, and God assigned this mission to wisdom. For she was His beloved, in whom He delighted, with whom He shared all His secrets, to whom He gave His entire love. On sending her among us, He could well have said: "This is My beloved in whom I am well pleased, hear ye her." He asks us, therefore, to welcome her as a mother and as the teacher of divine love.

The sages never hesitated to call wisdom a mother, for they believed that she had a right to the title. Indeed, no other title better suits her or better defines her mission to men. She herself, moreover, claims it, for she calls men her sons and she counsels them as if they were her children. "Now therefore, ye children, hear me; blessed are they that keep my ways." [268] The sages reveal wisdom's ways and her motherly methods of education.

She strives chiefly to arouse and then to develop perfect love in her children. Is this not every mother's ideal? So it

[266] Ecclus. 24:24.   [267] Ecclus. 4:12.   [268] Prov. 8:32.

is with wisdom. To accomplish this, she uses only love, a love of fathomless depth, of inexhaustible ingenuity, of exquisite tact. She begins by making her children look for her, but she sees to it that they can easily find her: "Wisdom is easily seen by them that love her, and is found by them that seek her. She preventeth them that covet her, so that she first showeth herself unto them." [269]

If her children do not succeed in finding her, then she herself, as a good mother, "goeth about seeking such as are worthy of her." [270] In calling them she speaks tenderly, persuasively, promising rewards. But the mother never forgets that she is also a teacher. The child must be docile and allow her to direct him. She is infinitely patient, but he must be willing and, in a way, "worthy of her." But what time and care is needed to complete his formation! And how long it takes the child to appreciate her attentions and to realize that beneath the strictness inherent in all true education can be found the mother's hand, steady and careful, gentle and vigorous. The fool ignores this.

How very unpleasant is wisdom to the unlearned, and the unwise will not continue with her. She shall be to them as a mighty stone of trial, and they will cast her from them before it be long. For the wisdom of doctrine is according to her name, and she is not manifest unto many.[271]

Even her most cherished child takes a long time to understand her deep love to which he owes everything. "Now all good things came to me together with her, and innumerable

[269] Wisd. 6:13–14. "But if any of you want wisdom, let him ask of God, who giveth to all men abundantly, and upbraideth not; and it shall be given him" (Jas. 1:5).

[270] Wisd. 6:17.   [271] Ecclus. 6:21–23.

riches through her hands . . . and I knew not that she was the mother of them all." [272]

Only those who have made some progress in love's ways or have at least desired to accept her invitation unconditionally can perceive her efforts to remove obstacles from the path, to rouse their courage, to sustain them in time of trial, and to relieve them of all worry. Throughout the journey, wisdom, which had first hastened to meet the child entrusted to her tender care, continues to protect him.

And she will meet him as an honorable mother.[273]

If wisdom shall enter into thy heart and knowledge please thy soul, counsel shall keep thee and prudence shall preserve thee, that thou mayest be delivered from the evil way. Then shalt thou walk confidently in thy way and thy foot shall not stumble; if thou sleep, thou shalt not fear; thou shalt rest, and thy sleep shall be sweet. Be not afraid of sudden fear nor of the power of the wicked falling upon thee. For the Lord will be at thy side and will keep thy foot that thou be not taken.[274]

As a good adviser she guides the child in times of weakness and uncertainty. She opens new horizons and vistas to his mind. What, indeed, could he do by himself alone? Wisdom's chief task is to accompany and support him step by step on the path of perfection, enabling him to climb its heights, to advance in the right direction, to find light in the darkness. If humility, trust and loving fear steadily increase in his heart, then wisdom will be for him a tabernacle where the Spirit will enlighten his mind and strengthen his heart for the perpetual new beginnings that are the secret of all sanctity. "She can do all things: . . . and through

[272] Wisd. 7:11–12.   [273] Ecclus. 15:2.
[274] Prov. 2:10–12; 3:23–26.

nations conveyeth herself into holy souls, she maketh the friends of God." [275]

The liberty she enjoys becomes also the prerogative of her sons and confirms them in glory and in grace. Her sweet influence, far from weakening those in her care, makes them more virile and enables them to become more fruitful. "Wisdom inspireth life into her children, and protecteth them that seek after her." [276] The day eventually comes when the child, worthy of the life bestowed on him and of the education he has received, will take pride in his mother and will understand the reason for all the trouble and effort endured at wisdom's school, about which he had long complained. He will welcome the close bonds of her care and will praise her fond vigilance and her tireless exhortations.

For in the latter end thou shalt find rest in her, and she shall be turned to thy joy. Then shall her fetters be a strong defense for thee, and a firm foundation, and her chain a robe of glory; for in her is the beauty of life, and her bands are a healthful binding. Thou shalt put her on as a robe of glory, and thou shalt set her upon thee as a crown of joy.[277]

These words found an echo in a much more authoritative and significant promise uttered in later times by Eternal Wisdom: "Take up My yoke upon you, and learn of Me, . . . and you shall find rest to your souls." [278]

Her have I loved, and have sought her out from my youth, and have desired to take her for my spouse.[279]

And she . . . will receive him as a wife married of a virgin.[280]

[275] Wisd. 7:27.   [276] Ecclus. 4:12.   [277] Ecclus. 6:29–32.
[278] Matt. 11:29.   [279] Wisd. 8:2.   [280] Ecclus. 15:2.

Wisdom chose to be called mother in order to show the constant tenderness and loving care she lavishes on those who love her and accept her guidance. But the intimacy of her love and the gifts she bestows inevitably suggested another title, expressive of her way of loving: the title of bride. What essential and vital yearning inspired this name? What was the loneliness that finally turned men's hearts to wisdom and emboldened them to discover that she was their hearts' desire, that she had the double power to arouse and to satisfy their yearning which nothing earthly could appease?

Adam's pain of loneliness was remedied when God gave him Eve, his helpmate, like to himself, made of his flesh and blood, charged with the mission of cooperating with him. Eve failed in her task. Since then, her daughters seem to have been deposed from their throne, though they still retain mysterious traces of the role assigned to them, the role of initiation into the secrets of love. Thus, men and women are isolated, incapable of communicating to each other the life which each should have made accessible to the other in their inmost hearts and in the mystery of their love. They are both deprived of the essential grace which could have directed and enlightened them, deprived of mutual discernment and loving understanding of the soul's inner depths, deprived of the imperishable and changeless dwelling where the soul might have rested, with all its spiritual longings appeased and amplified. And yet both of them yearn for an indissoluble union with "someone" able to liberate them from the flesh and from the world, someone infinitely admirable and lovable, someone possessing immaculate purity, perfect knowledge and love, someone willing to accompany them on their route. This companion that souls crave is wisdom. Once they have perceived her, therefore, they greet her with the name of bride. At a later time, when her dazzling beauty was clearly revealed to them in the person of Christ, they would recognize her as the fulfillment of their longings.

We must not suppose that the sages posit any opposition between wisdom viewed as a mother and wisdom viewed as a bride. This would be a total misunderstanding of their wholly spiritual concepts. On the contrary, in full accord with Old Testament tendencies, the richer and deeper and purer their notion of divine love becomes, the more apt is the union of these two themes, as if only their fusion could suggest wisdom's perfection. Therefore the sages, who had introduced wisdom to their disciples as a mother, also presented her as a bride to be won and loved.

This attitude is especially evident in Ecclesiasticus. First he had spoken of wisdom as a mother whose ambition was to "inspire life into her children" and to become for them "the mother of fair love." [281] Then the tone changes, as he praises wisdom's beauty and charms so fervently that the disciple cannot fail to realize that he is being invited to seek wisdom as a loving bride and wife.

> Blessed is the man that shall continue in wisdom. . . . He that considereth her ways in his heart and hath understanding in her secrets, who goeth after her as one that traceth, and stayeth in her ways; he who looketh in at her windows and hearkeneth at her door; he that lodgeth near her house, and fastening a pin in her walls shall set up his tent nigh unto her.[282]

To grasp the sage's attitude here, we must lay aside our habitual way of thinking, our human concepts, and rise to the level of purely spiritual reality. When Ben Sirah urges

[281] Ecclus. 4:12; 24:24.   [282] Ecclus. 14:22–25.

his disciple to stir up the flames of ardent love in his soul, does he mean to change the bonds which had already united him to wisdom? By no means. On the contrary, he must continue to love her and respect her as a mother, for the tribute of love which he offers now is not less pure or chaste then the filial sentiments already felt. And therefore wisdom does not refuse this homage. But in accepting it she takes care not to modify her own attitude toward the disciple. With queenly assurance she continues to guide and direct and lead into the path of divine love this soul that is now penetrated with loving admiration and respectful devotion. Two lines suffice to convey the inspired writer's subtle meaning: "And she will meet him as an honorable mother, and will receive him as a wife married of a virgin." [283] This reminds us of Mary, the Virgin Mother and the mystical bride of her Son; it also reminds us of her Son Himself, who called His disciples His "little children" and bestowed virgin purity upon the souls united to Him.

The sage then continues by describing what the bride brings to the one who has chosen her. "With the bread of life and understanding, she shall feed him, and give him the water of wholesome wisdom to drink." [284] He needs this bread in order to discern the mysteries promised to him; he needs the water in order to taste the sweetness and feel the gentle joy of the gifts bestowed. But on both sides the gift must be pure, complete and unconditional.

He who loves wisdom, who longs for her as for a chosen bride, must have a soul that is radically needy and poor, but is also subject to the pangs of an intense thirst for interior transformation and for the glory which is sensed as its des-

[283] Ecclus. 15:2.   [284] Ecclus. 15:3.

tiny, the glory of light and of charity. The lover of wisdom finds what he has longed for as he gazes on the beloved's face, as he hears her voice, sweet as honey. As she approaches, his heart thrills with a strange joy. Allured by her charms, he ardently desires her, wanting "to take her for my spouse." [285] His wishes are like those of the bride in the Canticle of Canticles. "I sat down under his shadow, whom I desired, and his fruit was sweet to my palate." [286]

Her have I loved, and have sought her out from my youth, and have desired to take her for my spouse, and I became a lover of her beauty.[287]

When I was yet young, before I wandered about, I sought for wisdom openly in my prayer. I prayed for her before the Temple, and unto the very end I will seek after her, and she flourished as a grape soon ripe. My heart delighted in her.[288]

The lover soon recognizes her as the perfect bride, the source and means of all his happiness. Then his only desire is to stay with her.

He shall set up his tent nigh unto her, where good things shall rest in his lodging for ever. He shall set his children under her shelter, and shall lodge under her branches; he shall be protected under her covering from the heat, and shall rest in her glory.[289]

He has cast aside the notion that such a love may impose unduly hard demands upon him; on the contrary, he gladly accepts Ben Sirah's advice: "Come to her as one that plougheth and soweth, and wait for her good fruits." [290]

[285] Wisd. 8:2.   [286] Cant. 2:3.   [287] Wisd. 8:2.
[288] Ecclus. 51:18–20.   [289] Ecclus. 14:25–27.
[290] Ecclus. 6:19.

His fidelity is unfaltering; his preference is constantly re-newed; his commitment to her is irrevocable. "She shall be made strong in him, and he shall not be moved; and she shall hold him fast, and he shall not be confounded." [291]

Even before wisdom's deep love had been revealed to her lover, he had sensed its delights and his intense desire was to dwell with her, to be bound to her by all the aspirations of his heart and mind, to share constantly through her in a life in which divine gifts become daily bread, but also to struggle for her sake, to work hard to become less unworthy of her. From this relationship, from this union, he expects happiness unalloyed and unchangeable happiness. "When I go into my house, I shall repose myself with her; for her conversation hath no bitterness nor her company any tediousness, but joy and gladness." [292] No boredom, monotony or weariness is experienced, but all is constant delight in the exploration of a world which appears ever more clearly as the only truth and the only real life. Such is life with the bride, a life filled with love which is inexhaustible because it is wholly divine.

THE ATTAINMENT OF WISDOM

Now all good things came to me together with her.[293]
And wisdom is justified by her children.[294]

Wisdom has given the sage the grace of her intimate love —a love so intimate, indeed, that he ventures to give the name of bride to her who fills his heart with joy. A man's wife is the woman whom he loves, with whom he is united,

[291] Ecclus. 15:3–4.   [292] Wisd. 8:16.   [293] Wisd. 7:11.
[294] Matt. 11:19.

whose whole life he shares, with whom he lives for always. Such a bride is given to the sages with all her infinitely tender love. She is a mother and a bride. If we are to grasp the spiritual realities to which these terms refer, we must cast off all material images, conceptions and representations. The union offered to the sages involves no limitations of space or time, no element of ownership or possession. It is total liberty along with total communion: a wholly spiritual union. And yet the bond uniting the sage to divine wisdom is as real as it is personal. It is a union within the framework of human experience; this is evident from the images instinctively chosen by the sages, images which imply the notion of an undivided and absolute gift, as of one person to another. Finally, the sages' biblical realism suggests that the union is direct and his communion with wisdom requires no intermediary.

However, every union presupposes and requires a certain similarity of nature. Indeed, it cannot become intimate or spiritually fertile except so far as a real interchange takes place. A bride and bridegroom find happiness if they share all their experiences: their interests and worries, and especially their deepest yearnings and their highest aspirations. That being so, how can we dare to speak of a true union of the sage with wisdom? Yet the Bible has not hesitated to do so.

The reason was that the sages possessed a deep and incommunicable certainty that this bride had come to open their souls to divine life and to communicate this life to them. By personal experience they knew how they had been transformed. Beneath her touch they became capable of divine action; they were born to a new life as new creatures.

Moreover, wisdom does not merely stamp her image upon the soul; she initiates a permanent change in it. She lives in the soul, establishing in it a true state of grace. Finally, wisdom is more than a medium of divine grace; she is a mediator. As she is of divine nature, she is omnipotent and acts upon the soul by virtue of the privileges of her nature. By her very presence men are transformed and "made divine." The sage's soul, to which she comes in union, is raised up and is born anew to the divine life which she possesses in fullness. As she is constant actuality, she never ceases communicating her very being. She is a permanent principle and source of divine life, a ceaseless life-process, an immediate experience.

Thanks to her, the sage henceforth sees, discerns and feels all things in a new way. His contacts with other men and even with all creation is renewed. He truly lives within the light of grace, and this affects his whole spiritual life. It is a fundamental reality which influences everything else. For wisdom does not come alone, but is accompanied by a retinue of virtues and gifts which adorn her and wafts sweet perfume round about. The virtues and gifts which the sages compared to precious gems and pearls are perhaps more like the diamonds of dew that glisten on the morning grass. Like the dew, they come from heaven, carried by wisdom who infuses them into the sage's soul, ennobling his labors, rewarding his efforts.

The sages extol these priceless treasures throughout the wisdom books. Their descriptions gradually lead us "farther into the thicket," [295] that we too may share their life of love, their union with wisdom. She comes to the soul bearing

[295] Cf. St. John of the Cross, *Spiritual Canticle*, stanza 36.

treasures richer and more rare than gold or silver, gems or pearls. "Now all good things came to me together with her, and innumerable riches through her hands, and I rejoiced in all these; for this wisdom went before me." [296]

However patient and strenuous human efforts may be, they can never obtain such treasure. Job, Baruch, Ben Sirah unanimously declare that wisdom, with her infused gifts and virtues, is beyond our grasp. But she gives herself, and in giving herself she is lavish with her other gifts. Her way of giving shows exquisite tact and delicate respect for the human efforts that may be awkward but at least are generous. Far from disregarding men's strivings, she improves them and elevates them, crowning them with new dignity and brilliance. From the painful labors of acquired virtues she brings forth a rich harvest. If it is true that grace does not destroy but perfects nature, it is all the more true that grace perfects the acquired virtues. They answer her summons.[297]

To explain wisdom's work, the sages multiply lovely images and amass their symbols: perfumes, fruits, fabrics, diadems, necklaces. All the wealth of the Orient enters into their picture. Similarly, centuries later, the angel of the Apocalypse was to say of the white tunic of the elect: "For the fine linen are the justifications of saints." [298] Men's humble efforts, when crowned by grace, become worthy of life in heaven.

[296] Wisd. 7:11–12.

[297] "But the wisdom, that is from above, first indeed is chaste, then peaceable, modest, easy to be persuaded, consenting to the good, full of mercy and good fruits, without judging, without dissimulation" (Jas. 3:17).

[298] Apoc. 19:8.

The first of the virtues displayed here is prudence, which the sage had taken care to instil into his disciple. Now prudence is marvellously bestowed from above.

Hardly do we guess aright at things that are upon earth; and with labor do we find the things that are before us. . . . And who shall know Thy thought, except Thou give wisdom, and send Thy Holy Spirit from above, and so the ways of them that are upon earth may be corrected and men may learn the things that please Thee? [299]

The most honorable title given to prudence is "companion of wisdom." "Wisdom hath been created before all things, and the understanding of prudence from everlasting." [300] It is one of wisdom's choicest gifts. "Counsel and equity is mine, prudence is mine, strength is mine." [301] The lessons of prudence demand close attention, for she is truly a communication from God Himself. "My son, attend to My wisdom and incline thine ear to My prudence." [302] "The knowledge of the holy is prudence." [303]

Prudence does not come alone, but brings with her the other cardinal virtues. "And if a man love justice, her labors have great virtues, for she teacheth temperance and prudence and justice and fortitude, which are such things as men can have nothing more profitable in life." [304]

Often the Old Testament extols justice as a beautiful princess, proud but gentle. The pages of the Book of Wisdom reveal how rarely men encountered justice and how anxiously they sought her, until at length they found her in the very heart of God, associated with wisdom in His gov-

---

[299] Wisd. 9:16–18.   [300] Ecclus. 1:4.   [301] Prov. 8:14.
[302] Prov. 5:1.   [303] Prov. 9:10.   [304] Wisd. 8:7.

ernment of the universe. Men learned the lessons of justice
set forth word by word in the divine alphabet of circumstances, in the development of historical events. "But Thou
hast taught Thy people by such works, that they must be
just and humane." [305] She has taught the sage to hate evil,
but with a holy hatred. "Thou hast loved justice and hated
iniquity." [306] Henceforth men can practice justice in a merciful and untroubled way, remembering that "he that keepeth
the commandment, shall find no evil. The heart of a wise
man understandeth time and answer. There is a time and
opportunity for every business, and great affliction for
man." [307]

Finally, we see temperance and fortitude with their happy
faces. "Strength and beauty are her clothing and she shall
laugh in the latter day." [308] They are so complementary to
each other that they cannot be separated in praise. One book
of the Old Testament particularly extols these two virtues
in all the episodes of a marvellous story: the Book of Daniel.
This story truly seems to verify the account of wisdom's attributes set forth in the Book of Wisdom. "And if a man
desire much knowledge, she knoweth things past and judgeth
of things to come; she knoweth signs and wonders before
they be done, and the events of times and ages." [309] The
Book of Daniel is indeed an uninterrupted succession of
visions, marvels, explanation of dreams, all to the glory of
Hebrew wisdom. The most amazing marvel is the way wisdom rewarded the virtue of the three young sages entrusted
to her loving care. Not only were they saved, but they were
also renewed and enraptured; all because of their temper-

[305] Wisd. 12:19.   [306] Ps. 44:8.   [307] Eccles. 8:5–6.
[308] Prov. 31:25.   [309] Wisd. 8:8.

ance, that invincible force which made their souls incorruptible and their bodies invulnerable. In the midst of torture they were filled with overwhelming joy—a joy which found expression in the most beautiful of thanksgiving hymns.[310] But Daniel remains humble in his strength and gives to God alone all the glory of the gifts conferred.

Blessed be the name of the Lord from eternity and for evermore, for wisdom and fortitude are His. And He changeth times and ages, taketh away kingdoms and establisheth them, giveth wisdom to the wise, and knowledge to them that have understanding. He revealeth deep and hidden things, and knoweth what is in darkness; and light is with Him. To Thee, O God of our fathers, I give thanks, and I praise Thee, because Thou hast given me wisdom and strength.[311]

But all these virtues form merely the retinue of another virtue or gift which dominates and embraces all the others: fear of God. It is a gift so great and noble that he who has it is beyond comparison. The disciple had been trained in it during his formation and it appeared to him as a goad and a yoke: a goad urging him to the way of prayer and adoration, a yoke preventing him from following the bypaths of self-will, guiding him on the straight but narrow path. Up to a certain point, he practiced this virtue in an exterior way, by means of discipline; it was an acquired virtue, though he knew it to be vital and essential. But at length, when divine wisdom infuses the fear of God into his heart, it develops wonderfully. Under its strong but gentle influence, he feels released from all slavery; he reigns like a king; his soul becomes accessible, easily opening its windows for the contemplation of divine things.

[310] Cf. Dan., chaps. 1 and 2.   [311] Dan. 2:20–23.

The state of soul initiated by fear of God could perhaps be expressed least inadequately by such terms as piety or the virtue of religion. It enables the soul to walk easily in the paths of fidelity and love. It makes duty easy and attractive, as for the psalmist, who declared: "I have run the way of Thy commandments, when Thou didst enlarge my heart." [312]

They that fear the Lord will not be incredulous to His word; and they that love Him, will keep His way. They that fear the Lord will seek after the things that are well pleasing to Him; and they that love Him shall be filled with His law. They that fear the Lord will prepare their hearts, and in His sight will sanctify their souls.[313]

There is no surer sign of divine wisdom's presence and influence in the sage's heart than this happy, filial fear, this loving fear. It cannot appear except in hearts that live in an intimate and trustful relationship with the bride who is both divine and near to them: wisdom. By infusing the fear of God into the sage's heart, wisdom implants profound peace, without which happiness is impossible. She is a bride whose presence assures stability and cloudless happiness. "I know from thence that it shall be well with them that fear God, who dread His face." [314] The man united to wisdom and living in the fear of God enjoys not only happiness, but also joy and safety, first here on earth, and then, so it seems, in another world after death.

Her conversation hath no bitterness nor her company any tediousness, but joy and gladness.[315]

The fear of the Lord shall delight the heart, and shall give joy and gladness and length of days.[316]

[312] Ps. 118:32.   [313] Ecclus. 2:18–20.   [314] Eccles. 8:12.
[315] Wisd. 8:16.   [316] Ecclus. 1:12.

Ye that fear the Lord, hope in Him, and mercy shall come to you for your delight. . . . For who hath continued in His commandment, and hath been forsaken? [317]

With him that feareth the Lord, it shall go well in the latter end, and in the day of his death he shall be blessed.[318]

On wedding wisdom, the sage realizes that all other treasures come gradually with her. She assures him of life, of happiness and of holiness. By union with her he is united to all that never passes away. He experiences the sanctity and eternity which belong to wisdom's very nature. He possesses wisdom herself as a life-companion, an eternal bride.

The fear of the Lord is holy.[319]
The fear of the Lord is unto life.[320]

The fear of the Lord leads to beatitude and its first fruits are tasted here below. "O how great is the multitude of Thy sweetness, O Lord, which Thou hast hidden for them that fear Thee!" [321]

Little by little, almost unawares, we have been led ever farther into the central regions toward that which is lasting, permanent, eternal. Thus we can understand that wisdom gives birth to the three virtues which even here below enable a man to possess the reality of heaven: faith, hope and charity. "I am the mother of fair love, and of fear, and of knowledge, and of holy hope." [322]

Stimulated by the gifts, these virtues acquire new vigor. How keen hope is in the sages' souls, eagerly scanning the horizon for the coming of the oft predicted Redeemer! To

[317] Ecclus. 2:9–12.   [318] Ecclus. 1:13.   [319] Ps. 18:10.
[320] Prov. 19:23.   [321] Ps. 30:20.   [322] Ecclus. 24:24.

the author of the Book of Wisdom it is so thrilling that he exclaims: "Hope is full of immortality." [323]

Nothing thwarts hope. The motives of her bold confidence are not derived from earthly reality, except perhaps so far as her understanding of things hidden from unbelievers gives her a discernment of providence and of mercy. She is sustained by grace, and flies toward God on eagle wings. It is a joyous hope in a living God who grants the desires of just men, who is sure to look after them in time of persecution. Thanks to hope, which is based on faith and is raised and exalted by love, the sage lives in a joy that no evil or trial can disturb. He possesses faith and charity, the knowledge and the love that are wisdom's crown. "The love of God is honorable wisdom. . . . To fear God is the fullness of wisdom, and fullness is from the fruits thereof." [324] Wisdom is a source of life and contemplation. "By the means of her I shall have immortality." [325] "They to whom she shall show herself love her by the sight, and by the knowledge of her great works." [326] Such illumination could well be expected from her who was described as "the brightness of eternal light." [327] As we see God in His Word—a brighter light than light itself—so the sage saw Him in wisdom. "I loved her above health and beauty, and chose to have her instead of

[323] Wisd. 3:4.   [324] Ecclus. 1:13, 20.   [325] Wisd. 8:13.

[326] Ecclus. 1:15. Love and knowledge are directed to the contemplation of divine things. St. Paul says: "We speak wisdom among the perfect; yet not the wisdom of this world. . . . But we speak the wisdom of God in a mystery, a wisdom which is hidden, which God ordained before the world, unto our glory. . . . But, as it is written, that eye hath not seen nor ear heard, neither hath it entered into the heart of men, what things God hath prepared for them that love Him" (I Cor. 2:6–9).

[327] Wisd. 7:26.

light; for her light cannot be put out." [328] Finally, this mother of fair love taught him how to love.

While it is true that neither the obscurity of faith nor the trials inherent in the practice of charity will be spared the sage, he dwells in love henceforth and he lives by mutual fidelity. He knows in whom he believes. He knows that he is loved. He lives in love and love lives in him. Storms may threaten, but he has nothing to fear. He is safely with the Lord, partaking of the banquet to which wisdom invited him. "Come, eat my bread, and drink the wine which I have mingled for you." [329]

Thus, little by little, guided by wisdom, the sage has transcended the temporal world to attain what is beyond time. He has passed from the sensual joy that was sometimes veiled by bitterness or fear, to the changeless, limpid joy that wells up from the depths of his soul. To be enthralled by such joy he had only to follow the attraction which wisdom exerts upon her friends. The author of the Book of Wisdom often points out a connection between his progress toward wisdom and his aspirations of immortality. "The keeping of her laws is the firm foundation of incorruption; and incorruption bringeth near to God." [330]

It is noteworthy that the gifts, as presented in the Old Testament, imply tranquillity of mind and confer permanence and stability wherever their influence is felt. However distorted and short-sighted Old Testament views of immortality may have been, it is nevertheless certain that the sages' contact and intimate association with wisdom gave them presentiments of the eternal life which Christ was to reveal and give to the world. In speaking of those whom the Lord

[328] Wisd. 7:10.   [329] Prov. 9:5.   [330] Wisd. 6:19–20.

has summoned back to Himself, the Book of Wisdom declares: "They that are faithful in love shall rest in Him." [331] As the sage knows the holy and incorruptible nature of the love binding him to wisdom, he confidently hopes that it will give him a share of the life of the spirit. Already here below he has a foretaste of its delight and its glory. Many texts referring to wisdom, the bride of the sage, emphasize this endlessness of love. "To be allied to wisdom is immortality, and there is great delight in her friendship." [332]

To find wisdom is to experience a stability and to enter a state that is no longer affected by fluctuating events and changeable human sentiments. "When thou hast gotten her, let her not go; for in the latter end thou shalt find rest in her, and she shall be turned to thy joy." [333]

In his life with wisdom the sage will enjoy a calm and happy security, sheltered from all storms. His soul will know perfect satisfaction as well as the certainty of unchanging peace after death. "All her paths are peaceable." [334] "The fear of the Lord is a crown of wisdom, filling up peace and the fruit of salvation." [335]

All the sages have emphasized the ineffable tranquillity attained by union with wisdom, but it must not be confused with a kind of artificial, passive beatitude. We are told indeed that "wisdom is more active than all active things, . . . for she is the unspotted mirror of God's majesty." [336] This tranquillity is a deeper development and a higher activity of a spirit unhindered by obstacles and marvellously free for total devotion to the one thing necessary. This supreme liberty produces great works of light and love. Wisdom's

[331] Wisd. 3:9. [332] Wisd. 8:17–18. [333] Ecclus. 6:28–29.
[334] Prov. 3:17. [335] Ecclus. 1:22. [336] Wisd. 7:24, 26.

tranquillity resembles the rest which the Church urges us to beg for the souls of the faithful departed; not eternal sleep by any means, but eternal life in peace and light. Rest of souls in God consists in an activity that has become so simple, so exempt from multiplicity and weakness, that it no longer causes any fatigue, but rather strengthens the soul. It becomes a source of such bliss and delight that the soul's only desire is to continue this way of life and to be completely absorbed by it.

The sages truly believed in the free and eager life of the spirit, the life proper to the children of God.[337] To have taught it as they did, they must have themselves experienced it to the full. Besides, could they have ventured to call wisdom a mother and a bride, if they had not known her as such, if they had not enjoyed her intimate love, if they had not welcomed the sweet perfume of her presence into their own souls and those of their disciples?

Hear me, ye divine offspring, and bud forth as the rose planted by the brooks of waters. Give ye a sweet odor as frankincense. Send forth flowers as the lily, and yield a smell, and bring forth leaves in grace, and praise with canticles, and bless the Lord in His works. Magnify His name and give glory to Him with the voice of your lips.[338]

In the life of friendship with God everything is directed to praise and thanksgiving. The Bridegroom's whole joy is in the beauty and charm and grace of His beloved. His whole delight is in her. Then again, what return can the soul make

[337] "Now we have received not the spirit of this world, but the spirit that is of God; that we may know the things that are given us from God" (I Cor. 2:12).

[338] Ecclus. 39:17–20.

to God after receiving so much? The happy soul cannot be silent, for the superabundance of divine bounty must overflow in praise. Such is, perhaps, the last lesson taught by the sages. Their final song is this serene and fervent hymn of thanksgiving, which keeps recurring as if it were the very breath of their souls. Of all the experiences they have shared with us, this is the most beautiful, the most humble and the most fervent testimony and the most joyful certainty. For indeed, unless the soul experiences within itself the divine gifts, the mystery of God's hidden desires and the secret of His ever-present love, it cannot maintain an attitude of serenity and praise. But the sage is united to wisdom and receives a profound knowledge of divine reality. If it brings a taste of bitterness or pain to his natural sensibilities, that no longer misleads him. He knows that all divine things are good,[339] and his whole joy is to extol them without cease.

[339] Ecclus. 39:21.

Chapter 3

✵ PURIFICATION

Why art thou sad, O my soul? And why dost thou disquiet me? [1]

I know thy tribulation and thy poverty, but thou art rich. . . . Fear none of those things which thou shalt suffer. . . . Be thou faithful until death, and I will give thee the crown of life. [2]

The Old Testament set souls on the pathway to truth when it supported faith in opposition to wonders, and divine wisdom against human wisdom. Thus it had already supplied the remedy to the errors that St. Paul was to denounce. "For both the Jews require signs and the Greeks seek after wisdom; but we preach Christ crucified, unto the Jews indeed a stumblingblock, and unto the Gentiles foolishness." [3] Suffering was Adam's lot first; no man since his time has been exempt from it. The Old Testament authors by no means ignored that suffering was the price of purification; still better, they knew it also as the means of purification. Though they sometimes stumbled when it proved a cause of

[1] Ps. 42:5.   [2] Apoc. 2:9–10.   [3] I Cor. 1:22–23.

scandal, they discovered that it was the supreme mystery of salvation.

The Bible shows that throughout the centuries God has always tested the souls of His servants by sending them afflictions, trials and humiliation. "Behold I have refined thee, but not as silver; I have chosen thee in the furnace of poverty." [4] The angel Raphael told old Tobias: "Because thou was acceptable to God, it was necessary that temptation should prove thee." [5] Here Scripture teaches by its usual method—not by abstract maxims, but by the portrayal of men suddenly struck by suffering, which persists throughout the rest of their lives and gradually leads them by successive purifications to divine union. First the disturbance of their snug lives by diverse unforeseen trials uproots their sin. It is a time of temptation, doubt, sometimes even rebellion. Nevertheless, once these souls are free of sin, they allow God to guide them into the narrow path where they learn patience; where, with the help of grace, they cast off their impurities and dross. For while the soul is no longer opposed to God, it still is radically dissimilar to Him. Just as divine initiative was necessary first to remove whatever blocked out the light, so it is required again to eliminate whatever cannot be assimilated by love.

To attain union with God, however, the ordinary sufferings of life, even though they be numerous and intense, are not sufficient. The soul must encounter the silence of God— a silence that is painful to the point of scandal. Treated by God in a way that seems as cruel as it is incomprehensible, it then enters the "dark night," which is the only way to bring about the great, transforming purifications.

[4] Isa. 48:10.   [5] Tob. 12:13.

These were not unknown to the Old Testament. In the Books of Jeremias and of Job they were so vividly described that mystics of every century have reverted to these texts as the truest account ever given. Jesus was to say: "Unless the grain of wheat falling into the ground die. . . ." [6] But the Old Testament already taught that life is born of death and that in God's hands suffering is the chosen instrument of resurrection. But did suffering have such power even before the Redemption? It is true, indeed, that suffering cannot be fully efficacious without participation in the grace flowing from the Cross, without incorporation into Christ. But even the purifications imposed by God in the Old Testament depended upon that same source for their effect. "For both He that sanctifieth, and they who are sanctified, are all of one." [7] The Bible portrays souls that became the quarry pursued by God. "Thou hast been stronger than I, and Thou hast prevailed." [8] These souls, like the burning bush, were enkindled by Yahweh's flame. "The bush was on fire and was not burnt." [9] In the proportion that they consent to die while still living, they are born to true life and experience union with God. Thus, they teach with amazing clarity that in God's hands suffering is a great mystery. "The Lord killeth and maketh alive." [10]

THE CRUCIBLE

Behold I have refined thee, but not as silver, I have chosen thee in the furnace of poverty. For My own sake, for My own sake will I do it. [11]

What men need first is to be purified of sin. [12] Scarcely had Adam and Eve committed their sin than they felt griev-

---

[6] John 12:24.　　[7] Heb. 2:11.　　[8] Jer. 20:7.
[9] Exod. 3:2.　　[10] I Kings 2:6.　　[11] Isa. 48:10–11.

ously burdened by it. Incapable of removing the defilement, they were afraid and hid. Adam told Yahweh: "I heard Thy voice in paradise, and I was afraid, because I was naked, and I hid myself." [13] Sin revealed to him his worthlessness and the need for expiation. This instinctive feeling was codified by the Law. One of the duties of the levitical priesthood was to carry out individual or collective purifications by means of carefully graduated sacrifices of expiation.

> And if any one of the people of the land shall sin through ignorance, . . . he shall offer a she goat without blemish. And he shall put his hand upon the head of the victim that is for sin, and shall immolate it in the place of the holocaust. And the priest shall take of the blood with his finger, and shall touch the horns of the altar of holocaust, and shall pour out the rest at the foot thereof. . . . And he shall pray for him, and it shall be forgiven him.[14]

In Israel every infraction of the Law, whether voluntary or not, required a purification,[15] which could be obtained by the offender himself or by his representative.

---

[12] Although Christ took men's sins upon Himself and redeemed them by His blood, although "where there is a remission of these [sins], there is no more an oblation for sin" (Heb. 10:18), purification and expiation are still necessary under the New Covenant. No other victim is needed since the sacrifice on Calvary, but Christians must be united to that sacrifice in order to receive its merits. By lovingly accepting whatever sufferings God sends and by carrying his cross after the Master, a Christian conformed to Christ allows God to accomplish His work in the soul. "That I may know Him, . . . and the fellowship of His sufferings, being made conformable to His death" (Phil. 3:10).

[13] Gen. 3:10.   [14] Lev. 4:27–31.

[15] Israel's history shows us the progress of conscience toward maturity. The Law was the pedagogue, but conscience was just as severe. St. Paul, who proclaimed the liberty of the spirit achieved by

Upon this day shall be the expiation for you, and the cleansing from all your sins. . . . You shall afflict your souls by a perpetual religion. And that priest that is anointed, and whose hands are consecrated . . . shall make atonement.[16]

The prophets reminded the people of the necessity of expiation. In their zeal they even demanded it of pagans. Jonas preached so forcefully that "the men of Ninive believed in God, and they proclaimed a fast, and put on sackcloth from the greatest to the least. And the word came to the king of Ninive; and he rose up out of his throne, and cast away his robe from him, and was clothed with sackcloth, and sat in ashes." [17] The prophet Daniel informed Nabuchodonosor that a terrible affliction was to strike him as a punishment and also as a purification from his sins, if he were willing to repent. The king's mind was deranged, so that he acted like an animal of the fields, but "after seven times had passed," [18] his sanity was restored and he blessed God "because all His works are true, . . . and them that walk in pride He is able to abase." [19]

There is, perhaps, no truth more emphatically reiterated in the Bible than the necessity of purification. It was required of Adam. The prophets kept insisting upon it. "Wash yourselves, be clean, take away the evil of your devices from My eyes." [20] The last of the prophets uttered the same cry to men:

Christ, who set men free of the Law, puts sin under the jurisdiction of conscience. "For all that is not of faith is sin" (Rom. 14:23). The practice of charity, which "covereth a multitude of sins" (I Pet. 4:8), replaced the oblations and sacrifices.

[16] Lev. 16:30–32.   [17] Jonas 3:5–6.   [18] Dan. 4:29.
[19] Dan. 4:34.   [20] Isa. 1:16.

Behold, I send My angel. . . . Behold he cometh, saith the Lord of hosts. . . . He is like a refining fire, and like the fuller's herb; and he shall sit refining and cleansing the silver, and he shall purify the sons of Levi, and shall refine them as gold, and as silver.[21]

The precursor, finally, taught that purification was the condition of salvation.

John was in the desert, baptizing and preaching the baptism of penance, unto remission of sins. And there went out to him all the country of Judea, and all they of Jerusalem, . . . confessing their sins.[22]

When he was asked by those who felt the need of purification: "Master, what shall we do?" he replied by requiring the practice of loyalty, justice and charity as an expiation of falsehood, fraud and extortion.[23]

Throughout the centuries the sacrificers raised their arms over countless substitute victims designated to represent sinners and to be immolated in their place. Throughout history men have felt the need to be cleansed from their sins. The fact that they could find no better way of expiation and purification than the killing of the victim representing them, proves how serious sin appeared in their eyes. In all times, too, they have been aware of the interdependence of all men.[24] This is illustrated by the tragic story of the deluge:

---

[21] Mal. 3:1–3.   [22] Mark 1:4–5.   [23] Luke 3:1–18.

[24] This solidarity was to gain new significance when St. Paul clarified the notion and the effects of original sin. "Wherefore as by one man sin entered into this world, and by sin death; and so death passed upon all men, in whom all have sinned. . . . By the offense of one, unto all men to condemnation. . . . For by the disobedience of one man, many were made sinners" (Rom. 5:12–19).

"I will destroy man, whom I have created, from the face of the earth." [25] So Yahweh declared, but the same text taught that one man could offer sacrifice in the name of all the guilty:

So Noe went out [of the ark]. . . . And Noe built an altar unto the Lord; and taking of all cattle and fowls that were clean, offered holocausts upon the altar. And the Lord smelled a sweet savor, and said: I will no more curse the earth for the sake of man.[26]

Similarly Job, fearing lest his sons may have sinned in the midst of their feasting, "sent to them, and sanctified them; and rising up early offered holocausts for every one of them. For he said: Lest perhaps my sons have sinned, and have blessed God in their hearts." [27]

Tobias did not fail to pray and to weep, asking God: "Neither remember my offenses nor those of my parents." [28]

Corresponding to this solidarity expressed by individuals, were the collective purifications imposed directly upon the people by God throughout their history.[29] A glance at the landmarks of Hebrew history shows the frequency of this kind of purification; it is an almost unrelieved succession of wars, foreign occupations, plagues, exile, captivity. Scarcely were the chosen people settled in Palestine when famine obliged them to emigrate to Egypt, where their life became "bitter with hard works," [30] so bitter, indeed, that God

[25] Gen. 6:7.   [26] Gen. 8:18–21.   [27] Job. 1:5.
[28] Tob. 3:3.

[29] When St. Paul said: "Who is weak, and I am not weak?" (II Cor. 11:29), he showed that this solidarity permitted an interaction which under the name of "the communion of saints" acquired its full spiritual fecundity.

[30] Exod. 1:14.

raised up a liberator for His people. But the sufferings endured in Egypt soon appeared easy by comparison with the forty years' living in the desert. "Would to God we had died by the hand of the Lord in the land of Egypt. . . . Why have you brought us into this desert, that you might destroy all the multitude with famine?" [31] Even after reaching the Promised Land, Israel continued to suffer, in a precarious situation, with constant war and frequent foreign domination.

And the children of Israel cried to the Lord; for he [Jaban] had nine hundred chariots set with scythes, and for twenty years had grievously oppressed them. . . . And the children of Israel again did evil in the sight of the Lord, and He delivered them into the hand of Madian seven years. And they were grievously oppressed by them. . . . And the Lord being angry with them, delivered them into the hands of the Philistines and of the children of Ammon. And they were afflicted and grievously oppressed for eighteen years.[32]

The last-mentioned affliction sent by God proved salutary.

The children of Israel said to the Lord: We have sinned, do Thou unto us whatsoever pleaseth Thee, only deliver us this time. And saying these things, they cast away out of their coasts all the idols of strange gods and served the Lord their God; and He was touched with their miseries.[33]

The most painful of these afflictions and the one that was to prove more fruitful spiritually was the exile in Babylon. Isaias had foreseen that it would be both a punishment and a purification. "You have not looked up to the Maker thereof,

[31] Exod. 16:3.   [32] Judg. 4:3; 6:1–2; 10:7–8.
[33] Judg. 10:15–16.

nor regarded Him even at a distance, that wrought it long
ago. . . . Surely this iniquity shall not be forgiven you till
you die, saith the Lord God of hosts." [34] Ezechiel announces
that the purifying expiation is imminent. "And they shall
know that I am the Lord, when I shall have made their land
waste and desolate, for all their abominations which they
have committed." [35] But the most dramatic picture of this
terrible trial is presented by Jeremias:

And I will make Jerusalem to be heaps of sand and dens of
dragons. . . . Behold I will feed this people with wormwood
and give them water of gall to drink. And I will scatter them
among the nations, which they and their fathers have not known;
and I will send the sword after them till they be consumed. . . .
Teach your daughters wailing; and every one her neighbor
mourning. For death is come up through our windows, it is
entered into our houses to destroy the children from without,
the young men from the streets. Speak: Thus saith the Lord:
Even the carcass of man shall fall as dung upon the face of the
country. . . . Therefore thus saith the Lord: Behold I will deliver this city into the hands of the Chaldeans and into the
hands of the king of Babylon, and they shall take it. And the
Chaldeans that fight against this city shall come and set it on
fire, and burn it. . . . It shall be delivered into the hands of
the king of Babylon by the sword, and by famine, and by
pestilence.[36]

And from the daughter of Sion [37] all her beauty is departed.
. . . Her filthiness is on her feet and she has not remembered
her end; she is wonderfully cast down, not having a comforter.

[34] Isa. 22:11, 14.   [35] Ezech. 33:29.
[36] Jer. 9:11, 15–22; 32:28–29, 36.
[37] That is to say, the city of Jerusalem, and with it the Jewish
people, whose lot is bound up in that of the Holy City.

. . . O all ye that pass by the way, attend and see if there be any sorrow like to my sorrow; for He hath made a vintage of me, as the Lord spoke in the day of His fierce anger.[38]

We must re-read the lamentations to form an idea of the tremendous sorrow and to imagine vividly the material suffering and moral humiliation of Israel at the time of the capture of Jerusalem and the exile to Babylon. The poignant melancholy of Psalm 136 conveys the intensity of this suffering:

Upon the rivers of Babylon, there we sat and wept; when we remembered Sion; on the willows in the midst thereof we hung up our instruments. For there they that led us into captivity required of us the words of songs. And they that carried us away, said: Sing ye to us a hymn of the songs of Sion. How shall we sing the song of the Lord in a strange land? [39]

These misfortunes were to continue under many forms until the end of the history of the chosen people. The Books of the Machabees intone a long hymn to the glory of the heroic resistance of Israel to those wishing to enslave her and snatch her away from her faith:

And Mathathias said: Woe is me, wherefore was I born to see the ruin of my people, and the ruin of the holy city? . . . Now Simon . . . exhorted them, saying: You know what great battles I and my brethren, and the house of my father, have fought . . . for all the heathens are gathered together to destroy us out of mere malice.[40]

The psalmists and the prophets have immortalized these sufferings and persecutions. Israel lived in this sombre at-

[38] Lam. 1:6, 9, 12.   [39] Ps. 136:1-4.
[40] I Mach. 2:7; 13:1-6.

mosphere, except for brief interludes of light. While every generation did not experience to the same extent the trials of civil war, Egyptian or Assyrian invasions, insecurity, plagues, or famine, yet all this is constantly recalled in the prophets' writings, like an undercurrent of terror.

Forasmuch as this people hath cast away the waters of Siloe. . . . Therefore behold the Lord will bring upon them the waters of the river strong and many, the king of the Assyrians, and all his glory. . . . As whirlwinds come from the south, it cometh from the desert from a terrible land. For it is a day of slaughter and of treading down, and of weeping to the Lord the God of hosts. . . . Arise, arise, stand up, O Jerusalem, which hast drunk at the hand of the Lord the cup of His wrath; thou hast drunk even to the bottom of the cup of dead sleep, and thou hast drunk even to the dregs.[41]

The senses of my heart are troubled within me. . . . Destruction upon destruction is called for, and all the earth is laid waste.[42]

But such catastrophes could not purify unless they were accepted without rebellion and borne in a spirit holier than indifferent passivity. To make the people realize that their sufferings were imposed as an expiation of sin was the role of the prophets—a thankless and difficult role which had been assigned to Moses long before. "And thou shalt remember all the way through which the Lord thy God hath brought thee for forty years through the desert, to afflict thee and to prove thee." [43]

The psalmist reminded the people that they had failed to

41 Isa. 8:6–7; 21:1; 22:5; 51:17.   42 Jer. 4:19–20.
43 Deut. 8:2.

learn the lesson thus taught by Moses: "Forty years long was I offended with that generation, and I said: These always err in heart. And these men have not known My ways." [44] Later Jeremias lamented because his contemporaries discerned God's ways no better than their ancestors:

Thou hast struck them, and they have not grieved; Thou hast bruised them, and they have refused to receive correction. . . . They have denied the Lord, and said, It is not He; and the evil shall not come upon us; we shall not see the sword and famine. The prophets have spoken in the wind.[45]

When Jeremias predicts divine punishment, the people answer: "Wherefore hath the Lord pronounced against us all this great evil? What is our iniquity? And what is our sin, that we have sinned against the Lord our God?" [46] In vain does the prophet urge that the punishment is imminent; none heed him.

Thus saith the Lord: Behold I frame evil against you, and devise a device against you, let every man of you return from his evil way, and make ye your ways and your doings good. And they said: We have no hopes; for we will go after our own thoughts, and we will do every one according to the perverseness of his evil heart.[47]

But the day came when the weight of adversity and the intensity of suffering forced Israel to open her eyes and discover how God's hand shaped all events. "The Lord is just, for I have provoked His mouth to wrath. . . . Who is he that hath commanded a thing to be done, when the Lord

[44] Ps. 94:10–11.   [45] Jer. 5:3–13.   [46] Jer. 16:10.
[47] Jer. 18:11–12.

commandeth it not? . . . Let us search our ways, and seek, and return to the Lord." [48]

But at length the divine process of purification produced fruit in abasement, humility and deep, sincere contrition.

To the Lord our God belongeth justice, but to us confusion of our face; as it is come to pass this day to all Juda and to the inhabitants of Jerusalem. . . . From the day that He brought our fathers out of the land of Egypt, even to this day, we were disobedient to the Lord our God; and going astray we turned away from hearing His voice. . . . And we have not harkened to the voice of the Lord our God according to all the words of the prophets whom He sent to us. . . . Therefore the Lord our God hath made good His word, that He spoke to us, . . . that the Lord would bring upon us great evils. . . . And we are brought under, and are not uppermost; because we have sinned against the Lord our God, by not obeying His voice. . . . And we have not entreated the face of the Lord our God, that we might return every one of us from our most wicked ways. And the Lord hath watched over us for evil, and hath brought it upon us; for the Lord is just in all His works which He hath commanded us. . . . And Thou hast made the Temple, in which Thy name was called upon, as it is at this day, for the iniquity of the house of Israel, and the house of Juda. And Thou hast dealt with us, O Lord our God, according to all Thy goodness, and according to all that great mercy of Thine, as Thou spokest by the hand of Thy servant Moses, . . . saying: I know that the people will not hear Me, for they are a people of a stiff neck; but they shall turn to their heart in the land of their captivity, and they shall know that I am the Lord their God; and I will give them a heart, and they shall understand; and ears, and they shall hear. And they shall praise Me in the land of their captivity, and shall be mindful of My name.[49]

[48] Lam. 1:18; 3:37, 40.   [49] Bar., chaps. 1, 2, *passim.*

My children, suffer patiently the wrath that is come upon you.[50]

But this principle of collective purification and expiation is most clearly stated by the author of the Second Book of the Machabees.

Now I beseech those that shall read this book, . . . that they consider the things that happened not as being for the destruction, but for the correction of our nation. For it is a token of great goodness when sinners are not suffered to go on in their ways for a long time, but are presently punished. . . . And therefore He never withdraweth His mercy from us; but though He chastise His people with adversity, He forsaketh them not.[51]

It may be thought that the purifications, collective or not, must touch each individual soul, so that the divine plan prospers or aborts in proportion as each individual accepts or rejects the trials sent by God. But this viewpoint is incomplete. Not only do the collective purifications have a definite value in themselves, but they also play a specially important role in Israel. The whole history of God's people tends toward one goal: the coming of the Messiah. This national event had to be prepared, not only by individuals, but also by the people as a whole. While it is true that God desired union with each soul, it was also the Jewish nation as such that was destined to be the cradle of the Redeemer. Likewise the whole nation, addressed as the "daughter of Sion," had to be purified, to expiate its faults and betrayals. That explains why, until the very dawn of salvation, collective purifications ever went hand in hand with the prophets' vehement pleas for individual conversion. The mission

[50] Bar. 4:25.   [51] II Mach. 6:12–16.

of the prophets, including the last and greatest of them, St. John the Baptist, consisted largely in helping each soul to derive from the calamities striking the nation its due measure of purification and expiation. The prophets showed what fruits a submissive and faithful heart could harvest from such trials.

Behold as clay is in the hand of the potter, so are you in My hand, O house of Israel. . . . Now therefore tell the men of Juda, and the inhabitants of Jerusalem, saying: Thus saith the Lord: Behold I frame evil against you; let every man of you return from his evil way, and make ye your ways and your doings good.[52]

Thus, the workings of grace in each soul are closely connected to the general plan that is God's secret. The collective story and the individual story keep pace with each other and control each other. So it is that in this crucible of purification and expiation salvation is prepared for the whole nation and for each soul. "Let the earth be opened, and bud forth a Savior." [53] By God's mercy, however, expiation is not the only benefit received through the purifications. Provided that sinners acknowledge their guilt and are able to accept suffering and humiliation, it will be possible for them to undergo the gradual process of transformation which God plans for them. In proportion as a soul is humble and welcomes the love which forgives, its purifications become fruitful. The Old Testament presents numerous examples of sinful souls that make progress by means of the punishments inflicted upon them, as they climb courageously up the narrow path to which they have been led.

[52] Jer. 18:6, 11.   [53] Isa. 45:8.

THE NARROW PATH

Perfect Thou my goings in Thy paths.[54]

After the soul is withdrawn from sin and cleansed of its defilement, the selfsame gesture of God's love continues the process of its regeneration. Purification is not absent from this work of sanctification; in fact, it then appears in its highest form. Sin is not the only obstacle that God encounters when He wishes to take full possession of a rational creature. The soul must be purified in its very substance, to the very roots of its faculties. The process must take place at a great depth. The Bible tells us that purification is not only for sinners, but also, and especially, for the good whom God wishes to draw into closer union with Himself. Particularly those called by God to a special mission feel the need of personal purification as a preparation for their task. Thus, when Judith, the widow famed for her exemplary life, considered saving her people by putting Holophernes to death, she "went into her oratory; and putting on haircloth, laid ashes on her head." [55] This was not intended as an expiation of her sins, but as a way of begging for the strength required for her formidable enterprise.

Others who seek divine graces have recourse to the same means. When Tobias and his bride, Sara, following the counsels of the archangel Raphael, consent to spend the first three nights of their marriage in penance and prayer, it is apparent that this purification is intended not only to chase away the devil Asmodeus, the demon of impurity and lust, but also and chiefly to sanctify their new state of life and to open their souls to heavenly blessings.

[54] Ps. 16:5.   [55] Judith 9:1.

But thou, when thou shalt take her, go into the chamber, and for three days keep thyself continent from her, and give thyself to nothing else but to prayers with her. And on that night lay the liver of the fish on the fire, and the devil shall be driven away. But the second night thou shalt be admitted into the society of the holy patriarchs. And the third night thou shalt obtain a blessing that sound children may be born of you.[56]

There is, then, all the more reason why those chosen by God as His mouthpieces feel the need to be free of all impurity. This is the prophets' spontaneous gesture; feeling incapable or unworthy, they take flight, like Balaam or Jonas, or they refuse, like Moses or Jeremias. They feel reassured only when they receive a preliminary purification, as was the case with Isaias.

And I said: Woe is me, because I have held my peace; because I am a man of unclean lips, and I dwell in the midst of a people that hath unclean lips, and I have seen with my eyes the King, the Lord of hosts. And one of the seraphims flew to me, and in his hand was a live coal, which he had taken with the tongs off the altar. And he touched my mouth, and said: Behold this hath touched thy lips, and thy iniquities shall be taken away, and thy sin shall be cleansed. And I heard the voice of the Lord, saying: Whom shall I send? And who shall go for us? And I said: Lo, here am I, send me.[57]

Several of the prophets felt the impulse to flee into solitude in search of purification; there they practiced voluntary penance before undertaking their mission. From the desert rang out the voice of the last and greatest of the prophets, John the Baptist, inviting the people to prepare the way for the Lord by conversion of heart. Finally, Christ Himself,

[56] Tob. 6:18–21.   [57] Isa. 6:4–8.

though He had no need of purification, enhanced the value of penance by His fast in the desert, which showed what preparation was required for any supernatural mission.

If men feel the need of purification whenever they are called—by God or by circumstances—to handle a task that transcends them, how much stronger the need becomes when they face, not just a task, but the one who infinitely transcends them: God Himself. Before Esther appeared before King Assuerus, who was but a man, however powerful, she had to undergo a long training.

Now when every virgin's turn came to go in to the king, after all had been done for setting them off to advantage, it was the twelfth month; so that for six months they were anointed with oil of myrrh and for other six months they used certain perfumes and sweet spices. And when they were going in to the king, whatsoever they asked to adorn themselves, they received.[58]

But greater still was her need of preparation when she uttered to God the wonderful prayer which obtained from Him remission of her people's doom:

Queen Esther also, fearing the danger that was at hand, had recourse to the Lord. And when she had laid away her royal apparel, she put on garments suitable for weeping and mourning; instead of divers precious ointments, she covered her head with ashes and dung, and she humbled her body with fasts; and all the places in which before she was accustomed to rejoice, she filled with her torn hair. And she prayed to the Lord the God of Israel, saying: O my Lord, who alone art our king, help me a desolate woman.[59]

[58] Esther 2:12–13.   [59] Esther 14:1–3.

Esther entered God's presence by means of prayer. Others come into His presence by a theophany, a vision. Little matters the manner of it, but as soon as men are face to face with God, they become aware of the divine majesty and sanctity.[60] Moses, though he ignored the divine presence in the burning bush, was commanded by Yahweh to purify himself before receiving the revelation of the incommunicable name. "Come not nigh hither, put off the shoes from thy feet; for the place whereon thou standest is holy ground." [61] So well did Moses understand the necessity for purity when men appear before God, that he, in turn, ordered all Israel to be purified when Yahweh was about to come down "in the sight of all the people upon Mount Sinai." [62] This necessity applies to all men, for even "in his angels He found wickedness." [63]

In God's presence no one is just or purified or justified; in the depths of the personality there stirs a vague consciousness of worthlessness, defilement, nothingness and sin.[64] Of course, sin immeasurably increases man's sense of unworthiness. But does this mean that in God's presence only the sinner feels the need of purification? The Bible shows the contrary. The just seek purification, not only that they may be cleansed from their hidden and unconscious faults (*Ab occultis meis munda me* [65]), but also that they may become less unworthy to appear before Him whose infinite sanctity is all the better known to them as their souls are less

[60] Cf. St. Peter's cry when Christ's power was revealed: "Depart from me, for I am a sinful man, O Lord" (Luke 5:8).

[61] Exod. 3:5.   [62] Exod. 19:11.   [63] Job 4:18.

[64] Cf. St. John the Baptist's attitude in Christ's presence (Matt., chap. 3; John, chap. 1).

[65] Ps. 18:13.

sullied by sin. While the sinner's regeneration is imposed
by the necessity of expiating the faults that still weigh him
down and prevent his enjoying God's friendship, the just
man's regeneration is related to the infinite purity of the
divine nature.[66]

The just man knows that he is radically unlike God and
this dissimilarity necessitates a real renewal. Even if he
were totally exempt from sin, the need would subsist all
the same, for it is required by and for the sake of the divine
transcendence and perfection. "Put off the shoes from thy
feet"—not only because you are defiled and sinful, but also
because you are *non-being* in the presence of *Him who is*.
Entirely aside from sin, the infinite distance between the
Creator and His creature invites the latter to purify himself
in order to attenuate the dissimilarity at least a little. Even
the holiest of men can still be considered sinners and the
attitudes of the sinner and of the just man display only
arbitrary differences. Never, under pain of presumption, can
the just man believe himself pure. He ever repeats the
psalmist's prayer: *Amplius lava me.*[67]

On the other hand, even the worst sinner's purification
is ordained from the very beginning with a view to its ulti-

[66] What David expresses negatively: "Wash me yet more" (Ps.
50:4), St. John depicted in high relief when he said in the Apocalypse: "He that is holy, let him be sanctified still" (Apoc. 22:11).
Christ offered a living symbol of this purification before the Last
Supper when He washed the feet of His disciples, though they were
already pure: "And you are clean" (John 13:10). He performed
this act—and its deeper significance eluded the apostles at the time
—and He ordered them to follow His example, because He knew
that the humility of such service would be a source of their deeper
purification.

[67] Ps. 50:4.

mate goal of union with God. That fact is certain. But while this notion always contains the same two elements, their proportion varies. For the farther man advances along the path of purification, the less attention he pays to himself. His sins impede him less and God attracts him more. Where once he kept looking backward ("My sin is always before me" [68]), now he ever looks forward: "As the Lord liveth, the God of Israel, in whose sight I stand." [69] The soul opens its doors ever wider to God's visit and His sanctifying influence. Purification, in its manifold forms and numerous stages, then tends to become an image of divine holiness and purity, as reflected in the soul. Of course the soul still must strive hard and painfully to follow divine guidance and to accept it actively. But to an increasing extent God takes man's ship in tow and it follows in the wake of divine purity and sanctity.

As the soul advances on this path of purification, it begins to breathe a different atmosphere. We can perceive this change if we examine what psalms of penance and contrition the Church chooses for the priest to say during the Mass. Even the order in which they occur is significant. The first psalm, *Judica me,* is all humility and compunction. "Why art thou sad, O my soul? And why dost thou disquiet me?" [70] The soul is bent down by the weight of its sins, as is indicated by the priest's posture at the foot of the altar and by his confession, followed by that of the people after the recitation of the psalm. When the words of pardon are spoken to those present (*misericordiam, indulgentiam*), it may seem that there remains no further need of purification. But dur-

[68] Ps. 50:4.   [69] III Kings 17:1.   [70] Ps. 42:5.

ing the Offertory, the priest recites Psalm 25, as he is cleansed anew:

I will wash my hands among the innocent; and will compass Thy altar, O Lord; that I may hear the voice of Thy praise and tell of all Thy wondrous works. I have loved, O Lord, the beauty of Thy house and the place where Thy glory dwelleth.[71]

The mood of this psalm is very different from the first. It is full of trust and joy, wholly centered upon God, for it is a prelude to the sacrifice of thanksgiving, the Eucharistic banquet, in which the soul is granted union with God.[72]

Many biblical texts show us this positive function of purification, its power to sanctify and to transform. Implicit in these pages are some of the richest truths of the Old Testament, as well as an account of the principal stages of the process by which God, in the past as in the present, has ever prepared souls for His coming and for their intimate union with Him.

Nothing is more mysterious than the way in which God, by an act of His will and by the power of His grace, enables a sinner to become guiltless. Where sin had reigned, God's purity enters in; where all was dark, the light shines; where

[71] Ps. 25:6–8.

[72] Until the very moment of Communion, however, humility and compunction remain with the soul that is still mindful of its sins. "Regard not my sins but the faith of Thy Church. . . . Never permit me to be separated from Thee. . . . Let not the partaking of Thy body . . . turn to my judgment and condemnation." So prays the priest, for only Christ, the Author of all holiness and source of all purification, can liberate and transform the soul. Therefore, even when it has been purified, it remains humbly conscious of its sin, worthlessness and nothingness.

the soul stood empty, a presence now dwells. God alone is the Author of this essentially positive and wholly divine work, of this *re-creation,* which is even more admirable than the original *creation.* This the Jews knew well and they set up a cry of "sacrilege" when Christ forgave sins: "Who can forgive sins, but God alone?" [73] Moreover, when grace swoops down upon a man, it makes a conquest of him. Of course, he still retains his own reactions, his temperament, his natural imperfections, the traces of his sin. But grace has radically changed him, converting his heart, winning him like a prize. In the past, perhaps even on the previous day, he had striven against God or He had ignored Him; now he works with God, cooperates in His enterprises.

This collaboration is indispensable. The free and responsible creature that has received God's grace must supply active concurrence and a positive response. Without this consent and response the divine work could not be done.[74] An episode from the Fourth Book of Kings emphasizes this cooperation of God and man, which was decreed from the very beginning:

Naaman, general of the army of the king of Syria, was a great man with his master, and honorable; for by him the Lord gave deliverance to Syria; and he was a valiant man and rich, but a leper. Now there had gone out robbers from Syria, and had led away captive out of the land of Israel a little maid, and she waited upon Naaman's wife. And she said to her mistress: I

[73] Luke 5:21.

[74] The necessity of active cooperation is stressed by these words of Christ from the Apocalypse: "Behold, I stand at the gate, and knock. If any man shall hear My voice and open to Me the door, I will come in to him, and will sup with him, and he with Me" (Apoc. 3:20).

wish my master had been with the prophet that is in Samaria; he would certainly have healed him of the leprosy which he hath. Then Naaman went in to his lord, . . . and the king of Syria said to him: Go, and I will send a letter to the king of Israel. And he departed, and took with him ten talents of silver, and six thousand pieces of gold, and ten changes of raiment, and brought the letter to the king of Israel. . . . And when the king of Israel had read the letter, he rent his garments, and said: Am I God, to be able to kill and to give life, that this man hath sent to me, to heal a man of his leprosy? Mark, and see how he seeketh occasions against me.

And when Eliseus the man of God, had heard this, to wit, that the king of Israel had rent his garments, he sent to him, saying: Why hast thou rent thy garments? Let him come to me, and let him know that there is a prophet in Israel. So Naaman came, with his horses and chariots, and stood at the door of the house of Eliseus. And Eliseus sent a messenger to him, saying: Go, and wash seven times in the Jordan, and thy flesh shall recover health, and thou shalt be clean. Naaman was angry and went away, saying: I thought he would have come out to me, and standing would have invoked the name of the Lord his God, and touched with his hand the place of the leprosy, and healed me. Are not the Abana, and the Pharphar, rivers of Damascus, better than all the waters of Israel, that I may wash in them, and be made clean? So, as he turned and was going away with indignation, his servants came to him and said to him: Father, if the prophet had bid thee do some great thing, surely thou shouldst have done it; how much rather what he now hath said to thee: Wash, and thou shalt be clean? Then he went down, and washed in the Jordan seven times, according to the word of the man of God, and his flesh was restored, like the flesh of a little child, and he was made clean.

And returning to the man of God with all his train, he came, and stood before him, and said: In truth, I know there is no other God in all the earth, but only in Israel; I beseech thee therefore take a blessing of thy servant. But he answered: As the Lord liveth, before whom I stand, I will receive none. And when he pressed him, he still refused. . . . So he departed from him.[75]

Naaman's bath in the river, even though repeated seven times, could not account for his cure. God intervened and performed a miracle. But it would not have occurred without the stipulated condition: Naaman's personal effort and good will. However paltry it may be, man's cooperation enters into the divine plan as an essential ingredient. In its own order it is as necessary as the divine activity.

God also prepares the soil for the planting of His grace, though the preparation is not always apparent from without. Until the very last moment the attitudes and words of the Syrian general betray his stupidity, impatience, irritation and inability to submit. "Naaman was angry and went away, saying: I thought he would have come out to me." All this is only too human and shows signs of a nature not yet invaded by grace. The sovereign power of grace is evident in the sudden change of this great leader, this haughty pagan who ceased his long struggle and followed his servants' opinion. The lasting conversion that followed his cure is also a tribute to grace.

However, the affectionate urging of the servants and their very manner of speaking to Naaman give pause for thought. The man whose servants called him "father" and to whom they ventured to give advice must certainly have possessed certain natural virtues and a real kindliness which

[75] IV Kings 5:1–19.

they knew by past experience. These attitudes were raised to a higher level by grace. But Naaman had to correspond with this grace and he could not be cured unless he bathed seven times in the Jordan. Thus it is evident that human activity is closely linked to the very act in which God manifests His omnipotent grace.

Is man purified by means of personal effort or does God purify him? The answer which the scriptural story gives to this question is indeed what we might expect. It fits into a thought pattern already familiar to us, as we have traced it in our study of faith and wisdom, which were revealed as human acts and, at the same time, as divine gifts. There is a duty to believe; and yet faith is received as a gift. There is a duty to acquire wisdom; and yet wisdom is communicated from above. The union of human acts and divine gifts is a constant law in the realm of the spirit. A new confirmation is found in the way that purifications take place. There, too, we see the fruit of an intimate and active collaboration of God and man.[76] This is not a transitory law, or one applicable only to certain stages of the spiritual life. It remains in effect on every level of spirituality, even to the highest peaks.

The sinner who wishes to emerge from his sin already realizes this necessity. When God punished Adam for his sin and expelled him from paradise, He obliged him to eat his

[76] St. Peter stresses this collaboration: "As all things of His divine power which appertain to life and godliness are given us, . . . and you, employing all care, minister in your faith, virtue; and in virtue, knowledge. . . . For if these things be with you and abound, they will make you to be neither empty nor unfruitful in the knowledge of our Lord Jesus Christ" (II Pet. 1:3–8). And St. Paul said: "We are God's coadjutors" (I Cor. 3:9).

bread by the sweat of his brow, while the first woman was to bring forth her children in pain. Thus, side by side with divine punishment, human effort also had its purifying value. The legal purifications and the voluntary sacrifices also took this law into account, for they always require active participation and effort on the part of man, who should generously offer to God his choicest possession.

The just man, too, discovers the same necessity. More than passive obedience was demanded of Abraham when he was ordered by God to sacrifice his only son, Isaac. He had to lead him to Mount Moriah, prepare the holocaust, and finally raise his arm to kill the well-loved child. Even when God seems to arrange all events, man is never wholly passive in the process of purification. The most unexpected and sudden blows which, it would seem, man can only sustain passively, still never can cancel the possibility and the obligation of cooperating with God, either by an external gesture signifying acceptance of what God sends or, more important, by the interior attitude of clinging to the divine will, as the soul utters its *Fiat* and actively consents to God. Purification is not achieved unless man's will is lost in God's. "My meat is to do the will of Him that sent Me," said Christ.[77] In actual fact, even if this meat is fully prepared, we still and always must lift it to our mouths, swallow it and assimilate it so that it may become our flesh and blood, the source of our everyday concrete activity.

It is not even enough to affirm that man's collaboration must continue throughout the whole process of purification. We must go farther by saying that it increases in proportion as God's work is carried on and becomes perfect. In this

[77] John 4:34.

respect the terms "active purifications" and "passive purifications" can sometimes be misleading if they give the impression that man begins the task and then reaches a point where God relieves him. This is not so at all. It is true that at the beginning of the spiritual life the sinner, striving painfully to be cleansed of his faults, has particular recourse to visible and external means of discipline and mortification. But later, when the purifications become more spiritual and the trials more interior, there is not any less activity and discipline required of him. Quite the contrary, for no form of spiritual activity is higher and no mortification sterner than the immediate and complete interior consent to God's wishes. It takes great courage to lead a truly mortified existence and to become purified by the daily repetition of external actions performed with unfailing fidelity. But it undoubtedly requires a higher and purer spiritual generosity to keep repeating, even when the soul writhes in pain or is crushed by God-sent trials: *Ecce* and *Fiat*.

While it is useful to continue referring to purifications as "active" and "passive," since ordinarily the one precedes the other, we must not forget that the two elements of the process are really inseparable. There is no purification, however trifling, that is exempt from passivity. On the other hand, activity is required more then ever in the midst of the greatest passive purifications. In order that God may achieve His purpose, the activity must even increase in proportion as the purification becomes more passive and more spiritual. Then, too, as activity and passivity increase and become intensified, they draw nearer to each other until ultimately they are indistinguishable in a simple attitude that contains them both. When at length the human will succeeds in being identified with and espoused to the divine will, unity is achieved. That is sanctity. This was explained by Christ when He said: "I do always the things that please Him" [78] and: "Not My will, but Thine be done." [79] But the Old Testament had already given a glimpse of the painful exertion demanded of the soul and of the long road it must follow to attain union.

THE STEEP ASCENT

Once a man has been conquered by grace and has undergone conversion of heart, he sets his foot on a path on which he must move ever forward. "Wash yourselves, be clean, take away the evil of your devices from My eyes; cease to do perversely, learn to do well." [80] But he is still very weak and, conscious of this weakness, he turns to God to implore His help.

I will praise Thee, O Lord my God, with my whole heart, and I will glorify Thy name forever. For Thy mercy is great toward me; and Thou hast delivered my soul out of the lower hell. . . . Give Thy command to Thy servant, and save the son of Thy handmaid. Show me a token for good, that they who hate me may see, and be confounded.[81]

Though cleansed by grace, yesterday's sinner is still strongly tempted. He calls for help, therefore, with tears and groans. As compunction opens his heart, he longs for deliverance from this tendency to evil that he discovers in himself. "Have mercy on me, O Lord, for I am weak; heal me, O Lord, for my bones are troubled. And my soul is

[78] John 8:29.   [79] Luke 22:42.   [80] Isa. 1:16–17.
[81] Ps. 85:12–17.

troubled exceedingly. . . . I have labored in my groanings, every night I will wash my bed; I will water my couch with my tears." [82] With humility comes strength. The soul no longer fears to speak up to its enemies, that is, the temptations that prowl about still seeking the prey that has escaped. "Depart from me, all ye workers of iniquity." [83]

But this generous determination initiates a weary time, for the soul realizes better each day that it is fundamentally wicked and that it is by nature, in many ways, an accomplice of the enemy. For now it sees its wounds better than it did when blinded by sin. Formerly it drifted on the current that carried it away; now that it tries to swim upstream, the violence of the current is felt.

And so it feels the need for purification in its inmost depths, at the very core of the self. "There is no health in my flesh, because of Thy wrath; there is no peace for my bones, because of my sins." [84] Remembering his past faults, the sinner asks to be protected against himself and liberated. He burns with the fire of repentance.

For my iniquities are gone over my head; and as a heavy burden are become heavy upon me. My sores are putrified and corrupted, because of my foolishness. I am become miserable, and am bowed down even to the end; I walked sorrowful all the day long. For my loins are filled with illusions; and there is no health in my flesh.[85]

The long wanderings in the paths of evil left their mark upon the soul. Now that it sincerely wishes to depart from such ways, it becomes the object of hostility and persecution from the companions of its former travels.

[82] Ps. 6:3–7.   [83] Ps. 6:9.   [84] Ps. 37:4.
[85] Ps. 37:5–8.

My friends and my neighbors have drawn near, and stood against me. And they that were near me stood afar off; and they that sought my soul used violence. And they that sought evils to me spoke vain things, and studied deceits all the day long. But I, as a deaf man, heard not; and as a dumb man not opening his mouth. And I became as a man that heareth not and that hath no reproofs in his mouth. For in Thee, O Lord, have I hoped; Thou wilt hear me, O Lord my God. For I said: Lest at any time my enemies rejoice over me, and whilst my feet are moved, they speak great things against me. For I am ready for scourges, and my sorrow is continually before me. For I will declare my iniquity and I will think for my sin.[86]

These last words prove that the purifying trials have brought the soul to a state of compunction. One clear sign of God's work in the soul is its ever-deepening desire for purification. "Wash me yet more from my iniquity, and cleanse me from my sin." [87] This was the sigh of the penitent king, David.

The soul, however, has voluntarily accepted the trial that falls upon it. And before long it tastes the fruit of the trial, understanding that it is the way by which God's mercy reaches it. "Have mercy on me, O God, according to Thy great mercy." [88]

As the sufferings and trials that veil the soul become more transparent, they permit a better view of divine mercy at work and this is a sure sign of its progress on the way of purification. Another sign is humility. As the soul draws nearer to God, it better realizes its worthlessness and ever more humbly implores divine help. "Forsake me not, O Lord

[86] Ps. 37:12–19.   [87] Ps. 50:4.   [88] Ps. 50:1.

my God; do not Thou depart from me. Attend unto my help, O Lord, the God of my salvation." [89] It now has a truer estimate of its enemies' strength: its external enemies and especially its internal enemies, the throng of evil tendencies hitherto ignored and only now revealed. "They are many that make war against me, . . . but I will trust in Thee." [90] Knowledge of its own weakness and trust in God: such are the fruits of purification. Like a man just pulled out of a chasm but still standing on the edge of it, the soul measures the extent of the mortal danger from which it has just been rescued by divine mercy.

But I have put my trust in Thee, O Lord. . . . My lots are in Thy hands. Deliver me out of the hands of my enemies, and from them that persecute me. Make Thy face to shine upon Thy servant.[91]

In order that a soul struggling in the midst of purifying trials may continue to hope for the coming of God after the defeat of its enemies, it must first experience some foretaste of His presence. The souls which have just returned to God are often granted an overwhelming delight in His presence. He wants to bind them to Him. Their faltering steps still need this divine support.

Make Thy face to shine upon Thy servant. . . . O how great is the multitude of Thy sweetness, O Lord, which Thou hast hidden for them that fear Thee. . . . Thou shalt hide them in the secret of Thy face, from the disturbance of men. Thou shalt protect them in Thy tabernacle from the contradiction of tongues.[92]

[89] Ps. 37:22–23.   [90] Ps. 55:3–4.   [91] Ps. 30:15–17.
[92] Ps. 30:17, 20–21.

Until this point the soul had reflected particularly upon itself and its past life. Realizing the need for purification, it added effort and mortifications [93] to these meditations. The soil thus ploughed was opened to divine action. Now the work bears fruit. The soul looks beyond its sin to find Him whom the sin had offended. The discovery of His goodness and infinite mercy brings keener pain at the thought of displeasing Him. It is still a prey of irksome struggles, shaken by crosscurrents of distaste, subject to discouragement. Without the sustenance of divine consolations, it might cease striving, through lack of courage to stay on the path and advance toward God.

Unless the Lord had been my helper, my soul had almost dwelt in hell. If I said: My foot is moved, Thy mercy, O Lord, assisted me. According to the multitude of my sorrows in my heart, Thy comforts have given joy to my soul.[94]

The soul that wants to stay faithful and yet realizes its own weaknesses has but one recourse: to cling to God. "In Thee, O Lord, I have hoped. . . . Be Thou unto me a God, a protector, and a place of strength, that Thou mayest make me safe. For Thou art my firmament and my refuge." [95] The sole purpose of the consolations was that the soul might become rooted in God, once it had a chance to "taste and see that the Lord is sweet." [96] Happy the man who does not seek them for their own sake, but rather uses them as a lamp to guide his steps and a support to strengthen his devotion. For the heavenly delight was but a short visit and a momen-

---

[93] "And every one that striveth for the mastery, refraineth himself from all things" (I Cor. 9:25).

[94] Ps. 93:17–19.   [95] Ps. 70:1–3.   [96] Ps. 33:9.

tary shining of the light. Once again darkness and trouble return, all the more painful by contrast with the time of delight and illumination. It is not surprising that the soul, not yet inured to war, utters a gentle complaint:

Why do I go sorrowful whilst the enemy afflicteth me? Send forth Thy light and Thy truth. They have conducted me, and brought me unto Thy holy hill, and into Thy tabernacles. And I will go in to the altar of God, to God who giveth joy to my youth. To Thee, O God my God, I will give praise upon the harp. Why art thou sad, O my soul? And why dost thou disquiet me? Hope in God, for I will still give praise to Him, the salvation of my countenance, and my God.[97]

But progress is impossible except by the path of purification. The time has come for the soul to be cut off from the consolations of the senses and to follow God by the arduous path of faith and fidelity.[98]

The next stage of the soul's journey is long and monotonous, a time of obscure struggle and modest plodding. It becomes exhausted in the constant repetition of humble, everyday striving; sometimes faltering, then starting off anew. This period of purification inevitably recalls an arduous mountain climb. When the last star fades at dawn, the snow on the peaks sings a welcome to the rising sun. The summit to be conquered stands clearly outlined, looking very near. Up the pathways, across colorful meadows and alpine fields, in the coolness of early morning, the wayfarer strides forward, full of confidence and enthusiasm. Suddenly every-

[97] Ps. 42:2–6.
[98] Cf. many passages of Psalm 118, showing that time is an essential factor of the spiritual life and of the process of purification. The virtue that it arouses in faithful souls is perseverance.

thing changes as he stumbles and strains on the long, hard climb over rocky ground. No longer is he cheered by any stimulus: the distant horizon has vanished; his view of the peak is blocked by the monotonous, interminable slopes that must be ascended step by step under the burning sun; a rigorous journey requiring effort, self-control and perseverance, while bringing no reward in return.

Such is the spiritual life during this period of the soul's purification, when it experiences no delight or consolation. Psalm 17 describes this state: "I have kept hard ways. Perfect Thou my goings in Thy paths; that my footsteps be not moved." [99] But by remaining true to God throughout this journey of approach, the soul makes tremendous progress. Often in unguarded moments comes the longing for a little rest, a welcome halt. But at the same time there is a realization that it is beneficial to lose sight of God for a time.[100] All those who have undergone these purifications have felt these opposite sentiments: on the one hand, the determination not to leave such a safe and profitable path; on the other hand, a hope that this hard road may soon end. Isaias expressed this state of soul: "If you return and be quiet, you shall be saved; in silence and in hope shall your strength be." [101]

And indeed, in God's good time a respite is granted the traveller who so courageously bore the fatigue of the road and the heat of the day. At length he reaches a spring of water, a shady corner, a moment's rest. After the long, weary hike, the soul avidly enjoys this relaxation, secretly consider-

[99] Ps. 16:4–5.
[100] "It is expedient to you that I go" (John 16:7).
[101] Isa. 30:15.

ing it "well-deserved." But is it able to be ever mindful that this is merely a halt, a brief rest, intended only to gain new strength and not to dissipate energy, for the real ascent has not yet started? There is a temptation to adopt the psalmist's words, somewhat distorting the meaning: "I have loved, because the Lord will hear the voice of my prayer. . . . I was humbled, and He delivered me. Turn, O my soul, into thy rest." [102]

How easy it is for the traveller to take this "rest in God" as a final stop, settling down to enjoy the spiritual delights encountered there. It is easier for him to thank God for granting them than to tear himself away from them. Unless precautions are taken, this time of respite tends, almost imperceptibly, to make him self-centered and, to some extent, self-satisfied. Of course, he thanks God for helping him and guiding him along the road, but he also measures the distance covered and more or less takes the credit for it himself.[103] Here again the temptation is strong to apply to himself the words uttered by King David when he was saved from danger by God and granted a victory over his enemies:

The Lord became my protector. And He brought me forth into a large place; He saved me, because He was well pleased with me. And the Lord will reward me according to my justice; and will repay me according to the cleanness of my hands; because I have kept the ways of the Lord and have not done wickedly against my God. . . . For by Thee I shall

---

[102] Ps. 114:1, 6–7.

[103] How often St. Paul's words can be applied to many penitential practices and even to instances of devotion to duty where much natural satisfaction is found! "Which things have indeed a show of wisdom in superstition and humility, and not sparing the body; not in any honor to the filling of the flesh" (Col. 2:23).

be delivered from temptation; and through my God I shall go over a well. . . . Thou hast enlarged my steps under me; and my feet are not weakened. I will pursue after my enemies, and overtake them; and I will not turn again till they are consumed. I will break them, and they shall not be able to stand; they shall fall under my feet. . . . And I shall beat them as small as the dust before the wind; I shall bring them to nought, like the dirt in the streets. . . . The Lord liveth, and blessed be my God.[104]

We may be tempted to think that this naive satisfaction presents no great danger. On the contrary, it invites disaster. Whatever excuse the soul may seek, the fact is that it has stopped; it no longer advances on the way; it has been halted by selfishness arising from temptations to cowardice or pride. The soul can make no progress in the path of purification unless it forgets itself and prepares for God's visit. The holier it becomes, moreover, the less does it look upon sanctification as a certain level that must be reached, for with greater progress comes a greater understanding that purification should be sought because of God and for His sake alone. The consciousness of sin obliges a man to be purified; an awareness of his status as a sinner includes the same obligation; but the knowledge of God and the hope of being admitted to the Lord's presence vastly increases the obligation. When he has been liberated from his sins and has been credited with some meritorious effort and some degree of knowledge of God, then hope arises that the purifications undergone may render divine control more effective.

We can well understand how critical this moment is. If a man refuse at this point to heed the voice calling him, if

[104] Ps. 17:19–47.

he declines to continue along the road, then all his spiritual progress is jeopardized. He faces a truly decisive choice. Should he cease longing for the summit he was seeking, should he selfishly judge that he has done enough and therefore refuse new effort, then he will never know what God, in His love, had prepared for him.[105]

On the contrary, if he consents to undergo deeper purifications with unflinching courage and to choose God, whatever the cost may be, then he will enter a new stage on the journey, a very hard stage, for it leads to unknown regions. This he knows, but he also knows that the road will emerge on heights where the air is pure and exhilarating. The Bible presents examples of souls that have reached this turning-point. The concrete terms of the problem must not deceive us concerning the real issue and the stakes of the option they face.

Solomon reached this crisis when, after making great progress in the paths of wisdom and receiving extraordinary divine illumination, he was urged by God to advance farther along the way. Because he was self-complacent and took pride in his knowledge and his progress, his heart was dimmed, and at the end of his life he was led astray and abandoned the straight path. "And his heart was not perfect with the Lord his God." [106] This occurred even though God "had appeared to him twice," [107] and had lavished wealth and glory upon him.

David, his father, had also known a time when, after so

[105] "Because thou sayest: I am rich, and made wealthy, and have need of nothing; and knowest not that thou art wretched, and miserable, and poor, and blind, and naked. I counsel thee to buy of me gold fire tried" (Apoc. 3:17–18).

[106] III Kings 11:4.   [107] III Kings 11:9.

many graces and so many years of fidelity, he was assailed by temptation. To succumb meant to abandon the forward march, to lose the graces of light and love with which he had been favored, to be cut off from the joy of divine intimacy. The psalms testify that this was the crucial point of David's spiritual life. Because he had not kept his heart intact for Yahweh, because he had left the straight path, this great king, who had advanced so far in divine love, had to beg God's pardon and again submit to atoning purifications.

Thus, the Bible shows us souls that had started out with great enthusiasm and courage, but then suddenly stopped, as if stumbling on a rock. Whether it be from weariness, cowardice, lack of faith or a renewed attack of pride, these souls, so long faithful and generous, cease to advance, lacking the energy needed to keep to the narrow road.[108] It may be but a temporary lapse, as in the case of Moses, but also it may be a final stop. But the Bible likewise gives us examples of generous souls that do not hesitate to persevere in their efforts and to bear the trials encountered on the path where God has led them. They make their way through the other stages of purification and thus gradually approach union with God.

[108] "I know thy tribulation and thy poverty, but thou art rich. . . . Fear none of those things which thou shalt suffer. Behold, the devil will cast some of you into prison that you may be tried; and you shall have tribulation ten days. Be thou faithful until death, and I will give thee the crown of life" (Apoc. 2:9–10). "Enter ye in at the narrow gate, for wide is the gate and broad is the way that leadeth to destruction, and many there are who go in thereat. How narrow is the gate, and strait is the way that leadeth to life; and few there are that find it" (Matt. 7:13–14).

GOD'S ACTION UPON THE SOUL

As we have just seen, what is required of the soul at this critical moment is a complete gift, an absolute self-surrender to divine influence. This attitude has tremendous consequences. By its interior consent, the soul enters the path of total dispossession, of spiritual poverty and nakedness. It gives itself into God's hands, accepting in advance whatever harsh treatment He may impose upon it in order that it may be purified in its very substance. This attitude is both decisive and necessary. Without it, nothing profound or lasting can be accomplished. Circumstances may differ, but at various periods of life God asks the same question of the soul: "Do you consent?" And each time the whole spiritual destiny of the soul depends upon the answer.

Although the Old Testament does not usually stress the personal reactions and subjective states of the actors in the various episodes it recounts, it has not failed to report some of their words which betray the commitment made once and for all and without regrets by a soul that surrenders itself. Whether it be in early childhood, like young Samuel, who cried out in all the innocence of his child-heart: "Here am I. . . . Speak, Lord, for Thy servant heareth"; [109] or in old age, like the highpriest Heli, who accepted God's decree with a sigh of distress: "It is the Lord, let Him do what is good in His sight"; [110] whether it be Moses or the prophets, whatever men God chose as His messengers had to make this absolute surrender and had to entrust themselves confidently to His guiding hand. On this condition they not only become capable of doing the task assigned to them but they

[109] I Kings 3:4, 10.   [110] I Kings 3:18.

are purified by the task itself. It is clearly evident that God requires this unconditional consent before He undertakes the work of purification, which may lead the soul to the frontiers of death, which, in any case, involves tremendous suffering. As God leads men to this path, He makes sure that they cannot complain afterward that they were forced there against their wills. And so, to ward off any surprise, God sees to it that His children are duly warned of what to expect:

Son, when thou comest to the service of God, stand in justice and in fear, and prepare thy soul for temptation. Humble thy heart, and endure; incline thy ear, and receive the words of understanding; and make not haste in the time of clouds. Wait on God with patience; join thyself to God, and endure, that thy life may be increased in the latter end. Take all that shall be brought upon thee; and in thy sorrow endure, and in thy humiliation keep patience.[111]

"Prepare thy soul for temptation." Acceptance, however generous, unconditional consent, the *Ecce* and the *Fiat* which surrender the soul to God and allow Him free entry: all this is not enough. There is also required a positive discipline, as taught in the wisdom literature and clearly described in the above text of Ecclesiasticus. The program comprises purity of intention, persevering courage, trust in God, serene fidelity and, finally, humility and patience. All who desire to enter the ways of spirituality and to undergo the mystical purifications should give thought to all this.

Elsewhere Ecclesiasticus shows, if further proof be necessary, that God's work presupposes advance preparation and that His handicraft always requires collaboration. We

[111] Ecclus. 2:1-4.

are reminded that while God is absolute master of His plans, yet human generosity makes the divine work possible and allows it to continue. How could God refrain from acting upon a soul that has courageously offered itself to be purified and transformed? The soul that makes the total gift of self becomes capable of ever deeper purification. Does this mean that such an act of surrender, of yielding oneself into the divine hands, brings the soul to an exceptional way of life? Does this unconditional consent cut it off from ordinary life and oblige it to be released from material contingencies?

A careful study of the Old Testament proves that this is by no means so. It is true that, regarding many biblical characters whose lives were very active, we have no knowledge of what point they reached in the process of purification or whether they had any truly personal and profound experience of God. They cannot answer our question. But there were others who undoubtedly experienced great purification. And these, far from being separated from society, led a life of intense activity. While their souls were especially cherished by God, this favor, however momentous in other ways, usually did not involve any peculiar form of life. These men chosen by God, whether it be Abraham, Moses or Jeremias, and destined to climb the loftiest spiritual peaks, remain closely implicated in external affairs. In fact, events have a very strong impact on them, as these servants of God have a mission to sway or to direct them. Thus they are indeed committed to God and to a definite course of action; but nevertheless this commitment isolates them. For their only rule is God's will, which sends them toward men and events. "Speak, Lord, for Thy servant heareth." "Do with me what Thou wilt." *Usque ad mortem.*

God is equally free to act in them and by them; this makes their souls wonderfully ready for purification. And how does this take place? Generally by means of their mission itself. The divine economy is thrifty and "to them that love God, all things work together unto good." [112] He, therefore, uses the life imposed upon His servants to bring about their profound purification. The Bible proves this very clearly.

The usual instrument of purification that God holds in His hand is life itself. Life, that is, the whole combination of situations that must be faced day by day, with all the consequent obligations. Nothing purifies men as well as life itself, if they are able to accept it and live it as it occurs. By nature it is unforeseeable and cannot be covered by any formula. It is real and must *really* be lived. It is all-inclusive and takes up the whole man, shaping him on every plane. No one can ever view it as a mere spectator, for sooner or later it involves even those who have refused to commit themselves. Life uses and intermingles every rhythm; often a sudden event transforms it in an instant. This forces men to adopt a new pace and to overcome difficulties which show them their inmost selves and purify them to the very core. No man, however prudent and wise, can ever arrange his life just as he pleases. On the contrary, it is life which, day by day traversing strange regions, must "lead thee whither thou wouldst not." [113] And always, mysteriously, invisibly, God is the weaver of life's fabric, the artist who places each tiny item in accord with His infinitely wise pattern. How then, can men venture to judge what is best for them or decide what they require? [114] Only life brings the answer, mo-

[112] Rom. 8:28.   [113] John 21:18.

[114] After listing in a concrete way the various trials which the

ment by moment. How can we fail to see that it is a royal road, a safe road? It is the chief means God uses to purify His servants. A few examples chosen from among many suffice to show how the principle is applied.

Abraham was the first to illustrate it and he did so magnificently. Was not his separation from his ancestral country and traditions a purification of his senses, as thorough as it was unexpected? Then came the purification of his will, as he learned to depend utterly upon God's direction. Nor was he spared the purification of his faith and hope. The final sanction came when he was asked to make the supreme sacrifice of his son's life. Life carried the process of purification to unsuspected depths in the soul of the father of all believers.

Moses' vocation is no less significant. He was timid by temperament, could not speak well, shunned responsibility. "I beseech Thee, Lord, send whom Thou wilt send." [115] But the mission God prescribed for him was that of leader of a whole nation and the herald of the divine word. He was naturally impulsive,[116] but he spent forty years learning the lesson of patient fortitude and meekness. His faith was harshly tested. The purification of his hopes was most painful, since, after all his labor and suffering, this man who was God's intimate friend, who proved admirably faithful and unselfish in the performance of an overpowering task, was

---

faithful may have to sustain, St. Paul cries out: "Who then shall separate us from the love of Christ?" (Rom. 8:35). Elsewhere he tells how what he judged to be best, to be freed of a certain "sting" of the flesh, was refused. God taught him to prefer his weakness, "for when I am weak, then am I powerful" (II Cor. 12:10).

[115] Exod. 4:13.   [116] Exod. 2:11–15.

to die without entering the Promised Land toward which he had ceaselessly directed and led God's people.[117] Truly, life purified him well.

Life also brought about David's purification, and at the cost of great pain. By causing the child of his sin to die, God opened the springs of humility and repentance in David's heart, cleansing "the concupiscence of the flesh, and the concupiscence of the eyes, and the pride of life." [118] The process was deepened by palace intrigues, rebellions, unsuccessful wars and desertions. Abandoned by his followers, betrayed by his son, he experienced terrible anguish, while his faith was fortified and his trust in God became heroic.

Life was likewise the chisel that sculptured the prophets' souls, as it exposed them to scorn, hostility, hatred and vengeance. It led them to persecution and to martyrdom. Thus, we have seen that God uses life as the supreme instrument of purification.[119]

Since the events of life are the fitting instrument of spiritual purification, let us see how profound and intense this process becomes in some instances. May God help us never to belittle the often intolerable burden of suffering and illnesses, or the still heavier burden of trials that touch souls in their dearest affections, in their reputation or their honor.

---

[117] Cf. Deut. 3:28; 31:23.　　[118] I John 2:16.

[119] Human life was for Christ Himself a school, certainly not of purification, but of subjection. "And whereas indeed He was the Son of God, He learned obedience by the things which he suffered" (Heb. 5:8). In this His life is an example for us even with regard to purifications, for we who are sinners and inclined toward evil cannot practice obedience and subjection without profound and constant sacrifices which are of great value in our purification.

We should not be deaf to their cries, which are recorded in the Bible and often show desperate anguish.

Agar's sorrow, though mute, was so profound that the Lord heard her affliction [120] and sent His angel to console her. Anna's poignant suffering was also expressed silently to God. When the highpriest Heli was astonished to see her moving her lips without making any sound, she answered him: "I am an exceedingly unhappy woman, . . . for out of the abundance of my sorrow and grief have I spoken till now." [121] The daughter of Jephte asked her father to let her "go about the mountains . . . and bewail my virginity," before being sacrificed, young as she was.[122] Rachel was so desperate because she was barren that she cried out: "Give me children, otherwise I shall die." [123] So heart-broken was Rachel that until the massacre of the Holy Innocents and even afterward, her desolation, of which the prophets sang, expressed the desolation of all mothers whose children were snatched from them. "A voice was heard on high of lamentation, of mourning and weeping, of Rachel weeping for her children, and refusing to be comforted for them, because they are not." [124]

David was betrayed by his son, Absalom, who expelled him from Jerusalem. "But David went up by the ascent of Mount Olivet, going up and weeping, walking barefoot, and with his head covered." [125] Later, when the death of this same son was announced, "the king, therefore, being much moved, went up to the high chamber over the gate, and wept. And as he went, he spoke in this manner: My son Absalom,

[120] Cf. Gen. 16:11.   [121] I Kings 1:15–16.   [122] Judg. 11:37.
[123] Gen. 30:1.   [124] Jer. 31:15.   [125] II Kings 15:30.

Absalom my son; would to God that I might die for thee, Absalom my son, my son Absalom." [126]

The prophets, in the winepress of persecution and indescribable suffering, cursed the day of their birth.[127] Elias, when pursued by Achab's men, his life threatened and his heart full of anguish, collapsed in the desert and prayed for death. "It is enough for me, Lord, take away my soul." [128] And finally, we can follow the poem of Job's unbearable martyrdom.

Thus, we see that the Bible does not underestimate the pain of such trials, but it also shows under what conditions they can become fertile. If a man is afflicted by pain and anguish, pursued by insults and calumny, overwhelmed by failure, crushed by disaster, and if he still refuses divine control, if he refuses to be formed by this process of "passive subtraction," as Teilhard de Chardin calls it, a process which disintegrates the soul and yet leads it to fulfillment, then he will never reach the goal to which God wanted to lead him. On the contrary, if he willingly and lovingly accepts these tortures, bearing them actively and entrusting himself to the hands of Him who is testing him by love, then he will know that his suffering can become a principle of transforming purification.[129]

THE GREAT TRIALS

Daily life, with its texture of diverse trials, suffices for the deep purification of faithful souls. But if God wishes

[126] II Kings 18:33.   [127] Cf. Jer. 20:14.
[128] III Kings 19:4.
[129] "Ought not Christ to have suffered these things, and so to enter into His glory?" (Luke 24:26.)

them to enjoy even closer union with Himself, then He leads
them by the way ordinarily called "the great purifications."
Their nature is indicated by a group of Old Testament texts
which later instinctively attracted the attention of spiritual
authors and mystics. Their extent and intensity are glimpsed
in an episode of the Second Book of the Machabees, containing a transparent symbolism of which the author himself has stressed the spiritual meaning and implication.

For when our fathers were led into Persia, the priests that
then were worshippers of God took privately the fire from the
altar and hid it in a valley where there was a deep pit without
water, and there they kept it safe, so that the place was unknown to all men. But when many years had passed, and it
pleased God that Nehemias should be sent by the king of
Persia, he sent some of the posterity of those priests that had
hid it, to seek for the fire; and as they told us, they found
no fire, but thick water. Then he bade them draw it up, and
bring it to him; and the priest Nehemias commanded the
sacrifices that were laid on, to be sprinkled wtih the same
water, both the wood and the things that were laid upon it.
And when this was done, and the time came that the sun
shone out, which before was in a cloud, there was a great fire
kindled, so that all wondered.[130]

The fire of divine life has been placed in our souls so
secretly that it takes us a long time to become conscious of
it. Some even run the risk of always ignoring the inward
treasure. But when God's good pleasure leads souls back
from the exile of sin, He inspires them to seek this fire deeply
hidden within themselves. But alas, nothing is found but
thick water, incapable of catching fire; it is the mud of sin-

[130] II Mach. 1:19–22.

ful tendencies. But God asks men to drain off this water to the point of utter emptiness and then, at the cost of great effort, to pour it upon the altar. These humble, irksome and persevering efforts teach souls the truth about themselves. Gradually all their evil substance is carried to the altar and thus offered as a holocaust. First the wood and the things required for the sacrifice had to be prepared; that is to say, the soul must come to God in true humility, with many acts of renunciation, surrender and spiritual poverty. At length a divine blessing descends upon these meritorious efforts; God's sun pierces the clouds and as its rays strike the altar, flames rise high and a great fire is kindled and consumes the holocaust.[131]

The work of purification is not yet complete, however thorough it may appear in this account. For the author of the Book of the Machabees continues as follows:

And when the sacrifice was consumed, Nehemias commanded the water that was left to be poured out upon the

[131] St. John of the Cross once explained what purifications the soul had to endure before it reaches transforming union. The image he used is very similar to that of the episode from the Book of the Machabees. "This purgative and loving knowledge of divine light whereof we here speak acts upon the soul which it is purging and preparing for perfect union with it in the same way as fire acts upon a log of wood in order to transform it into itself; for material fire, acting upon wood, first of all begins to dry it, by driving out its moisture and causing it to shed the water which it contains within itself. Then it begins to make it black, dark and unsightly, and even to give forth a bad odor, and, as it dries it little by little, it brings out and drives away all the dark and unsightly accidents which are contrary to the nature of fire. And finally it begins to kindle it externally and give it heat, and at last transforms it into itself and makes it as beautiful as fire (*Dark Night of the Soul,* Book II, chap. X, *op. cit.,* I, pp. 402–403).

great stones. Which being done, there was kindled a flame from them; but it was consumed by the light that shined from the altar. . . . And Nehemias called this place Nephthar, which is interpreted purification.[132]

The sacrifice and then the water were "consumed." The purification of this thick water was not limited to its burning on the altar. Even when the sacrifice has been consumed, there is more still to be done. The water that has been purified by the fire where it was thrown, must next be taken to a solitary place and poured out upon great bare stones. What does this mean, except that the soul must first give or relinquish all that it *has,* and then be purified and consumed in all that it *is*. Merely human trials, however intense, do not suffice for such a task. The flames of earthly fire cannot consume a soul or purify it in its very substance, for this requires the rays of a divine sun. Just as water absorbed by the sun can only rise as a pure distilled vapor, so also the soul that is drawn to God can reach union with Him only after it has recovered its essential purity by means of mystical purifications.

The episode of the Book of the Machabees allows us a glimpse of the great purifications. Can we know more about them? Following its usual method, the Old Testament does not define mystical purifications, but confines itself to depicting souls that undergo them. It brings us the cries they utter as they are crushed in the divine winepress or as they enter the dark night. By observing them, we can discern the nature of these purifications and the secret of their fecundity. We must take some note of this before allowing the texts to speak for themselves.

[132] II Mach. 1:31-36.

It would seem that the essential element of the great mystical purifications is the *night;* that is, a spiritual state explicitly willed by God, in which souls cease to understand the reason for the trials that afflict them and believe they are separated from Him forever. Previously they had been following a path which seemed to lead to a goal, so that every step, however painful, was an advance. But now the road seems to have no outlet. Previously such souls, even in their worst trials, never doubted God's mercy or His purifying treatment. But henceforth divine conduct seems utterly incomprehensible, even extremely arbitrary and unjust. Everything bewilders them, causing uneasiness, anguish, obscurity. The more they seek God, the more deeply hidden He remains; the more they desire Him, the more He rejects them. There is complete opposition and discrepancy between God's word and external events, between God's promises and the state of desolation in which souls are left. Sometimes they encounter a failure which He permits even though He has first assured victory; sometimes, for no apparent reason, they experience a reversal of God's relationship to them. They seem to be permanently abandoned or even rejected, though divine favor and friendship had been theirs before. They have not been guilty of the slightest infidelity, but they must become fit for the final mystery of faith. To reach this state and to gather its fruits, they must give up all human modes of action. Only in the *dark night* can they receive the revelation of what they could not and would not attain by their own minds.

God wishes to be possessed for His own sake, independently of all justice, all right, all reason. He brings souls to bay as they face scandal and injustice. He seems to act in a capricious, arbitrary way, following only His own good pleasure. Thus does He invite souls to enter the depths of spiritual love. For in His wisdom, He spurns all systems and He achieves His triumph by ways that to us seem utterly disconcerting. "He writes straight with crooked lines." He arouses such generosity and faith that souls must surrender their last self-defenses, and in spite of all struggle, the heart prevails against logic. He obliges them to attain absolute selflessness, to care for nothing but God's good pleasure, however incomprehensible it may be. This is the path by which they become like Him, transformed by the divine will. Examples of this contradiction between words and deeds are found in Jeremias and the psalmists. An admirable and poignant description of the worst of all trials, that of the just man crushed in the winepress of divine caprice, is contained in the Book of Job.[133]

From the time that he was still in the womb of his mother, the prophet Jeremias received his vocation, being claimed by the Lord and bound to Him. "Before I formed thee in the bowels of thy mother, I knew thee; and before thou camest forth out of the womb, I sanctified thee, and made thee a prophet unto the nations." [134] God assigned him to a difficult and thankless mission, but at least He promised help and protection:

Thou shalt go to all that I shall send thee; and whatsoever I shall command thee, thou shalt speak. . . . Lo, I have set

[133] Because he had reached this state, St. Paul was able to utter cries of joy and triumph even in the midst of intense affliction (cf. II Cor., chap. 4).

[134] Jer. 1:5.

thee this day over the nations, and over kingdoms, to root up and to pull down, and to waste and to destroy, and to build and to plant. . . . For behold I have made thee this day a fortified city, and a pillar of iron, and a wall of brass, over all the land, to the kings of Juda, to the princes thereof, and to the priests, and to the people of the land. And they shall fight against thee, and shall not prevail: for I am with thee, saith the Lord, to deliver thee.[135]

In fulfilling this mission, Jeremias shows heroic fidelity. When God asks him to renounce marriage in order that he may remain unattached among the people to whom he is sent, he obeys. "Thou shalt not take thee a wife, neither shalt thou have sons and daughters in this place." [136] Better still, as messenger of God's word, he himself is nourished most lovingly on that word. "Thy words were found, and I did eat them, and Thy word was to me a joy and gladness of my heart." [137]

Jeremias preaches God's message without heeding the opposition and the hatred and the stubborn attacks of his enemies. "And they said: Come, and let us invent devices against Jeremias. . . . Come, and let us strike him with the tongue,[138] and let us give no heed to all his words." [139] As he is defending God's cause, the prophet feels sure of divine support and calls on God to help him. "Give heed to me, O Lord, and hear the voice of my adversaries. Shall evil be rendered for good, because they have digged a pit for my soul? Remember that I have stood in Thy sight, to speak good for them, and to turn away Thy indignation

---

[135] Jer. 1:7–19.　　[136] Jer. 16:2.　　[137] Jer. 15:16.
[138] That is, let us find a serious accusation against him.
[139] Jer. 18:18.

from them." [140] But God is silent. Full of confident faith, Jeremias insists. "O Lord, Thou knowest, remember me, and visit me, and defend me from them that persecute me. . . . Know that for Thy sake I have suffered reproach." [141] The faithful servant who is the object of such persecution receives no answer, no help. God even seems to be protecting the persecutors:

Thou indeed, O Lord, art just, if I plead with Thee, but yet I will speak what is just to Thee: Why doth the way of the wicked prosper? Why is it well with all them that transgress and do wickedly? Thou hast planted them, and they have taken root; they prosper and bring forth fruit; Thou art near in their mouth, and far from their reins. And Thou, O Lord, hast known me, Thou hast seen me, and proved my heart with Thee. [142]

Jeremias' heart is tortured by misgivings and anguish. Could he have made a mistake in giving himself to God, in being allured by Him?

Why is my sorrow become perpetual? . . . It is become to me as the falsehood of deceitful waters that cannot be trusted. . . . Thou hast deceived me, O Lord, and I am deceived; Thou hast been stronger than I, and Thou hast prevailed. I am become a laughing-stock all the day, all scoff at me. For I am speaking now this long time, . . . and the word of the Lord is made a reproach to me, and a derision all the day. [143]

Then he feels dazed and he reaches the brink of rebellion: "Then I said: I will not make mention of Him, nor speak any more in His name." [144] His soul is submerged in pro-

[140] Jer. 18:19–20. [141] Jer. 15:15. [142] Jer. 12:1–3.
[143] Jer. 15:18; 20:7–8. [144] Jer. 20:9.

found obscurity. In heart-rending terms, later to be repeated by many mystics, he describes the desolation in which God leaves him, as well as the cruel and incomprehensible divine conduct:

I am the man that see my poverty by the rod of His indignation. He hath led me, and brought me into darkness, and not into light. Only against me He hath turned, and turned again His hand all the day. My skin and my flesh He hath made old, He hath broken my bones. He hath built round about me, and He hath compassed me with gall and labor. He hath set me in dark places as those that are dead for ever. He hath built against me round about, that I may not get out; He hath made my fetters heavy. Yea, and when I cry, and entreat, He hath shut out my prayer. He hath shut up my ways with square stones; He hath turned my paths upside down. He is become to me as a bear lying in wait, as a lion in secret places. He hath turned aside my paths, and hath broken me in pieces; He hath made me desolate. He hath bent His bow, and set me as a mark for His arrows. . . . And He hath broken my teeth one by one; He hath fed me with ashes. And my soul is removed far off from peace, I have forgotten good things. And I said: My end and my hope is perished from the Lord.[145]

A similar trial afflicted the psalmist, whose distress was expressed in almost the same terms:

O Lord, the God of my salvation, I have cried in the day, and in the night before Thee. . . . For my soul is filled with evils, and my life has drawn nigh to hell. . . . Like the slain sleeping in the sepulchres whom Thou rememberest no more, and they are cast off from Thy hand. They have laid me in

[145] Lam. 3:1–18.

the lower pit, in the dark places, and in the shadow of death. Thy wrath is strong over me, and all Thy waves Thou hast brought in upon me. Thou has put away my acquaintance far from me; they have set me an abomination to themselves. I was delivered up, and came not forth; my eyes languished through poverty. . . . Lord, why castest Thou off my prayer; why turnest Thou away Thy face from me? I am poor, and in labors from my youth; and being exalted have been humbled and troubled. They have come round about me like water all the day; they have compassed me about together. Friend and neighbor Thou hast put far from me; and my acquaintance, because of misery.[146]

Under such cruel treatment the soul feels its strength rapidly ebbing. Feverish and staggering, it collapses and is left in ruins. One by one its faculties fail and it helplessly witnesses its own dissolution. "My heart is broken within me, all my bones tremble; I am become as a drunken man, and as a man full of wine." [147] What recourse is left? None, since God Himself is the persecutor, striking without pity and then abandoning His servant, deaf to every plea. Soon all will be over.

Hear, O Lord, my prayer; and let my cry come to Thee. Turn not away Thy face from me, in the day when I am in trouble. . . . For my days are vanished like smoke, and my bones are grown dry like fuel for the fire. I am smitten as grass, and my heart is withered; because I forgot to eat my bread. Through the voice of my groaning, my bone hath cleaved to my flesh. I am become like to a pelican of the wilderness; I am like a night raven in the house. I have watched, and am become as a sparrow all alone on the housetop. . . .

[146] Ps. 87:1–9, 15–19.   [147] Jer. 23:9.

For I did eat ashes like bread, and mingled my drink with weeping. Because of Thy anger and indignation; for having lifted me up Thou hast thrown me down. My days have declined like a shadow.[148]

However, such distress never becomes despair. The hand that strikes is also the hand that sustains. Though God breaks his heart, though He offers the prophet neither support nor grounds for hope, yet the Lord enables Jeremias to trust Him wonderfully and to maintain this trust to the very end.

But the Lord is with me as a strong warrior. . . . The mercies of the Lord that we are not consumed, because His commiserations have not failed. They are new every morning, great is Thy faithfulness. The Lord is my portion, said my soul; therefore will I wait for Him.[149]

Tradition holds that Jeremias' life was sealed by martyrdom; in any case, it underwent constant purification by means of affliction, which enabled the prophet to advance very far along the path of union with God.

However enlightening the story of Jeremias or of the psalmists, there is another that is still more significant: that of Job. The Book of Job is undeniably one of the loftiest peaks of the Bible, but also one of the most mysterious. It must be admitted that of all the Old Testament characters, Job is the one whose sufferings are best known and most amply described. If we had to measure purification by the degree of suffering afflicting the soul, then Job would certainly be ahead of Jeremias. On the other hand, if sufferings are important primarily for the fruits produced in the soul,

[148] Ps. 101:1–12.   [149] Jer. 20:11; Lam. 3:22–24.

then the case of Job remains obscure. While the book is very explicit in its account of the hero's desolation and destruction, it is much less clear about the profit he derives from his sufferings. Not that the book does not obtain a very important spiritual result, but it is not the place to seek for the treasure which is the spiritual glory of other biblical books, particularly the psalms, that is, the positive fruits of God's purification of a soul, fruits which are called joy, peace, stability in God, friendship with Him and finally union. None of this appears in the Book of Job, which may seem astonishing.

Two observations may help us to understand why this is so. The Book of Job has a well defined purpose which is not so much to show us the progress of a soul along the path of purification, but rather to examine the subtle and appalling problem of the just man's suffering. This, in turn, prepared the way for a belief in a future life and eternal retribution. The author's particular purpose did not allow him the opportunity to dwell upon the spiritual benefits of the trials suffered by his hero, but we may be sure that he does not ignore this aspect. For the description of Job's sufferings and trials presupposes that the author speaks from experience, a singularly profound mystical experience. The greatest spiritual authors [150] have realized this and they instinctively have had recourse to the Book of Job when they seek to express in some degree the anguish they endure. Of all the inspired writings, therefore, it can and must be considered as the most valuable and significant contribution to the question of spiritual purification. Whatever this author did not see fit to explain is told in other biblical books. By singing of the

[150] Especially St. John of the Cross.

return of light after the darkness, they show what profit the soul derives from the mystical purifications, and so they usefully complete the Book of Job. But in describing the ultimate purifying trials, this book is unequaled, and descends much deeper than any other into this infernal region.

Moreover, when understood properly, Job contains far more than a negative and "nocturnal" experience of the purifications, as we shall see later. It would indeed be strange if an inspired book, showing such mastery of its subject and dealing at such length with purifications, did not teach men—in its own way, of course, but with extraordinary emphasis—to climb to the highest spiritual peaks.

Jeremias was purified in the course of his prophetic mission. God did not withdraw him either from his environment or from the vocation which, while overburdening him, also sustained him and spurred him on. The prophet was deserted by God, but his purification took place within the framework of his life. With Job things were quite different. It is true that the trial imposed by God came from without, but it did more than modify his way of life: trouble shattered it completely. Job lost everything ("The Lord gave, and the Lord hath taken away" [151]); he was deserted by all; he was exposed to his wife's sarcasm, his friends' criticisms and blame; even God rejected him. He was alone, absolutely and terribly alone. His illness, another trial permitted by God, which touched his flesh and irritated it to the very bone, inevitably heightened his awareness of himself and of his solitude. The burden of existence became intolerable to him. The pathos of Job's tragedy and the severity of his purification are inexpressible. No other book of the Old

[151] Job 1:21.

Testament creates such a stifling atmosphere or confines itself so completely to the interior realm. Once the characters
have taken their places, neither the background nor the
stage business, nor anything else can distract them from
their intense concentration on the wholly spiritual drama.
With faultless skill, the author has created an atmosphere in
which the hero rises to his full stature, facing alone the
problem of suffering, facing alone a mysterious and aveng-
ing God. The purifications described are in an unalloyed
state; therefore this book, perhaps better than any other,
conveys the sense of God's transcendence.

Like Jeremias, but even more clearly, Job knows that
God is responsible for his trials. Thus, there is no remedy,
since God Himself has become his persecutor. "For the arrows of the Lord are in me, the rage whereof drinketh up
my spirit." [152] In such a tempest of physical and spiritual
suffering, his life becomes unendurable.

The life of man upon earth is a warfare, and his days are
like the days of a hireling. As a servant longeth for the shade,
as the hireling looketh for the end of his work, so I also have
had empty months, and have numbered to myself wearisome
nights. As I lie down to sleep, I shall say: When shall I arise?
And again I shall look for the evening, and shall be filled
with sorrows even till darkness. My flesh is clothed with rot-
tenness and the filth of dust, my skin is withered and drawn
together. My days have passed more swiftly than the web is
cut by the weaver, and are consumed without any hope.[153]

The soul's paroxysm of suffering is so intense that it can
bear no more. All strength ebbs away. God has driven it to
such an extremity, to such abasement and prostration, that

[152] Job 6:4.   [153] Job 7:1–6.

it would infinitely prefer to die rather than live so oppressed by the divine hand. The soul is torn by intolerable physical pain and moral sufferings; then, as the climax, it is forsaken by God. Everything conspires to make this inexpressible state the ultimate trial. The very substance of the personality is crushed and begins to dissolve; the intensity of physical suffering is much worse because the soul also is tormented. God burns it alive by the direct contact of His fire. Thus, we can understand the cry of Job, whose pain is so extreme that he wishes to end his life.[154] Job has even more reasons than Jeremias to long for death and to curse the day of his birth.

Let the day perish wherein I was born, and the night in which it was said: A man child is conceived. Let that day be turned into darkness, let not God regard it from above, and let not the light shine upon it. . . . Why did I not die in the womb, why did I not perish when I came out of the belly? Why received upon the knees? Why suckled at the breasts? For now I should have been asleep and still, and should have rest in my sleep. . . . Why is light given to him that is in misery, and life to them that are in bitterness of soul? That look for death, and it cometh not, as they that dig for a treasure; and they rejoice exceedingly when they have found the grave. To a man whose way is hidden, and God hath surrounded him with darkness? [155]

Worse than his other sufferings is Job's dreadful impression that his life is devoid of all meaning and purpose and hope. Hope and faith provide for even the most unfortunate

[154] St. Paul admitted the same: "We were pressed out of measure above our strength, so that we were weary even of life" (II Cor. 1:8).

[155] Job 3:3–23.

of men a landmark in their distress, a light in their darkness. But when God extinguishes the soul's last light by withdrawing His presence, then the soul feels the terrible disgust with all things, the *taedium vitae,* which is completely different from neurotic anxiety or the pain of self-dissatisfaction. The soul feels uprooted from reality, deprived of all guidance, utterly alien, rejected by both heaven and earth. Henceforth life becomes a blind alley and contains only baleful nonsense.

"Can an unsavory thing be eaten, that is not seasoned with salt? Or can a man taste that which when tasted bringeth death? The things which before my soul would not touch, now, through anguish are my meats." [156] So grievous, so loathsome, is this state that the soul would far prefer to die once and for all instead of bearing this slow and helpless sinking as into quicksand.

Who will grant that my request may come; and that God may give me what I look for? And that He that hath begun may destroy me, that He may let loose His hand, and cut me off. . . . So that my soul rather chooseth hanging, and my bones death. I have done with hope, I shall now live no longer; spare me, for my days are nothing.[157]

For one whose life was based on God, is it not hell on earth [158] to be thus forsaken and disowned, and that per-

---

[156] Job 6:6-7.   [157] Job 6:8-9; 7:15-16.

[158] Apparently Job's greatest pain was the terror caused by the vision of God. Job yearns for friendship with God, and while his faith remains intact, his whole experience forces him to despair of attaining that friendship. His self-defense proves that he will not be resigned to this ultimate despair. He prefers to die rather than to surrender to a tyrant whose law is arbitrary, to a God who is not his friend.

manently, as it seems? Job would have agreed with St. Paul that "if in this life only we have hope in Christ, we are of all men most miserable," [159] for Job experienced the mystical suffering of being divested of all hope, truly an indescribable torture.

O that my sins, whereby I have deserved wrath, and the calamity that I suffer, were weighed in a balance. As the sand of the sea this would appear heavier; therefore my words are full of sorrow.[160]

Only those who have in some way, even on the human level, experienced a truly hopeless situation, a distress that nothing can relieve, can understand Job's cries of bitter despair. The inspired author, who even dares to address words of abuse to the Almighty, exceeds all tragedy, for we see here a declaration of human dignity, the portrait of a man rising above the destiny that crushes him. For God wills that at the very moment when His servant is about to succumb, the very essence of the man's nobility and greatness should issue forth from the winepress of suffering. Thus, creatures can continue to glorify their Creator, even though it be by vehement reproaches, in the depletion of their last reserves of strength. A heart that breaks displays to the full light of day the divine image and resemblance which it contains.

Job knows that he is about to die. But against the blind force that relentlessly crushes him, he opposes the indestructible strength of his spirit, which is sure of rising above all that overwhelms and destroys him. All complaint is useless and in no way relieves the suffering. No illusion is left to

[159] I Cor. 15:19.   [160] Job 6:2–3.

him. "If I speak, my pain will not rest; and if I hold my peace, it will not depart from me. But now my sorrow hath oppressed me, and all my limbs are brought to nothing." [161] And yet he continues to speak, not to justify himself, but to reproach the Almighty for treating him thus. "Wherefore I will not spare my mouth, I will speak in the affliction of my spirit; I will talk with the bitterness of my soul." [162] The Creator certainly knows, better than all others, the weakness and misery of His creatures. Why then does He show such incomprehensible severity and cruelty?

He hath gathered together His fury against me, and threatening me He hath gnashed with His teeth upon me; my enemy hath beheld me with terrible eyes. . . . I that was formerly so wealthy, am all on a sudden broken to pieces; He hath taken me by my neck, He hath broken me, and hath set me up to be His mark. He hath compassed me round about with His lances. My face is swollen with weeping, and my eyelids are dim. These things have I suffered without the iniquity of my hand, when I offered pure prayers to God.[163]

Does God seek to destroy him by this constant affliction?

In the night my bone is pierced with sorrows; and they that feed upon me, do not sleep. . . . I am compared to dirt, and am likened to embers and ashes. I cry to Thee, and Thou hearest not; I stand up, and Thou dost not regard me. Thou art changed to be cruel toward me, and in the hardness of Thy hand Thou are against me. Thou has lifted me up, and set me as it were upon the wind, and Thou has mightily dashed me. I know that Thou wilt deliver me to death, where a house is appointed for every one that liveth.[164]

[161] Job 16:7–8.   [162] Job 7:11.   [163] Job 16:10–18.
[164] Job 30:17–23.

Since all is lost, since nothing more is to be expected from this merciless God who seems to be playing with His quivering creature that He is leading to death, since the die has been cast, Job seizes a final opportunity and stands up to face his executioner with bitter but supremely noble irony.[165]

What is a man that Thou shouldst magnify him? Or why dost Thou set Thy heart upon him? Thou visitest him early in the morning, and Thou provest him suddenly. How long wilt Thou not spare me, nor suffer me to swallow down my spittle? I have sinned; what shall I do to Thee, O Keeper of men? Why hast Thou set me opposite to Thee, and I am become burdensome to myself? Why dost Thou not remove my sin, and why dost Thou not take away my iniquity? Behold now I shall sleep in the dust; and if Thou seek me in the morning, I shall not be.[166]

We should not be deceived by these last words, for Job knows that he is just. What he says to his wretched consolers, he says also to God Himself: "Teach me, and I will hold my peace; and if I have been ignorant in anything, instruct me." [167] But he has renounced begging for compassion from the one whom he no longer hopes to move. It is true that God has strength and right on His side. Who could be bold enough to try to teach Him a lesson?

Indeed I know it is so, and that man cannot be justified compared with God. If he will contend with Him, he cannot

---

[165] In the lines that follow, Job implies that God, from whom he had expected tokens of love and friendship, is plotting to destroy him. Only by recalling that Job had formerly enjoyed God's friendship, can we measure the intensity of his suffering and the depth of his despair (cf. Job 29:1–5).

[166] Job 7:17–21.   [167] Job 6:24.

answer Him one for a thousand. . . . If He examine on a
sudden, who shall answer Him? Or who can say: Why dost
Thou so? . . . If strength be demanded, He is most strong;
if equity of judgment, no man dare bear witness for me.[168]

But is that a reason why God should use this power according to His good pleasure, which Job contends really
verges on arbitrary treatment? "Although I should be simple, even this my soul shall be ignorant of, and I shall be
weary of my life. One thing there is that I have spoken, both
the innocent and the wicked He consumeth. If He scourge,
let Him kill at once, and not laugh at the pains of the innocent." [169] But to demand an accounting of God is a wasted
effort.

Behold I shall cry suffering violence, and no one will hear;
I shall cry aloud, and there is none to judge. He hath hedged
in my path round about, and I cannot pass, and in my way
He hath set darkness. He hath stripped me of my glory, and
hath taken the crown from my head. He hath destroyed me
on every side, and I am lost, and He hath taken away my
hope, as from a tree that is plucked up. His wrath is kindled
against me, and He hath counted me as His enemy. His troops
have come together, and have made themselves a way by me,
and have besieged my tabernacle round about.[170]

Thus, there is no appeal possible, since God Himself
openly violates the law and acts like a prejudiced and unjust
judge.

But if so also I am wicked, why have I labored in vain? If
I be washed as it were with snow waters, and my hands shall
shine ever so clean; yet Thou shalt plunge me in filth, and

[168] Job 9:2–19.   [169] Job 9:21–23.   [170] Job 19:7–12.

my garments shall abhor me, for I shall not answer a man that is like myself, nor one that may be heard with me equally in judgment. . . . My soul is weary of my life, I will let go my speech against myself, I will speak in the bitterness of my soul. I will say to God: Do not condemn me; tell me why Thou judgest me so. Doth it seem good to Thee that Thou shouldst calumniate me and oppress me, the work of Thy own hands, and help the counsel of the wicked? Hast Thou eyes of flesh or shalt Thou see as man seeth? Are Thy days as the days of man, and are Thy years as the times of men? That Thou shouldst inquire after my iniquity and search after my sin? And shouldst know that I have done no wicked thing, whereas there is no man that can deliver out of Thy hand.[171]

Like dead leaves in the autumn gusts, so do Job's thoughts whirl in his mind. But in spite of himself he turns to this God who rejects him. He believes in God's justice even while accusing Him of injustice. He continues to expect everything of God, even though he knows that God has forsaken him. Though he is battered and crushed by this inflexible Judge, yet he appeals to His mercy. Who indeed could understand Job's feelings, the confusion of contrary sentiments that perturbed and agitated his heart? Before his scandalized contradictors he reproached God for His cruelty. "Why do I tear my flesh with my teeth and carry my soul in my hands? Although He should kill me, I will trust in Him; but yet I will reprove my ways in His sight." [172] And shortly afterward, when he has lost all hope of surviving the affliction, he appeals to God with absolute trust: "O earth, cover not thou my blood, neither let my cry find a hiding

[171] Job 9:28–31; 10:1–7.   [172] Job 13:14–15.

place in thee. For behold my witness is in heaven, and He that knoweth my conscience is on high. . . . My eye poureth out tears to God." [173]

Who could bear for long such a grievous, inhuman affliction? Indeed, Job's strength fails him; his days are running out; he knows that death is approaching. "Only the grave remaineth for me." [174] He even hopes that death may come quickly, before his mind is deranged. For this God on whom he calls in vain, this cruel and heedless God, surely cannot be the God in whom he used to believe. This seems to be the conclusion of all that is happening.

If this were merely the desperate struggle of a man against forces that outnumber and overwhelm him, Job would long before have been defeated. But here he is fighting both *for* God and *against* God. The one who strives against him until he is led to the very gates of death is also the one who upholds him. Over and over again Job should have expired. But God takes care to rekindle the flame before it vanishes. Just when it seemed to be extinguished, it flares up once more from the ashes. What brings Job back to life is the very thing which a moment before was leading him to his end.

Other souls have also known the mystery of this startling return of faith and trust, this impulse of trembling and indefectible love, just when the soul had been plunged into the abyss and felt helplessly lost. But never as impressively as in the Book of Job do we find a soul held on the brim of the precipice by a single tiny thread of tenuous trust.

Who will grant me that I might know and find Him, and come even to His throne? I would set judgment before Him,

[173] Job 16:19–21. [174] Job 17:1.

and would fill my mouth with complaints. That I might know the words that He would answer me, and understand what He would say to me. I would not that He should contend with me with much strength, nor overwhelm me with the weight of His greatness. Let Him propose equity against me, and let my judgment come to victory.[175]

How close to Job's heart is this hidden God! How touching it is that the victim continues to hope in his executioner! "But He knoweth my way, and has tried me as gold that passeth through the fire." [176]

However, in order that hope may survive such torment, and in order that the work of purification may truly take place, one thing is indispensable for the soul: fidelity. The soul that has persevered in the straight path even in the midst of the darkest shadows and desolation finds comfort, enjoys peace, waxes strong in the hope of emerging unscathed from the wildest tempests.[177] So it is with Job. "My foot hath followed His steps, I have kept His way, and have not declined from it. I have not departed from the commandments of His lips, and the words of His mouth I have hid in my bosom." [178] This fidelity is not only the soul's safeguard; it is also its consolation in distress. "And this may be my comfort, that afflicting me with sorrow, He spare not, nor I contradict the words of the Holy One." [179]

To the very end, Job experienced this strange state of soul: he was torn between trust in God and the conviction

[175] Job 23:3–7.   [176] Job 23:10.

[177] "We glory also in tribulations, knowing that tribulation worketh patience; and patience trial; and trial hope; and hope confoundeth not" (Rom. 5:3–5).

[178] Job 23:11–12.   [179] Job 6:10.

of being rejected by Him. To the very end, nothing seems to attenuate the almost desperate suffering he experiences. The most he attains by way of consolation is the occasional memory of former days that were bathed in the light of peace and joy, radiant with that divine presence whose friendship was a sheer delight, fragrant with the tenderness of God's caress.

Who will grant me, that I might be according to the months past, according to the days in which God kept me? When His lamp shined over my head, and I walked by His light in darkness? As I was in the days of my youth, when God was secretly in my tabernacle? When the Almighty was with me, and my servants round about me? [180]

But is this really a consolation? No, for the memory of a lost paradise is the worst of all sufferings. Thus it is that nothing in the way of affliction has been spared Job. Until the end, until God appears and imposes silence upon him— a silence thrilling with humble fear and adoration—Job remains torn between his trust that refuses to die and the despair of seeing that God rejects him. Until the end also, his cries alternate between two extremes: the accents of one who persists in seeing God as a Creator and a Father, and the rebellious protests of a wounded soul in the pangs of unbearable pain.

Thy hands have made me, and fashioned me wholly round about, and dost Thou thus cast me down headlong on a sudden? Remember, I beseech Thee, that Thou hast made me as the clay, and Thou wilt bring me into dust again. Hast

[180] Job 29:2–5.

Thou not milked me as milk, and curdled me like cheese? Thou hast clothed me with skin and flesh; Thou hast put me together with bones and sinews; Thou hast granted me life and mercy, and Thy visitation hath preserved my spirit.[181]

Although Thou conceal these things in Thy heart, yet I know that Thou rememberest all things. If I have sinned and Thou hast spared me for an hour, why dost Thou not suffer me to be clean from my iniquity? And if I be wicked, woe unto me; and if just, I shall not lift up my head.[182]

This alternating light and darkness—the most subtle of tortures—was unhesitatingly decreed by the Almighty to afflict the soul of one who never ceased proclaiming his justice and innocence before the face of heaven. "Although He should kill me, I will trust in Him; but yet I will reprove my ways in His sight." [183]

As we have said, the purpose of the Book of Job is to show the just man who suffers, and thus to arouse in Israel a hope and then a demand for retribution in the after-life. But it is also noteworthy that no other Old Testament book presents such apt descriptions of the sufferings endured by souls in contact with the divinity. While the book does not treat primarily of the spiritual fruits to be derived from such an encounter with God, we may be sure that this great purification could not have failed to produce a harvest. There is at least a succinct description of its results, the first fruits of a harvest that ripens fully in other biblical books, particularly the psalms. Several details indicate that suffering purified Job's soul. In the first place, he gives proof of submission even in speeches which voice his rebellion. "As God liveth, who hath taken away my judgment, and the Almighty,

[181] Job 10:8–12.   [182] Job 10:13–15.   [183] Job 13:15.

who hath brought my soul to bitterness, as long as breath remaineth in me, and the spirit of God in my nostrils, my lips shall not speak iniquity, neither shall my tongue contrive lying." [184] His marvellous fidelity is also evident; such unfaltering fidelity that even in the time of black despair, he never transgressed the divine law. Other authentic fruits of the purification wrought by suffering were humility, compunction, absolute submission to the divine will, even when it was utterly incomprehensible and apparently unjust. It is true that we could well expect much more of a soul so carefully sculptured by God's chisel, but we must never forget the particular and limited purpose in the writing of the Book of Job. Nor should we hope for an exact prototype of the supremely just man, as we seek in Job for sentiments that directly prefigure those of Christ. And yet we are not mistaken in striving to hear overtones in this stirring poem that defines, with profound truth, the sufferings of a truly great soul that meets God as it undergoes the great mystical purifications.

The impression that gradually emerges from the Book of Job is that there exists, beyond all human horizons and schemes, a divine plan that determines all the events in which creatures are involved. Without this plan, life has no meaning. For there truly exists a divine mystery that infinitely transcends the mysteries of the material world and confers a new dimension on the realities in which we are immersed. That is the mystery of divine wisdom, the mystery of God Himself. This mystery it is that the Almighty, at the end of the Book, urges Job to consider and to adore in all humility. "Gird up thy loins like a man; I will ask thee, and

[184] Job 27:2–4.

do thou tell Me. Wilt thou make void My judgment; and condemn Me, that thou mayest be justified?" [185] Once Job "saw," that is, understood something of this plan, he bowed down in respectful fear of the Lord. "I know that Thou canst do all things, and no thought is hid from Thee. . . . I have spoken unwisely. . . . With the hearing of the ear, I have heard Thee, but now my eye seeth Thee." [186]

"My eye seeth Thee." It may be that for Job, as well as for Elias, Jeremias, the prophets, and all who lovingly and faithfully reached God through suffering, as they experienced the pain of the winepress and the night of mystical purifications, the shadow of the Almighty was already assuming the shape of a cross.

[185] Job 40:2–3.   [186] Job 42:2–5.

Chapter 4

✤ GROWTH IN SANCTITY

When the Bible describes the painful purifications of God's friends, it also allows a glimpse of the security and the joys that they receive along the way. In their darkness there gleams a light; in the midst of their trials, they harbor peace. Only God, who knows the secrets of all hearts, can grasp the living reality of the union which none suspect and the soul itself ignores. It is a union of light and darkness, of trouble and peace, of fear and confidence, of hopelessness and trust. Everyday difficulties often call for bloodshed, tears and heroic efforts. But who suspects this at the time? And the way God visits men in the midst of affliction is likewise hidden from all eyes. Just as the Bible afforded glimpses of the sufferings of souls that lie in the crucible of purification, so also it casts its light upon the joys and certainties that they experience at times. After alarming us by the

303

description of the trials required in order to attain the goal, it dazzles us by a glimpse of the treasure to be found there.

Christ recalled this double aspect of the process of purification and He emphasized its positive value and its fecundity.

Amen, amen, I say to you, unless the grain of wheat falling into the ground die, itself remaineth alone. But if it die, it bringeth forth much fruit. . . . Every branch in Me that beareth not fruit, He will take away; and every one that beareth fruit, He will purge it, that it may bring forth more fruit.[1]

Old Testament men had already experienced this fruitfulness; they describe it to us and tell of the great satisfaction the soul receives from it. The Bible shows what peace and joy pervade the souls that have been tested and proved true. Through their suffering and trials they become implanted in God, admitted to His friendship, totally His. Thus they advance toward union with Him and they produce the fruits of a sanctity which unites their will to God's will and conforms them to the divine plan.

The Bible allows us a glimpse of the fruits gathered by faithful souls along the path of purification, while the account of progress accomplished displays signs that herald the coming of union with God. Like the ears of grain that already contain the future harvest and remain in the summer sun to complete their ripening, so the souls that have received the pledge of union with God and already taste the first fruits of this union, continue to dwell in the sun of purifications. But the time is close when these souls that already are "white to harvest" [2] will gather in the rewards of the sanctity

---

[1] John 12:24; 15:2.   [2] John 4:35.

acquired by their tears. After their exile they will be welcomed in their homeland and united to God forever. "They that sow in tears shall reap in joy. Going they went and wept, casting their seeds. But coming they shall come with joyfulness, carrying their sheaves." [3]

THE FIRST FRUITS

The soul that is reborn to grace after suffering in expiation, or that once more sees that light on emerging from the pain of long transforming purifications, experiences abundant joy, often expressed by the inspired authors. With great delight the soul exults in its cure or its rescue and its return to life.

Sing to the Lord, O ye His saints, and give praise to the memory of His holiness. For wrath is in His indignation, and life in His good will. In the evening weeping shall have place, and in the morning gladness. And in my abundance I said: I shall never be moved. O Lord, in Thy favor, Thou gavest strength to my beauty. Thou turnedst away Thy face from me, and I became troubled. To Thee, O Lord, will I cry, and I will make supplication to my God. . . . Thou hast turned for me my mourning into joy; Thou hast cut my sackcloth and hast compassed me with gladness, to the end that my glory may sing to Thee, and I may not regret. O Lord my God, I will give praise to Thee forever. [4]

I will give glory to Thee, O Lord, O King, and I will praise Thee, O God my Savior. . . . For Thou hast been a helper and protector to me, and hast preserved my body from destruction. . . . Thou hast been my helper. And Thou hast delivered me, . . . out of the hands of them that sought my life,

[3] Ps. 125:5–7.   [4] Ps. 29:5–16.

from the oppression of the flame which surrounded me; and in the midst of the fire I was not burnt, from the depth of the belly of hell. . . . My life was drawing near to hell beneath. They compassed me on every side, and there was no one that would help me. I looked for the succour of men, and there was none. I remembered Thy mercy, O Lord, . . . how Thou deliverest them that wait for Thee, O Lord. . . . I called upon the Lord, the Father of my Lord, that He would not leave me in the day of my trouble, and in the time of the proud without help. . . . And my prayer was heard. And Thou hast saved me from destruction, and hast delivered me from the evil time. Therefore I will give thanks, and praise Thee, and bless the name of the Lord.[5]

I will extol Thee, O Lord, for Thou hast upheld me, and hast not made my enemies to rejoice over me. O Lord my God, I have cried to Thee, and Thou hast healed me. Thou hast brought forth, O Lord, my soul from hell; Thou hast saved me from them that go down into the pit.[6]

Is it then necessary to be rescued from sin or to undergo purifying suffering in order to experience joy? Indeed not, for it should ever dwell in our souls. "Rejoice in the Lord always," [7] as St. Paul said. But it is a fact that the joy of the pardoned sinner and the purified soul seems nobler and more keenly felt. Is it not because the soul then experiences God's wholly gratuitous love with a foreglimpse of the mystery of His mercy? Thus the prophet Baruch cried out:

Be of good comfort, my children . . . for as it was your mind to go astray from God, so when you return again you shall seek Him ten times as much. For He that hath brought evils

---

[5] Ecclus. 51:1–17.   [6] Ps. 29:1–4.   [7] Phil. 4:4.

upon you, shall bring you everlasting joy again with your salvation.[8]

The reason why this joy is so pure and so delightfully refreshing is that it flows from the springs of divine mercy. Scripture's constant refrain is mercy, and all who have experienced it continue to invoke it.

Turn to me, O Lord, and deliver my soul. O save me for Thy mercy's sake. . . . According to Thy mercy remember Thou me; for Thy goodness' sake, O Lord. . . . Hear me, O Lord, for Thy mercy is kind; look upon me according to the multitude of Thy tender mercies.[9]

Psalms 105, 106 and 107 extol God's mercy, while Psalm 135 tirelessly repeats with every line, "for His mercy endureth forever." The sages and the prophets likewise praise divine mercy. "Therefore the Lord waiteth that He may have mercy on you; and therefore shall He be exalted sparing you." [10]

All God's visits are effects of His mercy, and nothing brings greater joy to the soul than to receive this mark of love that is reserved to God alone. Mercy is compounded of compassion, gentleness, a vast and tender kindness and charity. By mercy the sinner feels the boon of love that pardons; he feels that even in his wretchedness he is loved. As soon as he consents to turn to God and appeal to His mercy, his soul is filled with joy; a vast, calm joy, immense and complete, peaceful and pacifying. "Thus saith the Lord thy Redeemer: . . . Thy peace had been as a river." [11] The

[8] Bar. 4:27–29.   [9] Ps. 6:5; 24:7; 78:17.   [10] Isa. 30:18.
[11] Isa. 48:17–18.

soul is humble and quiet, as it entrusts itself utterly to the God of mercy. "Lord, my heart is not exalted. . . . As a child that is weaned is toward his mother, so reward in my soul." [12] Joy brings peace; peace brings joy. In spite of all the suffering and tribulation, God's mercy has prevailed and the soul is safe. "Thou wilt keep peace; peace, because we have hoped in Thee." [13]

Shall not my soul be subject to God? For from Him is my salvation. For He is my God and my Savior; He is my protector, I shall be moved no more. . . . In God is my salvation and my glory; He is the God of my help, and my hope is in God.[14]

The soul feels like a ship on the open sea, sailing on the tranquil waters of peace, carried by the currents of mercy.

When I called upon Him, the God of my justice heard me, when I was in distress, Thou hast enlarged me.[15]

Give praise to the Lord, for He is good; for His mercy endureth forever. Let Israel now say that He is good; that His mercy endureth forever. . . . In my trouble I called upon the Lord, and the Lord heard me, and enlarged me. . . . The Lord is my strength and my praise, and He is become my salvation. . . . I shall not die, but live; and shall declare the works of the Lord. The Lord chastising hath chastised me; but He hath not delivered me over to death.[16]

The soul tastes peace; not the peace which the world gives, but the peace of God, which springs from suffering itself. All who have known it in the midst of their trials can cry out with King Ezechias:

[12] Ps. 130:1–2.　　[13] Isa. 26:3.　　[14] Ps. 61:1–2, 8.
[15] Ps. 4:1.　　[16] Ps. 117:1–2, 5, 14, 17–18.

O Lord, if man's life be such, and the life of my spirit be in such things as these, Thou shalt correct me and make me to live. Behold in peace is my bitterness most bitter; but Thou hast delivered my soul that it should not perish.[17]

Not only does the soul find joy and peace in the midst of suffering, but it emerges from it greatly strengthened. A tree can resist squalls and tempests only by thrusting its roots deep down into the soil. Similarly, the soul that encounters purifying trials becomes more deeply rooted in God. Its dependence upon God not only assures it of salvation but also permits progress in knowledge and love of Him. It is true that during the time of affliction the soul could not see these fruits, much less pluck them. Its whole striving was just to weather the storm. "For my heart hath been inflamed, and my reins have been changed; and I am brought to nothing, and I knew not." [18] But at length fidelity is recompensed; the soul belongs entirely to Yahweh and henceforth feels firmly rooted in Him. "I am always with Thee. Thou hast held me by my right hand; and by Thy will Thou hast conducted me, and with Thy glory Thou hast received me." [19] Being rooted in God means also belonging to Him. What tender love the psalmist shows as he expresses his absolute preference for God:

For what have I in heaven? And besides Thee what do I desire upon earth? For Thee my flesh and my heart hath fainted away; Thou art the God of my heart, and the God that is my portion forever. . . . It is good for me to adhere to my God, to put my hope in the Lord God.[20]

[17] Isa. 38:16–17.   [18] Ps. 72:21.   [19] Ps. 72:23–24.
[20] Ps. 72:25–28.

The soul is committed to God in life and in death. The soul had already chosen God, but affliction brought it completely into His hands.[21] "For God only and always" is the refrain of Psalm 15, which is the psalm of religious vocation, of God's call and the soul's response. The commitments of youth acquire their full meaning only when the fragrant spring breezes have made way for the hot blasts of summer and the harsh storms of autumn, that is to say, when the soul has undergone a long process of divine purification.

Preserve me, O Lord, for I have put my trust in Thee. I have said to the Lord: Thou art my God, for Thou hast no need of my goods. . . . The Lord is the portion of my inheritance and of my cup; it is Thou that wilt restore my inheritance to me. The lines are fallen unto me in goodly places, for my inheritance is goodly to me. I will bless the Lord, who hath given me understanding; moreover my reins also have corrected me even till night.[22]

As the bride of the Canticle declared: "I sat down under his shadow, whom I desired," [23] so also the soul's wish is to dwell in the shadow of her chosen Love. Rooted in God and belonging to God, the soul then produces the good fruit of a firm hope of living with God. St. John of the Cross was to declare that sweet fruits ripen in a fertile, cold land. The soul needed the harsh climate of purification in order to reach maturity. Henceforth it has passed beyond the stage of merely sighing: "How lovely are Thy tabernacles, O Lord of hosts! My soul longeth and fainteth for the courts of the

[21] Thus, St. Paul wished to teach the first Christians to belong entirely to God. "For all things are yours. . . . And you are Christ's; and Christ is God's" (I Cor. 3:22–23).

[22] Ps. 15:1, 5–7.   [23] Cant. 2:3.

Lord." [24] It has passed beyond the stage of exclaiming, with a note of envy: "Blessed are they that dwell in Thy house, O Lord, . . . blessed is the man whose help is from Thee." [25] The soul has already undertaken the climb, the arduous ascent that cost such effort. It has received God's visitation, even in the midst of its struggles down in the valley of tears.

Blessed is the man whose help is from Thee; in his heart he hath disposed to ascend by steps, in the vale of tears, in the place which he hath set. For the lawgiver shall give a blessing, they shall go from virtue to virtue; the God of gods shall be seen in Sion.[26]

The soul's strength increases as the goal looms nearer. "I rejoiced at the things that were said to me: We shall go into the house of the Lord. Our feet were standing in thy courts, O Jerusalem." [27] What a thrill of happiness it is to reach the threshold of God's house.

For better is one day in Thy courts above thousands. I have chosen to be an abject in the house of my God, rather than to dwell in the tabernacles of sinners. . . . He will not deprive of good things them that walk in innocence; O Lord of hosts, blessed is the man that trusteth in Thee.[28]

But how infinitely greater is the joy of crossing the threshold and entering the state of divine friendship! The soul's yearning has been satisfied; it is admitted to God's home and dwells with Him. "I have loved, O Lord, the beauty of Thy house, and the place where Thy glory dwelleth." [29] That dwelling becomes familiar to the soul, which feels perfectly

[24] Ps. 83:1.   [25] Ps. 83:5–6.   [26] Ps. 83:6–8.
[27] Ps. 121:1–2.   [28] Ps. 83:11–13.   [29] Ps. 25:8.

at ease there. "For Thy mercy is before my eyes; and I am well pleased with Thy truth." [30] Now it can say from personal experience: "Come and hear, all ye that fear God, and I will tell you what great things He hath done for my soul." [31] Since the whole self has been purified, the whole self now receives life and satisfaction from God. The inspired authors, whose painful voyage of purification finally brings them to the shores of divine happiness, describe it by an accumulation of words like exultation, rest,[32] trust, joy, delight. So great is this happiness that it cannot be kept hidden in the heart; a fraternal voice speaks out, inviting those who are still in suffering and affliction to be hopeful and confident. If only they knew how they would soon be recompensed for their trouble, they would no longer fear the trials.

I will bless the Lord at all times, His praise shall be always in my mouth. In the Lord shall my soul be praised; let the meek hear and rejoice. O magnify the Lord with me; and let us extol His name together. I sought the Lord, and He heard me; and He delivered me from all my troubles. Come ye to Him and be enlightened; and your faces shall not be confounded. This poor man cried, and the Lord heard him; and saved him out of all his troubles. The angel of the Lord shall encamp round about them that fear Him; and shall deliver them. O taste, and see that the Lord is sweet. Blessed is the man that hopeth in Him. Fear the Lord, all ye His saints, for there is no want to them that fear Him. . . . The Lord is nigh unto them that are of a contrite heart; and He will save the humble of spirit. Many are the afflictions of the just; but out of them all will the Lord deliver them. The Lord keepeth all their bones, not one of them shall be broken.[33]

[30] Ps. 25:3.   [31] Ps. 65:16.   [32] Cf. Heb. 4:1–13.
[33] Ps. 33:2–10, 19–21.

The psalmist gives us another testimony of this intimacy with God. It is a psalm that is unique for its fresh loveliness, like the song of the bride gladly resting in the arms of the lover whom she trusts and cherishes. The notes of tender affection still retain the memory of the grievous pangs which God permitted for the sake of purification, but the soul has emerged from all fear and has learned the lesson of perfect surrender and unfailing trust.[34] Henceforth the soul lives in friendship with God and follows the divine guide wherever He may lead.

The Lord ruleth me; and I shall want nothing. He hath set me in a place of pasture. He hath brought me up, on the water of refreshment; He hath converted my soul. He hath led me on the paths of justice, for His own name's sake. For though I should walk in the midst of the shadow of death, I will fear no evils, for Thou art with me. Thy rod and Thy staff, they have comforted me. Thou hast prepared a table before me, against them that afflict me. Thou hast anointed my head with oil; and my chalice which inebriateth me, how goodly is it. And Thy mercy will follow me all the days of my life. And that I may dwell in the house of the Lord unto length of days.[35]

UNION WITH GOD

We need hardly stress that perfect union with God far transcends even the most intimate friendship with Him. For the soul to be united to Him is far more than to be His close friend. By union the soul is not only loved by God and promised to the divine Bridegroom; it is finally wedded to

[34] Thus does St. John define perfect love (cf. I John 4:17–19).
[35] Ps. 22.

Him. While such a union must await the completion of purification, the seeds of it are already present in the first purifying trials, which even in the early stages prepare the soul for God's coming. The Old Testament confirms this fact. So eager is God for union with His creatures that after awakening love in their hearts, He enables them to "pass by the mighty and cross the frontiers," [36] and to stop only when they rest in Him. But how were men to learn that such a union requires the most drastic purifications? The Bible teaches this by showing that even on the human level the deepest and most richly blessed unions must be purchased at the cost of hard trials and long preparation.

Such was the case with Jacob, who had to work for seven years, and then for another seven years before obtaining Rachel's hand in marriage. Young Tobias attained union with his love only after long delay and purifying trials. Many a time Old Testament women had to suffer and to weep before receiving the blessing of children, the fruit of union.

Of course, these images bear only a remote resemblance to the soul's union with God and to the sacrifices that must be accepted to achieve such union. But the Old Testament frequently uses such images as a way of leading the mind gradually toward the understanding of spiritual realities. Thus, the Canticle of Canticles, under a veil of human feelings and loves, teaches us to discover the supreme mysteries of divine love. The Bible's teaching goes yet farther, for the mystery of the covenant demonstrates the necessity of purifications. No Jew could ignore it. All who had striven to ratify or to deepen the covenant, God's union with Israel, His bride, had been profoundly purified by trials. This is

[36] St. John of the Cross, *Spiritual Canticle, op. cit.,* II, p. 26.

true of Noe first, then of Abraham. So linked is Abraham's story to that of the covenant, so bound up is his destiny with that of Israel, that the purifications that made up the fabric of the great patriarch's life had double effects as they united both him and his people to God.

To confirm and to renew the covenant likewise demanded purifications, as we see in the history of Jacob and of Joseph. Moses' heavy burden of affliction can be understood if we remember that he was destined to carry out the promises of the covenant. In him, too, suffering and purifications accomplish both his own intimate union with God and Israel's covenant with Yahweh. It is enough to hear his exhortations to the people to understand how inseparable he considered these two aspects: "But the word is very nigh unto thee, in thy mouth and in thy heart, that thou mayest do it. . . . Choose therefore life, that both thou and thy seed may live. And that thou mayest love the Lord thy God, and obey His voice, and adhere to Him (for He is thy life)." [37] Moses could never have spoken so effectively nor worked so hard to establish the covenant in Israel, had he not been so intimately united to God; had he not suffered to attain both unions. This suffering made him one of the men who attained the highest understanding and experience of divine reality.[38]

Thus, we see that union always requires preliminary purification and trial, whether it be marriage and fecundity on the natural level, or the union of Yahweh with His people by the covenant. We can, therefore, expect that the supreme and most intimate of all unions, that of God and the soul, should also involve great suffering, the means of profound

[37] Deut. 30:14–20.   [38] Cf. Exod. 33:18; 34:9.

purification. The lessons that were to be fully developed in the New Testament were already contained in the Old Testament, but in embryonic form. For the significance of the actions of Old Testament men and of the events in which they were involved is not limited to their own day; their mission continues throughout all the centuries.[39]

St. Paul strikingly declared, in speaking of Sara and Agar: "For these are the two Testaments." [40] Thus, he not only authorizes us but invites us to seek out prophetic and spiritual meanings in the biblical stories. God seems to have planned to nourish our spiritual life by means of these inspired texts, and the Church has always permitted us to use them in this way.

In considering the Bridegroom's love for His bride, we encountered the great poem of mystical love, the Canticle of Canticles. This is not the only text of the Old Testament which extols the union of the soul with God. The Book of Ruth contains lessons of the same kind. In its allegorical and spiritual overtones this short but admirable tale sings of the purifying trials that precede union, of the long journeying to that goal. Its theme is well worth recalling.

Noemi was forced to leave Judea because of the hardship of famine there. She settled in Moab, where she was soon left a widow and had to bring up her two sons. But the sons both died, a few years after their marriage to Moabite women. Noemi then thinks of returning to her native land

[39] "Of which salvation the prophets have inquired and diligently searched, who prophesied of the grace to come in you. Searching what or what manner of time the Spirit of Christ in them did signify; when it foretold those sufferings that are in Christ, and the glories that should follow" (I Pet. 1:10–11).

[40] Gal. 4:24.

and advises her two daughters-in-law, who are still young, to return to their families, where they would probably find greater opportunity to start life over again after their premature misfortunes. Noemi will return alone to Judea. "Return, my daughters; why come ye with me?" [41]

One of the daughters-in-law is convinced by this reasoning, but the other, Ruth, voluntarily renouncing all worldly hopes, decides to cling to Noemi and to follow her.

> Be not against me, to desire that I should leave thee and depart; for whithersoever thou shalt go, I will go; and where thou shalt dwell, I also will dwell. Thy people shall be my people, and thy God my God. The land that shall receive thee dying, in the same will I die; and there will I be buried.[42]

And so they returned together to Noemi's native town of Bethlehem.[43] "They returned into Bethlehem, in the beginning of the barley harvest." [44]

As the two women were destitute, Ruth went to glean in the field of Booz, a rich relative of Noemi. When Booz noticed this modest and reserved young stranger, he inquired about her and treated her well.

> And Booz said to Ruth: Hear me, daughter, do not go to glean in any other field, and do not depart from this place, but keep with my maids. . . . And if thou art thirsty, go to the vessels, and drink of the waters whereof the servants drink. . . . All hath been told me, that thou hast done to thy mother-in-law after the death of thy husband; and how thou hast left thy parents, and the land wherein thou wast born, and art come to a people which thou knewest not here-

[41] Ruth 1:11.   [42] Ruth 1:16–17.   [43] Ruth 1:19.
[44] Ruth 1:22.

tofore. The Lord render unto thee for thy work, and mayest thou receive a full reward of the Lord the God of Israel, to whom thou art come, and under whose wings thou art fled. And she said: I have found grace in thy eyes, my lord, who hast comforted me and hast spoken to the heart of thy handmaid, who am not like to one of thy maids.[45]

Ruth, therefore, stayed and gleaned in Booz' field until the end of the barley harvest and the wheat harvest. When Noemi heard of Booz' compassionate kindness to Ruth and of his interest in the young woman, she began to entertain great hopes, because as a kinsman he had a claim upon her. "Noemi said to her: My daughter, I will seek rest for thee, and will provide that it may be well with thee." [46] And Noemi instructed her daughter-in-law how to act in the whole affair. One night a short time later, Booz went to the threshing floor to winnow barley and then lay down to sleep by the heap of sheaves. Ruth also followed and did all that Noemi had ordered.

She came softly, and uncovering his feet, laid herself down. And behold, when it was now midnight the man was afraid, and troubled; and he saw a woman lying at his feet. And he said to her: Who art thou? And she answered: I am Ruth thy handmaid; spread thy coverlet over thy servant, for thou art a near kinsman. And he said: Blessed art thou of the Lord, my daughter, and thy latter kindness has surpassed the former; because thou hast not followed young men either poor or rich. Fear not therefore, but whatsoever thou shalt say to me I will do to thee. For all the people that dwell within the gates of my city, know that thou art a virtuous woman. Neither do I deny myself to be near of kin, but there

[45] Ruth 2:8–13.   [46] Ruth 3:1.

is another nearer than I. Rest thou this night; and when morning is come, if he will take thee by the right of kindred, all is well; but if he will not, I will undoubtedly take thee, as the Lord liveth; sleep till the morning.[47]

The next day in the presence of the people and the ancients of the city, Booz assured his claim to the young woman and declared:

You are witnesses this day, that I have bought all that was Elimelech's . . . of the hand of Noemi; and have taken to wife Ruth the Moabitess. . . . Then all the people that were in the gate, and the ancients answered: We are witnesses. . . . Booz therefore took Ruth, and married her.[48]

The charm and limpid beauty of the biblical tale shows the goal toward which a purified soul tends, as well as the path to be followed in seeking it. The union of Ruth and Booz is truly appreciated if we realize how long and painful were the trials preceding it. Ruth's life was difficult and harsh. Suffering, exile, solitude, generous and unselfish service kept emptying her soul. Truly, for her, life was a stern lesson of purification, as we have shown to be the usual process. And always she, who did not even consider herself equal to one of the master's maidservants, in her heart was faithful, gentle and humble. In the midst of affliction she was true to God, preferred Him above all else, and found union with Him in the events of her life. But even this long and painful purification were in nowise proportionate to the marvellous recompense that was to be awarded: marriage with Booz, a rich, just, good man. Exercising toward the poor servant his kinsman's right to claim her, he stood as an

[47] Ruth 3:7–13.   [48] Ruth 4:9–11, 13.

image of the Savior, whose mercy was infinite and wholly gratuitous. "For thus saith the Lord: You were sold gratis, and you shall be redeemed without money." [49]

While the soul may desire friendship with God, it could neither hope for nor even glimpse what God, in His infinite generosity, planned to offer: a union of love with Him. St. John of the Cross has used this biblical story in a beautiful prayer: "Ah, how sweet will Thy presence be to me, Thou that art the highest good. I will approach Thee with silence and will uncover my feet before Thee that Thou mayest be pleased to unite me unto Thee in marriage and I will not take mine ease until I have fruition of Thyself in Thine arms." [50]

ACCEPTANCE OF GOD'S PLAN

We have seen that union with God is the fruit of a process of purification. This union is destined to be fertile, as Christ asserted: "Every branch in Me, that beareth not fruit, He will take away; and every one that beareth fruit, He will purge it, that it may bring forth more fruit." [51] What does this mean, except that even when the union is achieved, purification continues to play a role and produce effects. For the union with God should bear fruit in good works,[52] and these good works encounter many obstacles. Moreover, the life of charity must be constantly perfected, and this is done by further purification. Thus, little by little the soul approaches holiness, as it is purified in reaching and in maintaining union with God, and purified also by the practice of

[49] Isa. 52:3.
[50] St. John of the Cross, *op. cit.*, III, p. 254.   [51] John 15:2.
[52] "Faith . . . worketh by charity" (Gal. 5:6).

the charity that has been infused into it. The Bible shows this holiness achieved in a few souls pure of heart. Perhaps the finest example is Tobias, who was so docile to God's Spirit and so eagerly open to the influence of grace, that he deserves to be called something more than just; only the word *holy* truly suits him. The deep piety and heroic charity which made up Tobias' authentic holiness was not, however, acquired without many trials. In his person and in his life he verifies the truth often repeated in Scripture:

For gold and silver are tried in the fire, but acceptable men in the furnace of humiliation.[53]

The souls of the just are in the hand of God. . . . Afflicted in few things, in many they shall be well rewarded, because God hath tried them and found them worthy of Himself. As gold in the furnace He hath proved them, and as a victim of a holocaust He hath received them.[54]

As silver is tried by fire, and gold in the furnace, so the Lord trieth the hearts.[55]

Trials and purifications have made Tobias a saint whom the Bible sets up as an example. First the inspired author portrays Tobias' eminent virtues:

Even in his captivity, [he] forsook not the way of truth. But every day gave all he could get to his brethren, his fellow captives. . . . When all went to the golden calves . . . he alone fled the company of all, and went to Jerusalem to the Temple of the Lord, and there adored the Lord God of Israel, offering faithfully his firstfruits and his tithes. . . . He took to wife Anna of his own tribe, and had a son by her, whom he called after his own name. And from his infancy he taught him to fear God and to abstain from all sin. And when by the

[53] Ecclus. 2:5.   [54] Wisd. 3:1, 5–6.   [55] Prov. 17:3.

captivity he with his wife and his son and all his tribe was come to the city of Ninive (when all ate of the meats of the Gentiles), he kept his soul and never was defiled with their meats. . . . He . . . went to all that were in captivity, and gave them wholesome admonitions. . . . And when king Sennacherib . . . fleeing from Judea by reason of the slaughter that God had made about him . . . being angry slew many of the children of Israel, Tobias buried their bodies.[56]

Later these virtues were ratified in time of trial. "When it was told the king, he commanded him to be slain, and took away all his substance. But Tobias fleeing naked away with his son and with his wife, lay concealed, for many loved him." [57] A short time afterward, Tobias, whose goods had been restored to him on the death of King Sennacherib, was informed that an Israelite lay assassinated in the street.

And he forthwith leaped up from his place at the table, and left his dinner, and came fasting to the body; and taking it up carried it privately to his house, that after the sun was down, he might bury him cautiously.[58]

Tobias, like Job, received no earthly recompense for his heroic virtue, but was blamed by others.

Now all his neighbors blamed him, saying: Once already commandment was given for thee to be slain because of this matter, and dost thou again bury the dead? But Tobias fearing God more than the king, carried off the bodies of them that were slain, and hid them in his house, and at midnight buried them.[59]

When God saw such great fidelity, He sent a still more painful trial. One day when Tobias was tired after his work

[56] Tob., chap. 1, *passim.*   [57] Tob. 1:22–23.   [58] Tob. 2:3–4.
[59] Tob. 2:8–9.

of burying his brothers, he came home and cast himself down by the wall and slept.

And as he was sleeping, hot dung out of a swallow's nest fell upon his eyes, and he was made blind. Now this trial the Lord therefore permitted to happen to him, that an example might be given to posterity of his patience, as also of holy Job. For whereas he had always feared God from his infancy, and kept His commandments, he repined not against God, . . . but continued immoveable in the fear of God, giving thanks to God all the days of his life. For as the kings insulted over holy Job; so his relations and kinsmen mocked at his life. . . . But Tobias rebuked them, saying: Speak not so; for we are the children of saints, and look for that life which God will give to those that never change their faith from Him.[60]

Then, since his wife also rebuked him angrily, Tobias sighed and began to pray with tears. This prayer reveals the depth of his inner union with God. That was the secret of his heroic virtues:

Thou art just, O Lord, and all Thy judgments are just, and all Thy ways mercy, and truth, and judgment. And now, O Lord, think of me, and take not revenge of my sins, neither remember my offences, nor those of my parents. For we have not obeyed Thy commandments. . . . And now, O Lord, great are Thy judgments, because we have not done according to Thy precepts. . . . And now, O Lord, do with me according to Thy will, and command my spirit to be received in peace; for it is better for me to die, than to live.[61]

But God leaves him in life, in order to bring him to a still higher stage of virtue. Tobias bears his afflictions so patiently that he becomes wonderfully gentle. This man who

[60] Tob. 2:10–22.   [61] Tob. 3:2–6.

is blind and dying, rejected by his friends, repaid for his
fidelity by nothing but increasing trials from God, utters
only peaceful, gentle, loving words. He attains the supreme
wisdom and the supreme serenity of the saints, for already
he dwells in the land of love.

When Tobias thought . . . that he might die, he called to
him Tobias his son, and said to him: Hear, my son. . . . Thou
shalt honor thy mother all the days of her life; for thou must
be mindful what and how great perils she suffered for thee in
her womb. . . . All the days of thy life have God in thy mind;
and take heed thou never consent to sin. . . . Turn not away
thy face from any poor person. . . . According to thy ability,
be merciful. If thou have much, give abundantly; if thou have
little, take care even so to bestow willingly a little. . . . Take
heed to keep thyself, my son, from all fornication, and beside
thy wife never endure to know a crime. Never suffer pride to
reign in thy mind, or in thy words; for from it all perdition
took its beginning. . . . See thou never do to another what
thou wouldst hate to have done to thee by another. Eat thy
bread with the hungry and the needy, and with thy garments
cover the naked. . . . Seek counsel always of a wise man.
Bless God at all times; and desire of Him to direct thy ways.[62]

With sanctity the purpose of purifications seems to be accomplished, so that all is achieved. But sanctity is the supreme goal of each individual destiny only because thereby
God's plans can be carried out perfectly. For sanctity demands that a man's personal viewpoint, even though it be
very noble, must be transcended so that his whole life serves
God's plan. This integration shows God's control better than
all the rest and it offers great glory to Him. The Old Testa-

[62] Tob. 4:1–20.

ment well knows this; sanctity is its guiding star and the goal of the soul's journey. The soul that transcends all selfishness responds completely to God's desires and to the urgings of grace. No soul is truly purified until this takes place. For a soul that is purified is a soul that has left itself behind and surrendered to God. Nothing personal can then attract or trouble its inner attitude. At every moment it clearly perceives God's will and complies with His plans.

There is a continuous process of evolution from egotism to sanctity, that is to say, from the point of departure to the ultimate arrival. But as the soul more completely loses itself, it clings more surely to the mind of God. This spiritual itinerary was followed by Abraham, Moses, Isaias, Jeremias, the author of the Book of Job, and many others. We see them subjected to countless despoilments and purifications, as they abandon their possessions, their country, their way of life, their personal opinions and interests, in order to enroll in God's service. These victories allow them to cooperate ever more fully in God's plan and to produce fruits for Him. In spite of surface appearances, the Book of Job is very enlightening on this point, showing the positive spiritual value of the purifications suffered by the book's hero.

With admirable patience, Job bore God's treatment of him. In neither thought nor word did he sin, and this heroic generosity and fidelity at length were rewarded. While Job appears throughout the book as a just man, yet something was still lacking in him, for he was wholly concentrated upon his personal problem and worried by his own individual fate. He seemed unable to escape from it or transcend it. But toward the end of the book the whole atmosphere suddenly changes. Perhaps without his being conscious of it, the effect of purification is to cause Job's soul to die to it-self and to be born to a new reality. Until this point Job sought only one thing: justice from God. Beyond that, he discerned nothing. But henceforth God grants him a truly contemplative viewpoint. As the psalmist had said: "In Thy light we shall see light." [63]

By this light Job now discovers the existence of a divine plan which transcends all creation. He understands that for the sake of this plan everything in himself should subside and be silent. Indeed, the ultimate purpose of all his trials was to reveal "the King's secret" to him, to show him the divine pattern in order that he might fit himself into it. But God first had to take possession of Job's soul sufficiently to be able to use it in a scheme far transcending the ideal of personal perfection. As the prologue informs us, the purpose of Job's life was to serve as the stakes of a contest between God and Satan. God will not permit hell to prevail against Job; this satisfies divine justice and mercy. But in all else God is free. As He is sure of His servant's love and unselfish-ness, He will use him as He pleases, according to the divine good pleasure and for His greater glory. Here we are no longer in a realm where accounts, even spiritual accounts, are settled by the recognition of legal rights; we are in a realm of infinite generosity, which the soul must learn from God Himself, if it is to advance little by little to such a state.[64]

With God's help, Job first caught a glimpse of his own

[63] Ps. 35:10.

[64] "And Christ died for all; that they also who live, may not now live to themselves, but unto Him who died for them, and rose again" (II Cor. 5:15).

inadequacy in knowledge as well as in wisdom and love. But then it was revealed to him that man is permitted to collaborate in the infinite divine plan. That is the whole lesson of God's answer. He gives no reply to Job's anguished questioning about his own situation or about the issues involved, which would seem to require settlement. He even reproaches Job for wasting his time on such matters, on the limited universe of a single individual. "Who is this that wrappeth up sentences in unskillful words?" [65] Yahweh is about to open Job's mind to insights as yet quite unsuspected.

From this moment the poem's proportions change as it takes on magnificent scope. Whatever subject is touched— and does not the inspired author seem overwhelmed by the abundance of images suggested to him?—the constant concern is to cast off private interests and to rise higher, so that mind and heart may behold wider vistas and exult in admiration. God forces Job's heart to expand to divine proportions, to lose itself at length in a greater than itself, to forget itself in the vast glory of God the Creator. Job, therefore, feels that he is poor, wretched, unworthy of God's call. "Who is this that hideth counsel without knowledge? Therefore I have spoken unwisely, and things that above measure exceeded my knowledge. Hear, and I will speak: I will ask Thee, and do Thou tell me." [66]

The naive descriptions of fantastic animals in chapters 39 to 41 emphasize how unimportant is the explanation demanded. We have here one of the playful "tricks" customarily used in the Old Testament when it cannot or will not reveal God's secrets. Job is not deceived by it, for already he perceives something else. God is not knocking at

[65] Job 38:2.   [66] Job 42:3–4.

the door of his imagination, but at that of his heart and his soul. God is treating him as a friend who cannot be duped by words. Beyond the words lies the divine silence where Job's soul finds satisfaction, as he accepts his ignorance and loses his thirst.

Job's heart drinks deep in the heart of God. Gone are all his self-assertion, his self-defense, his reservations. His liberated soul has acquired a capacity for the eternal. Though Job lies on dust and ashes here below, his inward gaze is fixed on heaven; he is united to God and henceforth sees all things in God. "I know that Thou canst do all things, and no thought is hid from Thee. . . . With the hearing of the ear, I have heard Thee, but now my eye seeth Thee." [67] His eyes opened by so much suffering and so many purifying trials, Job perceives that beyond his personal plight there exists a divine plan that infinitely transcends him. This is a discovery of major importance, affecting and controlling the whole course of spiritual life. Without it there can be no true maturity or full spiritual development.

The day when any man has been purified and illuminated by God sufficiently to perceive that his union with God and his personal perfection, far from being ends in themselves, must be used to carry out the divine plan, he must then so far outreach personal interest that he totally forgets himself. This resistance to the downward pull, this death to self and voluntary adaptation of the creature to God's plan constitute the surest signs of God's action on the soul. But how can it be possible for men to fit into the divine plan, that mystery which, as St. Paul says, "in other generations was not known to the sons of men"? [68] How could Old Testa-

[67] Job 42:2, 5.   [68] Eph. 3:5.

ment men acquire knowledge of this "eternal purpose, which He made, in Christ Jesus our Lord"? [69] Moreover, in view of the Jews' notion that God's kingdom was exclusively reserved to themselves, were they not thereby prevented from discovering the divine plan or accepting its true dimensions?

It is true that the just men and the saints of times before Christ did not enjoy the full light, but already they were inspired by the expectation of the Messiah. Their actions and their whole life were controlled by this dominant theme. Though their concept of God's kingdom was imperfect, already they were contributing to its coming. Though much of God's plan remained dim or hidden, yet they worked with all their hearts to carry it out. Thus, they served obscurely, perhaps without knowing it, but truly and efficaciously, to prepare the realization of the great and unique divine plan which was eternally foreseen and was in process of accomplishment from the very beginning of the world.

Reaching a point where it becomes habitual to transcend all personal interests and where sufferings, trials and persecutions are held of no account in the service of the cause they have embraced, these just men—and they are numerous in the Old Testament—show that they have reached the summit of the spiritual life. It is noteworthy also that in the same journey they have also attained their own full development. Man is made in the image of God and for God, but formed from the dust of the earth and rooted in the earth for a while, to work there and bear fruit. He cannot attain full maturity unless he is constantly directed toward his last end and employed in an enterprise of eternal scope.

Only when man can give free rein to the two essential

[69] Eph. 3:11.

tendencies of his nature, uniting them perfectly, only then
does he experience the joy of perfect supernatural stability.
These two tendencies which unite in perfect harmony are
called the service of God and praise. They constitute the
true vital rhythm of man. By the first, he strives to find his
proper place and play his true role in God's great plan; by
the second (which is likewise a form of service, the purest
of all) he tries to keep ever in the divine presence, extolling
divine reality in a voice that utters his increasing adoration,
with a heart that thrills with constantly growing love. To
serve in the achievement of the divine plan and to praise
God: this double rhythm is the very heartbeat of a soul that
is united to God once and for all. We may say that this is
the Old Testament's *last word,* its choicest and purest message to the soul, the principle that contributes most to man's
maturity, joy, and life.

Indeed, it would be impossible to find any other human
rhythm. Can we not recognize therein the double theme of
the *Our Father,* the divine prayer, the perfect prayer? "Hallowed be Thy name. Thy kingdom come." We can hear this
rhythm beating in the hearts of the Old Testament saints
who knew it and lived it.

Chapter 5

❦ AT HOME
WITH GOD

At the end of the day, when the farmer's work is finished, he stops a while before returning home, to contemplate the field that he has ploughed all day. His gaze rests on the scene which he knows and loves. As night comes on, the noises gradually subside and silence reigns. Then there rises from the earth a voice which the ploughman hears and with which he communes.

After our long examination of the Bible, let us pause at last to grasp the essential harmony that emerges from the sacred text. Let us listen to the rhythm beating in the hearts of the faithful souls of Old Testament times. Whether they journeyed by the path of faith, of wisdom or of purification, their hearts eventually sang in unison. All aspired to serve God and to praise Him. This double theme of service and praise is the secret of their satisfaction and their joy. It is likewise the ultimate treasure which they offer to us.

SERVICE

Lo, here am I, send me.[1]

Once a man has understood that there exists a general plan far transcending himself, which God means to follow, and in which his own soul is one element, like a cell in a body or a stone in a building, then he desires to be used in the divine plan and to work for its accomplishment. Henceforth he has finished with "walking wherever he pleases." [2] Now he allows himself to be guided and led. He no longer belongs to himself; his life has been surrendered, and doubtless sacrificed. He will encounter many trials and must attain utter unselfishness. But he will also experience the exhilarating joy of serving a cause that constantly raises him above his own level. All the Old Testament souls that reached a permanent state of union with God made this discovery.

We see this first in souls dedicated to faith. Of course, if faith is strong enough to inspire the believer to make his whole life a testimony to the one in whom he believes, it must be a living faith. "The just shall live in his faith," [3] said Habacuc, which means that faith must be to him a source of interior life. But we see also in the Old Testament that the just man lives not only *in* but also *for* his faith. As soon as a man forms an intimate and personal relationship with the living God, he realizes that he belongs to God and depends upon Him. And as soon as the light of faith reveals that God is the Creator, the Master and the Father, as well as transcendent and merciful Being, this light also governs

[1] Isa. 6:8.   [2] Cf. John 21:18.   [3] Hab. 2:4.

the creature's attitude. What else can he do but leave all things to enter God's service?

The patriarchs faithfully followed this ideal. In all of them the full development of the life of faith produced the fruits of obedience and service. All of them call themselves *servants of Yahweh* and they prove it by their deeds.[4] All are aware of being called by God to carry out His will and to work on a plan which to some extent has been both revealed and entrusted to them. We have seen that the covenant was concluded at the beginning of Genesis. And the covenant was an early manifestation of the divine will and of the plan which Christ was to carry to completion.

Hardly does the light of faith penetrate to the depth of a soul, hardly does the soul surrender to God, when He sends it out to work in His vineyard, binding it to His service. He does not allow His servants to remain inactive. On revealing Himself to them, He also shows them their role and their duties in the world. For here below, everything functions for a purpose, tends toward a goal. There takes place the constant building and forming of something that infinitely surpasses man, but to which it is his duty to contribute. God, by intervening in the world, has accepted the laws of time; His eternal plan is realized progressively and each man must follow it in accord with the directions addressed to him personally.[5]

In the perspective of faith each man is a simple link in an immense chain, but he is directly attached to God. Thus,

[4] St. Peter claimed the title of *servant* even before that of *apostle* (II Pet. 1:1). St. Paul referred to himself as *God's servant* (Tit. 1:1) and even considered himself *a prisoner of Christ* (Eph. 3:1).

[5] "And let our men also learn to excel in good works for necessary uses; that they be not unfruitful" (Tit. 3:14).

he ever keeps the sense of his littleness and the sense of his greatness. He has his own place; though his role may be humble, he should not shirk it, for the entire divine epic is expressed through him and by him. Again and again in Israel the patriarchs, the judges, the kings, the prophets and the ordinary people enrolled in Yahweh's service, thus enabling Him to realize His plan and to build His kingdom, stone by stone. In return, God constantly confirms that He is with them and accompanies them wherever they go. "As I have been with Moses, so will I be with thee; I will not leave thee, nor forsake thee. Take courage, and be strong; for thou shalt divide by lot to this people the land, for which I swore to their fathers, that I would deliver it to them." [6] So spoke Yahweh to Josue before the people entered the Promised Land.

One after the other, God's servants learn that they have been chosen for a great mission, enrolled in what should be called the one great adventure that continues throughout all generations. After all, what is the Old Testament but the accomplishment of God's plan? In all its epochs—the covenant, the people's exodus to the Promised Land, the conquest, the promulgation of the law, the building of the Temple, the defense of the living faith and its preservation in the captivity or in the *diaspora*—loyalty, and often heroism, were demanded of men of faith. They had to muster all their courage to serve the cause which God entrusted to them.

The men presented as models all worked without respite for God, or did not hesitate to make the supreme sacrifice for the sake of His kingdom. "But I, like my brethren, offer

[6] Jos. 1:5–6.

up my life and my body for the laws of our fathers; calling upon God to be speedily merciful to our nation." [7]

Like the men of faith, the disciples of wisdom also devoted themselves to the achievement of God's plan. The paths they follow may seem different, but they lead to the same destination. Their mentality and their fundamental tendencies led them to discover first the order that governs this world. The order displayed in material creation deserves admiration; it is the work of divine wisdom, but is not its only manifestation. If the sages sought wisdom so eagerly, it was because the divine thought was disclosed to her. And if they even desire to possess her as a bride, it is because "she glorifieth her nobility by being conversant with God; yea, and the Lord of all things hath loved her." [8]

He who becomes a lover of wisdom hopes, if not to penetrate God's secrets, at least to know His will, to become part of His plan. This is the fruit he seeks from his intimacy with wisdom. He also seeks thereby the meaning of the Law and the Scriptures. Without wisdom he cannot serve God usefully, for "wisdom knew what was agreeable to Thy eyes, and what was right in Thy commandments." [9] Happy the disciple who discovers by wisdom's light something of God's plan and of His intentions for humanity. "We are happy, O Israel, because the things that are pleasing to God, are made known to us." [10]

At length there comes a time when the purpose of all things and their role in the divine plan becomes apparent to the sage. Henceforth he becomes capable of rising above contingencies, transcending all appearances, tracing all

[7] II Mach. 7:37.   [8] Wisd. 8:3.   [9] Wisd. 9:9.
[10] Bar. 4:4.

things back to their source in the divine mind which arranges them and determines their value and meaning. Henceforth he believes that "all the works of the Lord are good, and He will furnish every work in due time." [11]

The wise man is then detached from all egoistic and personal interests, free of all purely human viewpoints, caring only to know God's intention and to conform to it. So he becomes a reliable instrument of infinite wisdom. He acts by the power of the Spirit which "ordered all things in measure, and number, and weight." [12] His soul is "in the hand of God," [13] and he cooperates, therefore, in the divine purposes and the eternal pattern. "In His commandments they [all creatures] shall feast, and they shall be ready upon earth when need is, and when their time is come they shall not transgress His word." [14] Thus the sage too, as a man of faith, works to realize the prayer: "Thy kingdom come."

"Thy kingdom come!" The same cry springs from the lips of those who have sacrificed everything for God's sake. In particular it summarizes the whole life and spirit of the prophets. Purified by their trials and sufferings, the prophets have been extricated from temporal concerns and narrow-minded nationalism. They espoused the divine cause and worked for God's plan, which their contemporaries failed to discern because they lacked the proper spiritual integrity and purity of intention. While it is true that the call they heard and the mission they received included a certain illumination, their merit lies in having answered: "Lo, here am I, send me." [15] They were not satisfied merely to hear the heavenly voice and to answer, like Samuel: "Here am I, for Thou

[11] Ecclus. 39:39.   [12] Wisd. 11:21.   [13] Wisd. 3:1.
[14] Ecclus. 39:37.   [15] Isa. 6:8.

calledst me," [16] but they abandon everything: their position, their family and their country, in order to serve God. "And Amos answered and said to Amasias: I am not a prophet, nor am I the son of a prophet; but I am a herdsman plucking wild figs. And the Lord took me when I followed the flock, and the Lord said to me: Go, prophesy to My people Israel." [17] In the end they take leave of themselves and "lose" their souls. "O Lord, . . . Thou hast been stronger than I, and Thou hast prevailed." [18] Their immense merit lies in their having preserved the limpid purity of their spiritual vision. And so the divine pattern was not concealed from their eyes and they could work on it profitably. By their actions they were already saying the prayer: "Thy will be done. Thy kingdom come." Their entire self enters into the divine purpose as it is revealed to them.

Thus, little by little they come to see as God sees, to will as He wills, to love as He loves. By their total self-forgetfulness, they have risen to the level of the mission entrusted to them. They knew well what price they had to pay if they were to participate fully in God's task and work for the establishment of His reign. Since they prepare the way for the Redeemer, it is not surprising that the shadow of the Cross should darken their existence. So it is that throughout the Bible are found souls, often very lowly but always royal in spirit, for whom only one thing matters: God's service and the founding of His kingdom. These good servants have left all things in order to come and work in the Father's field. "I will keep my strength to Thee." [19] God is their all: the source of their life, the support and the goal

16 I Kings 3:6.   17 Amos 7:14–15.   18 Jer. 20:7.
19 Ps. 58:10 (Vulgate).

of their actions. They are so intimately and constantly united to Him that this intimacy is often indicated by a single word or even a gesture.

For how could a soul share God's views, desires and intentions, unless it stays closely united to Him? And how could it resist all relapse or self-interest, unless it is uplifted and urged onward by a mighty inspiration? These souls were already living the ideal that would soon be proposed to Christians: "For none of us liveth to himself. . . . Let no man therefore glory in men. . . . You are Christ's." [20] And so, since they all are united to the same divine will, they cannot remain isolated. Always their minds are fixed and their faculties are concentrated on the same goal, whether it be the establishment of God's kingdom, the advent of the coming King, the restoration of the Holy City, or the recovery of the bride's beauty. Their unity in effort gives a foreglimpse of the figure of the Messiah, and of the cells of His mystical body. This is so because the Old Testament saints are enrolled in God's service, and God, throughout the centuries, ever seeks the accomplishment of His one eternal plan: to form the Church of Christ, which St. Epiphanius called the aim of all things. In this sense the men of the Old Testament also worked to build up the Church.

PRAISE

O Lord, . . . Thou art my praise.[21]

And they were always in the Temple, praising and blessing God.[22]

[20] Rom. 14:7; I Cor. 3:21–23.   [21] Jer. 17:14.
[22] Luke 24:53.

The Bible, which has showed us that the service of God was one essential attitude of the faithful soul, presents praise as still more essential. For is it not an earthly participation in eternal life, a prototype of the ultimate form of service? To emphasize its primacy, Christ makes it the first petition of the *Our Father:* "Hallowed be Thy name." [23] In the Old Testament, too, praise occupies the first place. It rises spontaneously from souls united to God and dwelling in His love. It flourishes at the end of each of the pathways leading to Him.

Faith ever invites men to intensify their praise of God, for it opens their eyes to invisible realities and reveals countless proofs of divine omnipotence and mercy. Unlike those who keep complaining and lose sight of divine benefits, the just never forget to give thanks. The faith that animates them enables them to recognize God's presence and control in all things; this urges them to praise Him. Even here below, is it not characteristic of noble souls to be readily grateful? At first they saw God principally in the benefits He heaped upon them and they thanked Him for them. But gradually they learned to see the Giver, to love Him for Himself alone, [24] to delight in His infinite perfections. They find their whole happiness in praising Him for being what He is. Faith,

[23] St. Paul also declares that praise is the ultimate secret of God's plan for mankind. "In whom we also are called by lot, being predestinated according to the purpose of Him who worketh all things according to the counsel of His will. That we may be unto the praise of His glory, we who before hoped in Christ, . . . who is the pledge of our inheritance, unto the redemption of acquisition, unto the praise of His glory" (Eph. 1:11–14).

[24] "For I seek not the things that are yours, but you" (II Cor. 12:14).

which gave them "eyes" to see God and to discover that only the divine reality is worthy of praise, puts the seal of objectivity on the spiritual life of such souls. For them that is a means of perfection.

Wisdom likewise helps to discern and to display the very soul of praise. "Praise shall be with the wisdom of God, and shall abound in a faithful mouth, and the sovereign Lord will give praise unto it." [25]

Finally, the trials and sufferings that purify the just man's soul also purify praise itself. A particularly beautiful prayer of praise is uttered by Anna, who was sterile for such a long time, but was finally satisfied after many fervent petitions. Her words are dear to us for a special reason, since they were repeated, in part, by the Virgin Mary in her *Magnificat*.

My heart hath rejoiced in the Lord. . . . There is none holy as the Lord is, . . . for the Lord is a God of all knowledge. . . . The Lord killeth and maketh alive. . . . The Lord maketh poor and maketh rich, He humbleth, and He exalteth. He raiseth up the needy from the dust, and lifteth up the poor from the dunghill. . . . For the poles of the earth are the Lord's, and upon them He hath set the world. . . . And He shall give empire to His king, and shall exalt the horn of His Christ.[26]

If Anna's praise is characterized by humility, that of Tobias is the chant of a saint, offering thanks to God in the evening of a long life filled with trials:

Thou art great, O Lord, for ever, and Thy kingdom is unto all ages. . . . Give glory to the Lord, ye children of Israel, and praise Him in the sight of the Gentiles. . . . With fear

---

[25] Ecclus. 15:10.   [26] I Kings 2:1–10.

and trembling give ye glory to Him; and extol the eternal king of worlds in your works. As for me, I will praise Him in the land of my captivity; because He hath shown His majesty toward a sinful nation. . . . Bless ye the Lord, all His elect, keep days of joy, and give glory to Him. Jerusalem, city of God, the Lord hath chastised thee for the works of thy hands. Give glory to God for thy good things, and bless the God eternal. . . . My soul, bless thou the Lord, because the Lord our God hath delivered Jerusalem His city from all her troubles. . . . The gates of Jerusalem shall be built of sapphire, and of emerald, and all the walls thereof round about of precious stones. All its streets shall be paved with white and clean stones; and Alleluia shall be sung in its streets. Blessed be the Lord, who hath exalted it, and may He reign over it for ever and ever. Amen.[27]

Frequently praise attains its highest form at the very end of life, as if its purity and beauty proceeded from the experience of trials and anguish. Thus Moses, as he was about to die, uttered the admirable canticle which we read in the Book of Deuteronomy. "I will invoke the name of the Lord; give ye magnificence to our God. The works of God are perfect, and all His ways are judgments." [28]

But to learn praise does not always require a long life. The three youths cast into the furnace sang such a beautiful hymn of praise that the Church places it on the lips of her priests as they return from offering the Mass, the supreme sacrifice of thanksgiving:

Blessed art Thou, O Lord the God of our fathers, and worthy to be praised, and glorified, and exalted above all for ever: and blessed is the holy name of Thy glory: and worthy

[27] Tob., chap. 13, *passim*.   [28] Deut. 32:3–4.

to be praised, and exalted above all in all ages. Blessed art
Thou in the holy Temple of Thy glory: and exceedingly to be
praised, and exceeding glorious for ever. . . . Blessed art
Thou that beholdeth the depths and sittest upon the cherubims:
and worthy to be praised and exalted above all for ever. Blessed
art thou in the firmament of heaven: and worthy of praise,
and glorious for ever. All ye works of the Lord, bless the Lord:
praise and exalt Him above all for ever. . . . O ye sons of
men, bless the Lord: praise and exalt Him above all for ever.
O let Israel bless the Lord: let them praise and exalt Him
above all for ever. O ye priests of the Lord, bless the Lord:
praise and exalt Him above all for ever. O ye servants of the
Lord, bless the Lord: praise and exalt Him above all for ever.
O ye spirits and souls of the just, bless the Lord: praise and
exalt Him above all for ever. O ye holy and humble of heart,
bless the Lord: praise and exalt Him above all for ever.[29]

But however perfect it may be, individual praise does not
suffice. To praise God is such an essential activity that it
should take place always and unceasingly. The levitical
priesthood was instituted for the purpose of carrying out this
great duty of praise. "The Levites are to stand in the morning to give thanks, and to sing praises to the Lord; and in
like manner in the evening, as well as in the oblation of the
holocausts of the Lord." [30] This taught everyone that the
duty of praise was an absolute necessity and should be
undertaken for its own sake alone. For the praise that rose
continuously to God, independent of all particular intentions, could have no other reason or purpose but God Himself. This prayer, therefore, was clothed in pure and radiant
beauty. What is it, indeed, but a wholly unselfish hymn

[29] Dan., chap. 3, *passim.*   [30] I Par. 23:30–31.

rising from the earth toward the supreme Being? And what does it mean to be a soul of praise? It means to strive to remain in the presence of that living and loving reality, to stay in the rays of that bright sun, to bathe in the ocean of His love.

Praise occupies the crossroads of all our spiritual tendencies; it is the focus of all the light that we receive; it is the destination on which all paths converge: the whole of divine revelation, our knowledge of God's love for us, all the aspirations of our soul. In a soul united to God, praise reaches the surface and gushes forth, like water in saturated soil.[31]

Indeed praise, which offers God his due, which offers thanks, is *the* essential function, the ultimate goal of all others. Even the service of God, however noble it may be, is linked to our earthly state and inscribed in the book of time. Its purpose will vanish when time is over and the pattern is complete. Or rather, it will then be transformed into its supreme form: praise, that motionless, perfect activity, directed to God alone and sharing His eternity and His perfection.[32]

Only in eternal life will praise be clothed in its perfect form. Then it will display absolute simplicity, as dazzling as the sun. Here below our human state and imperfection shade the light or split it, like the rays in a prism. And yet what beauty still is found in that praise, diffused throughout the

[31] So did it constantly spring from the lips of Christ. "I confess to Thee, O Father, Lord of heaven and earth" (Matt. 11:25).

[32] The Apocalypse shows all creatures busy at this activity. "And I heard as it were the voice of a great multitude, and as the voice of many waters, and as the voice of great thunders, saying, Alleluia; for the Lord our God the Almighty hath reigned. Let us be glad and rejoice, and give glory to Him" (Apoc. 19:6–7).

sacred books! But especially in the psalms does its fire burn
with the loveliest glow, and the symphony of its variegated
tones attains its purest beauty. And so on these final pages
we shall seek some of the rays which they reflect.

Often the Creator is praised for the beauty and magnificence of the works formed by His hands:

The heavens show forth the glory of God, and the firmament declareth the work of His hands. Day to day uttereth
speech, and night to night showeth knowledge. There are no
speeches nor languages, where their voices are not heard. Their
sound hath gone forth into all the earth; and their words unto the
ends of the world.[33]

Others praise His greatness, His might and His royalty:

Come let us praise the Lord with joy; let us joyfully sing to
God our Savior. Let us come before His presence with thanks-
giving; and make a joyful noise to Him with psalms. For the
Lord is a great God, and a great King above all gods. . . .
Come let us adore and fall down.[34]

The earth is the Lord's and the fullness thereof; the world,
and all they that dwell therein. . . . Lift up your gates, O ye
princes, and be ye lifted up, O eternal gates, and the King of
glory shall enter in. Who is this King of glory? The Lord of
hosts, he is the King of glory.[35]

Many psalms, affected particularly by the benefits God
always bestows, extol the Father's goodness and the Savior's
mercy:

O bless our God, ye Gentiles; and make the voice of His
praise to be heard. Who hath set my soul to live.[36]

[33] Ps. 18:2–5.   [34] Ps. 94:1–6.   [35] Ps. 23:1, 9–10.
[36] Ps. 65:8–9.

Sing joyfully to God, all the earth; serve ye the Lord with gladness. Come in before His presence with exceeding great joy. Know ye that the Lord He is God; He made us, and not we ourselves. We are His people and the sheep of His pasture. Go ye into His gates with praise, into His courts with hymns, and give glory to Him. Praise ye His name, for the Lord is sweet, His mercy endureth forever, and His truth to generation and generation.[37]

The mercies of the Lord I will sing for ever. I will show forth Thy truth with my mouth to generation and generation. For Thou hast said: Mercy shall be built up for ever in the heavens.[38]

This praise of God is not assigned exclusively to a few men. All should sing in unison. With truly prophetic enthusiasm, the psalmist emphasizes this catholicity of praise:

The Lord hath reigned, let the people be angry; He that sitteth on the cherubims, let the earth be moved. The Lord is great in Sion, and high above all people. Let them give praise to Thy great name; for it is terrible and holy. . . . Exalt ye the Lord our God.[39]

Let all the earth adore Thee, and sing to Thee; let it sing a psalm to Thy name. . . . O bless our God, ye Gentiles; and make the voice of His praise to be heard.[40]

O praise the Lord, all ye nations; praise Him, all ye people.[41]

Behold now bless ye the Lord, all ye servants of the Lord.[42]

All men are invited to join the psalmists in extolling Him who alone is worthy of all praise and blessing.

Sing ye to the Lord a new canticle; sing to the Lord all the earth. Sing ye to the Lord and bless His name; show forth His salvation from day to day. Declare His glory among the Gen-

[37] Ps. 99.   [38] Ps. 88:2-3.   [39] Ps. 98:1-3, 9.
[40] Ps. 65:4, 8.   [41] Ps. 116:1.   [42] Ps. 133:1.

tiles; His wonders among all people. For the Lord is great, and exceedingly to be praised. . . . Praise and beauty are before Him; holiness and majesty in His sanctuary. Bring ye to the Lord, O ye kindreds of the Gentiles, bring ye to the Lord glory and honor; bring to the Lord glory unto His name. Bring up sacrifices, and come into His courts; adore ye the Lord in His holy court. Let all the earth be moved at His presence. Say ye among the Gentiles, the Lord hath reigned.[43]

But the psalmist gazes yet higher, seeking a universal vista, uniting heavenly and terrestrial praise. So all creatures, "on earth, . . . as in heaven," will praise God and hallow His name.

Praise ye the Lord from the heavens, praise ye Him in the high places. Praise ye Him, all His angels; praise ye Him, all His hosts. Praise ye Him, O sun and moon; praise Him, all ye stars and light. Praise Him, ye heavens of heavens; and let all the waters that are above the heavens praise the name of the Lord. For He spoke, and they were made; He commanded, and they were created. . . . Kings of the earth and all people, princes and all judges of the earth, young men and maidens, let the old with the younger, praise the name of the Lord.[44]

At length the psalter draws to a close on a note of utterly pure praise, the praise of God because He is God.

Praise ye the Lord in His holy places; praise ye Him in the firmament of His power. Praise ye Him for His mighty acts; praise ye Him according to the multitude of His greatness. Praise Him with sound of trumpet; praise Him with psaltery and harp. Praise Him with timbrel and choir; praise Him with strings and organs. Praise Him on high sounding cymbals; praise Him on cymbals of joy; let every spirit praise the Lord. Alleluia.[45]

[43] Ps. 95:1–10.   [44] Ps. 148:1–5, 11–13.   [45] Ps. 150.

The psalms are the highest expression of praise. Countless lips repeated them in the days of the first covenant. Mary, and Jesus Himself, used them and consecrated them in their prayer to the Father. What more could the Old Testament offer us after such a gift? It has only to bring forth the praise which infinitely surpasses all other praises, for which all its inspired pages were merely a preparation. The voices which the whole earth has long yearned to hear, at last speak forth. "Praise ye the Lord from the heavens; praise ye Him in the high places. Praise ye Him, all His angels." [46] And these angelic voices lead the humble, the simple, all "men of good will" to a crib. "The Word was made flesh." Eternal praise came down among us and dwells with us in silence. And henceforth, in that Word, the songs of praise uttered by God's children of both the Old and the New Testaments can rise in perfect unity. "O Lord, . . . Thy magnificence is elevated above the heavens. Out of the mouths of infants and of sucklings Thou hast perfected praise." [47]

"For what things soever were written, were written for our learning; that through patience and the comfort of the Scriptures, we might have hope. Now the God of patience and of comfort grant you to be of one mind one toward another, according to Jesus Christ; that with one mind and with one mouth you may glorify God and the Father of our Lord Jesus Christ." [48]

[46] Ps. 148:1–2.   [47] Ps. 8:2–3.   [48] Rom. 15:4–6.